Shantung
Compound

Shantung Compound

THE STORY OF MEN AND WOMEN UNDER PRESSURE

by Langdon Gilkey

HarperSanFrancisco

A Division of HarperCollins*Publishers*

First Harper & Row paperback edition published in 1975.

Library of Congress catalog card number: 66-15040
ISBN: 0-06-063112-0

92 93 94 95 CWI 25 24 23 21 20

*To
my
love
Sonja*

CONTENTS

Drawings by the author follow page 146

PREFACE

This book is about the life of a civilian internment camp in North China during the war against Japan. Unlike some other volumes dealing with such a subject, this one has no horrors to relate. We in the Weihsien camp suffered no extreme hardships of limb, stomach, or spirit. As the quotation from Brecht hints, our problems were created more by our own behavior than by our Japanese captors. Thus, compared to many other internment camps, both in Asia and in Europe, ours was in fact nearly an ordinary life. That is precisely what gives the story its interest and excitement, and why it is here told.

This was a life almost normal, and yet intensely difficult, very near to our usual crises and problems, and yet precarious in the extreme. Thus my story relates an experience within which one of those rare glimpses of the nature of men and of their communal life is possible. In our internment camp we were secure and comfortable enough to accomplish in large part the creation and maintenance of a small civilization; but our life was sufficiently close to the margin of survival to reveal the vast difficulties of that task. Had we been continually tortured and starved, no representative communal existence would have been possible; had our life been more secure, the basic problems of our human lot might not have manifested themselves so clearly. Thus, as the laboratory reveals the structure of what is studied by reducing it to manageable size and subjecting it to increased pressure, so this internment camp reduced society, ordinarily large and complex, to viewable size, and by subjecting life to greatly increased tension laid bare its essential structures. Because internment-camp life seems to reveal more clearly than does ordinary experience the anatomy of man's common social and moral problems and the bases of human communal existence, this book finally has been written.

The reader may well wonder how anyone can remember details and episodes of an experience twenty years in the past.

The answer is that I kept a rather lengthy journal during the internment in which were set down every fact and happening, every problem and its resolution, that came to my attention. Thus the main resource for these chapters stands very close to the life described, for the journal was largely written in camp and was completed shortly after my return to the United States in November, 1945.

I have often been asked why we did not try to escape. The reason was simple: a Westerner cannot wander unrecognized through the Chinese countryside as he might in Europe. His face and color identify him at once to any onlooker. He is thus infinitely vulnerable to any Chinese seeking the reward for his capture. To escape successfully, he must join a guerrilla band at once, who can hide and protect him. But guerrilla bands only wish to care for those who are strong, who possess some special skill that can help the group, and who speak fluent Chinese. Contacts with the guerrillas were, moreover, difficult and rare. Consequently, only two men were able to make such contacts as to allow them to escape; those of us who spoke little Chinese or had no special skills were never even considered.

Finally, it is inevitable that in attempting an analysis of our problems I should describe the "sins" as well as the virtues of the people in the camp. For this is essentially the subject of our story. Necessarily, therefore, this book seems to be describing the foibles, weaknesses, lapses, and selfishness of other folk, so that the impression might be given that I alone trod a saintly path through the life of the camp. At the outset it is important to state that any such impression would be false: no one stood apart from our common weaknesses and our common sins, and certainly I least of all. Different temptations beset and conquer different persons. While as an unencumbered bachelor of twenty-four, I may not have been as concerned as some others about space, food, and security, and so have been able to resist many of the temptations described in the following pages, nevertheless, I had my own moral problems in which I failed as miserably as others did in theirs. All men—each in his own way—need the forgiving grace of God if they would be whole. This is an essential note of the Christian gospel, and it has certainly been the continual lesson of my own life. If then the "sins" of other men seem to be described and analyzed in this volume, let it be remembered that another book on the camp could easily tell our tale with a different cast (doubtless including me, too), playing slightly different roles but enacting ultimately the same story. To save embarrassment all around, I have changed the name of every person mentioned in the book.

LANGDON GILKEY

Shantung
Compound

For even saintly folk will act like sinners
Unless they have their customary dinners.

     —BERTOLT BRECHT, *The Threepenny Opera*

I ✒ Into the Unknown

The letter arrived in late February, 1943, at the door of the house I shared with five bachelor teachers in Peking. Rumors had been going around for weeks that the Americans and the British who were then in Peking would be sent "somewhere to camp." Some said we would be shipped to Japan; some said Manchuria; some, a Chinese prison. These stories increased in volume and in flavor; something was going to happen soon, we knew. So it was with anxious concern that I tore open the long, white envelope.

In stilted English sentences, the official letter announced that "for your safety and comfort" all enemy nationals would be sent by train to a "Civilian Internment Center" near Weihsien. This was a city in Shantung Province, two hundred miles to the south. The letter went on to declare that "there every comfort of Western culture will be yours." For our own well-being we could send ahead a bed or cot and one trunk apiece. We were to bring our eating utensils with us. Beyond these items we were allowed *only* what we could carry by hand. Meanwhile, the letter concluded, we were all to make preparations for this "rare opportunity" which the Japanese government was providing us.

How do you prepare for an internment camp? No one in the British or American communities knew—nor did anyone know exactly where we were going or what life would be like when we got there. Further rumors told us that the camp would be in an old Presbyterian mission compound, but beyond that we had no information. I pictured a life of monotony spent in a prison cell, and so rounded up copies of Aristotle, Spinoza, and Kant.

1

Another man, who took seriously the travel-brochure promises of the letter, lugged his golf clubs along. We were both wrong. Wiser heads in the community advised us all to bring blankets, towels, and basic camping and household equipment. They did say to be sure to pack some books, and if possible, musical instruments in our trunks. We were advised also to take our share of necessary medicines. Committees made up of the few doctors and nurses among us were formed to see that the latter items were bought and distributed so that each of us would bring some medicines with us. Everyone tacitly agreed that since the trunks might not arrive for weeks at this remote spot, we had better carry with us as much in the way of extra warm clothing and woolens as we could.

On March 25, we Americans met in the former United States Embassy compound. On the great lawn surrounded by the empty and mindless buildings of an officialdom long since fled, a motley crowd had gathered with all their varied equipment. There must have been about four hundred or so, males and females of all shapes and sizes, from every segment of society, ranging in age from six months to eighty-five years. The only thing we all seemed to have in common—besides our overloads of possessions—was a queer combination of excitement and apprehension. Were we bound for a camping vacation or the torturer's rack? Because of the uncertainty, our emotions see-sawed, voices were loud and tempers short.

The group of teachers from Yenching University of which I was a part, were, of course, familiar to me. Yenching was a privately owned Anglo-American university near Peking, one of ten "Christian Colleges" in China, with Chinese students and about one-third Western faculty. In our group were older professors, some young instructors in their twenties like myself, graduate students of Chinese like Stanley Morris, as well as numerous women professors. I also recognized the doctors from the Peking Union Medical College, the missionary families from the leading Protestant Boards, and some of the businessmen. The latter had been helping to provide leadership for the Americans in Peking since the beginning of hostilities a year and a half before, when we found ourselves captives of the Japanese and confined within the city walls of Peking.

But most of this varied crowd was new to me. There, a few feet away, for example, stood Karl Bauer, tall, straight, strong and sour, an ex-marine and ex-pro baseball player. Karl was never known to smile; for him everything that happened was an irritant, and everyone hostile. As we came later to know, he was capable of generating with less reason, more unhappiness in himself and others than anyone I have encountered before or since. Standing near him was a wan, paper-thin ghost of a man, with dirty, torn clothes, scraggly beard and sea-green complexion. His name proved to be Briggs, and he was the captive of a dope addiction that was slowly eating away what flesh remained his own.

By way of contrast, near the steps of the deserted Embassy office building was a knot of what were obviously wealthy older women. All wore furs and elegant hats. A few, I was told, were wealthy widows who had been living in retirement in Peking many years, and some were world travelers who happened to be caught and held in North China by the suddenness of the attack on Pearl Harbor. Further away, by the long-deserted American Ambassador's residence, were what seemed to be hundreds of Roman Catholic priests, monks, and nuns. They were missionaries, who had been seized in Mongolia, and brought here from their monasteries to go to camp with us. The panoply of civilian life in all its wonderful and amazing variety seemed to be represented here.

We stood waiting for orders. Each child clutched his teddy bear; single persons and families alike stood surrounded by the miscellaneous heaps of bags, duffles, coats, potties, and camp chairs—all this assorted gear, in spite of the stern Japanese warning that we must bring only what we could carry.

That warning had been issued in earnest. At noon sharp, a Japanese officer shouted through a megaphone that everyone must pick up his own belongings and carry them by hand to the railway station. A horrified gasp swept through the crowd. Every elderly person, every father of a family, every single woman thought of the station a mile away and then looked in near panic at the mountain of his own stuff at his feet. In the group were a goodly number of men alone—many of whom had sent their families home the year before—but since each of them had already brought as much as he could manage, they could not carry it all. Even the old and the very young had somehow to drag their things. Everything was a necessity. How could anyone bear to leave anything behind when he was bound to a strange life of indeterminate duration in a faraway concentration camp?

The Japanese officer again barked out his order to march.

There was nothing to do but to pick up the things and start moving. Every man, with the exception of those over seventy, carried the bags of at least two other persons. So, by a process of dragging and resting, of dragging some more and resting again, the march began. Slowly we crawled out of the Embassy compound and onto the main streets of Peking.

Here we found that the Japanese had lined up most of the city's Chinese population along the street to view our humiliation. The Chinese had been our allies against the Japanese; they had done much for us since the beginning of the war. And yet, because they themselves had been ruled so long by the West, they must have had mixed emotions as they impassively watched these four hundred white Westerners stagger weakly through their streets. We knew the Japanese intended that these marches, which took place throughout the cities and ports of China, be the symbol of the final destruction of Western prestige in the Orient. For that reason, we tried our best to walk erect and to present a dignified mien. But that is a hard enough job for a young man carrying four of five heavy bags. It was hopeless for the elderly. So on that sad mile we provided precisely the ridiculous spectacle that the Japanese hoped for. From this late vantage point, it is plain that the Japanese had guessed correctly: the era of Western dominance in Asia ended with that burdened crawl to the station.

A full hour had passed before that march was finally over. It was a great relief to hear that it had caused no more than one fatal heart attack and two fainting spells.

At the station we were told that a train would be ready to take us to Weihsien in another hour or so. Meanwhile we were ordered not to move from the platform or to make contact with the Chinese. This latter proscription was far from welcome since it meant that no more food and no more liquid could be purchased from the hawkers, who now stared at us wistfully from another platform with a look of disappointment matched only by our own. We would have to make do on the long trip to Weihsien with the little that each of us had brought along. So we all sat down on our belongings and waited. We sipped from our canteens and nibbled on our sandwiches.

The train ride itself was no improvement. We were jammed into the straight, wooden seats of Chinese third-class carriages, some of us standing, some sitting on luggage. In this comfortless state, we lurched and bounced for twenty-four hours two hundred miles into the south. For the old people, exhausted from the march, for infants and young children, that night on the hard boards of the jolting smelly train must have been a nightmare. Every rattle of the loose windows, or screech of the old-fashioned whistle was accompanied by the cries of those miserable youngsters suffering from hunger, from thirst, and from just plain fright.

No one could sleep. We talked endlessly about what might lie ahead. Would we be in cells? If so, what would we do there? Would they work younger men to death, as we had heard? Would there be enough food? Again our thoughts were a strange brew of excitement, apprehension, and curiosity. What *would* camp be like?

We were well into the long night when the sound of singing drifted in from the coach behind us. It came softly at first and then grew loud enough to drown out the cries of the children around us. We looked back to see a car filled with pipe smoke through which we could discern dim, monastic, bearded figures. These monks, cheerful and certainly untroubled by discomfort, were loudly singing Dutch and Belgian student drinking songs. After a moment's surprise and delight at this totally unexpected aura of easy good humor, some of us moved back to their car, joined in lustily, and sang ourselves hoarse as the train lurched over the dark plains and into the darker unknown ahead.

Our food and water ran out early in the night; no one had any sleep to boast of, so it was a dirty, stiff, tired, and hungry crew that arrived at the Weihsien city station in the middle of the next afternoon. On hand to greet us was a British businessman from Tientsin who had been sent to camp four days before when the first Tientsin group arrived. We were pleased to hear that army trucks would come shortly to take us to the camp, some three miles outside the city walls. But his second statement gave us all a jolt. No Chinese would be allowed in camp. No *Chinese?* Who, then, would be the No. 1 boys in this new world? Who would cook the food and feed the fires necessary for life and warmth? And with that thought, I could *feel* the years of being waited on and served, both at home and at college, going down the drain. I could feel the familiar comforts of being provided with heat, food, warm water, and clean clothes peeling off—and a quite new life beginning.

Soon, however, the trucks arrived and we clambered into them with our baggage. After a forty-minute ride through the cobbled streets of the city, through the massive gates in the city walls and out across three miles of countryside, we arrived at the compound. Curious as to what our future would be inside those walls, we climbed stiffly out of the trucks and looked around.

The compound looked like any other foreign mission station in China, dull gray and institutional. It seemed roughly the size of most of them—about one large city block. There were the familiar six-foot walls that surround everything in China; there were the roofs of Western-style buildings appearing above the walls; there was the welcome sight of a few trees here and there inside the compound; and, of course, the familiar great front gates. Stretching endlessly on either side, was the bare, flat, dusty Shantung farmland over which we had just come. We turned to take a last glance at that landscape. The guard on our truck barked at us, and we started up the slope toward the gate.

The first sight that greeted us was a great crowd of dirty, unkempt, refugeelike people, standing inside the gate and coldly staring at us with resentful curiosity. Their clothes looked damp and rumpled, covered with grime and dust—much as men look who have just come off a shift on a road gang.

"My God," I thought, as I stared back at them with disgust, "they look like real freight-yard bums. Why haven't they cleaned themselves up a little bit?"

A feeling of utter dreariness came over me as I looked at them. Would we, in time, become as drab and disheveled as this crowd? Was this dull dirtiness to be the character of our life here?

Who were these people? I wondered. With some distaste, we learned that they were earlier arrivals. Some came from Tsingtao, a nearby port city, and some from Tientsin. It had never really occurred to me that there would be anyone in camp besides our small Peking group. At this sudden confrontation with total strangers, I felt excitement as well as antipathy. Paradoxically, the camp might offer a wider, livelier universe for a young man than our small world of academicians, business people, and missionaries in Peking. Immediately I found myself "checking the crowd," searching eagerly for a pretty face or a rounded figure—and, sure enough, even among that scruffy-looking lot there were three or four.

Still looking about us curiously, we were led from the gate past some rows of small rooms, past the Edwardian-style church, out onto a small softball field in one corner of the compound. Here we were to be lined up and counted. For the first time I noticed the guard towers at each corner or bend of the walls. I felt a slight chill as I noticed the slots for machine guns, and the electrified barbed wire that ran along the tops of the walls.

Then a considerably greater chill swept me as I saw that the machine guns were pointing our way.

And a sense both of complete change and of utter reality came over me. Suddenly I felt what it was like to be *inside* something, and stuck there; and what is more, inside an internment camp from which one could not get out for any reason whatsoever, a camp run under the iron discipline of an enemy army.

With this awareness I could feel my world shrink: the countryside beyond the walls receded and became unreal—like the pictured scenery of a stage set. The reality in which I had now to exist seemed barely large enough to stand on, let alone large enough to be alive in. With a feeling of genuine despair I thought, "How can anyone *live* enclosed in this tiny area for any length of time? Will I not go wild with cramp, with boredom? What can there be to do in this dreary place?"

I moved dejectedly toward a doctor I knew, who was talking to the "leader" of the Peking Americans, William Montague, of the British American Tobacco Company. Seated on a small mound on the edge of the diamond, Montague was the cheerful center of animated chatter and amused laughter. This able man, undismayed by any misfortune, seemed more like a happy old grad at a homecoming game in his soft camel's hair topcoat, than the responsible head of an internment-camp community. Apparently the Japanese had told him to pick one man to be in general charge of our group (Montague, needless to say, had regarded himself as already appointed to this post!), one other person to handle housing, and another to organize our food and cooking. This group of lively participants was suggesting names of men suitable for these our first political positions. I do not know what prompted me, a young teacher of English and philosophy barely twenty-four, to enter this world of affairs. Anyway, I blurted out the name of Dr. Arnold Baldwin for the housing job. I was aware that he had been head of an American Quarters Committee formed in Peking after the start of war to help homeless Americans. Montague looked up at me at this—he hardly knew me—and said quickly and coldly: "Oh, no, Baldwin has much more important work than that to do here. There will be more sickness in this mess than any number of doctors can take care of!"

Knowing he was absolutely right in his observation, I felt

ashamed for having put in my two cents. I started to turn away, when, to my amazement I heard Baldwin say, "All right, I'll accept that—but how about young Gilkey here for housing?"

Montague looked at me again, narrowed his eyes, and said, "All right, Gilkey, you help me with this housing stuff, and I'll take over the general charge of the group—Dr. Foster can handle medicine, and we'll find someone for cooking when we've had a look at the kitchen setup."

I swallowed hard and said nothing. I had no knowledge of housing and had hardly any administrative experience. But still, I thought, who did know how to house people in an internment camp? Surely working with the effervescent Montague would be more diverting than staring dolefully at my shoes from the side of a bed! So I said I would take a crack at the housing job, and went back to join my friends.

Just then we were lined up in rows to be counted and harangued. We found ourselves listening to a set speech on the rules of camp life, and on our good fortune at being there. At the end we had to swear to cooperate with our overlords in anything that they might ask of us. It sounded grim enough. The March wind was becoming freezing cold. But something new had entered into this drab scene. I remembered my glimpse of two or three shapely girls in the motley crowd at the edge of the ballfield. Also as we parted, Montague had said that tomorrow night there was to be a meeting of "leaders," and I could help him by going along with him and taking notes.

When this initial roll call was finished, one of the earlier arrivals in camp, another British businessman from Tientsin, gathered the men of our Peking group together. He was natty in a plaid wool shirt, bow tie, gray tweed coat and checkered hunting cap, but all of this elegant ensemble was slightly soiled from a solid week's wear. He led us over to our temporary quarters, while others conducted the families and the single women to theirs.

"Ours" turned out to be the basement of one of the two school buildings. We were ushered into a large room without furniture, its cement floor damp and dirty. There were naked bulbs hanging from the ceiling, and great wet splotches showing through the broken plaster on the walls. We were told that in the corridor were rush mats for us to sleep on, and that we ought to hang onto them since the beds we'd sent weren't likely to arrive for several weeks. Meanwhile, we were to wash up and in half an hour get our first meal at the kitchen run by earlier arrivals from Tsing-tao. By the following day we were to get our own Peking kitchen in operation, for it would have to feed the next batch of internees from Tientsin who were due in a couple of days.

We deposited our gear on the cold cement floor, and found mats, for our beds. Then some of us went out to look for the toilet and washroom. We were told they were about a hundred and fifty yards away: "Go down the left-hand street of the camp, and turn left at the water pump." So we set off, curiously peering on every side to see our new world.

After an open space in front of our building, we came to the many rows of small rooms that covered the camp except where the ballfield, the church, the hospital, and the school buildings were. Walking past these rows, we could see each family trying to get settled in its little room in somewhat the same disordered and cheerless way that we had done in ours. In contrast to the unhappy mutterings of miscellaneous bachelors, these rooms echoed to the distressed cries of babies and small children.

Then we came to a large hand pump under a small water tower. There we saw a husky, grinning British engineer, stripped to the waist even though the dusk was cold, furiously pumping water into the tower. As I watched him making his long, steady strokes, I suddenly realized what his presence at that pump meant. We ourselves would have to do all the work in this camp; our muscles and hands would have to lift water from wells, carry supplies in from the gates. We would have to cook the food and stoke the fires—here were neither servants nor machinery, no running water, no central heating. Before we passed on into the men's room, the British pumper, whose back was rising and falling rhythmically, fixed us as best he could in that situation with a cheerful and yet hostile eye, and reminded us with as much authority as his gasps would allow, "Every chap will be taking his full share of work here, chaps, you know!"

As we entered the door of the men's room, the stench that assailed our Western nostrils almost drove us back into the fresh March air. To our surprise, we found brand-new fixtures inside: Oriental-style toilets with porcelain bowls sunk in the floor over which we uncomfortably had to squat. Above them on the wall hung porcelain flushing boxes with long, metal pull-chains, but— the pipes from the water tower outside led only into the men's showers; not one was connected with the toilets. Those fancy pipes above us led nowhere. The toilet bowls were already filled to overflowing—with no servants, no plumbers, and very little running water anywhere in camp, it was hard to see how they would ever be unstopped. We stayed there just long enough to do our small business—all the while grateful we had not eaten the last thirty-four hours—and to wash our hands and faces in the ice-cold water that dribbled out of the faucets.

Back outside, we strolled around for our first real look at the compound. I was again struck by how small it was—about one hundred and fifty by two hundred yards. Even more striking was its wrecked condition. Before the war, it had housed a well-equipped American Presbyterian mission station, complete with a middle, or high, school of four or five large buildings, a hospital, a church, three kitchens, bakery ovens, and seemingly endless small rooms for resident students. We were told that, years before, Henry Luce had been born there. Although the buildings themselves had not been damaged, everything in them was a shambles, having been wrecked by heaven knows how many garrisons of Japanese and Chinese soldiers. The contents of the various buildings were strewn up and down the compound, cluttering every street and open space; metal of all sorts, radiators, old beds, bits of pipe and whatnot, and among them broken desks, benches, and chairs that had been in the classrooms and offices. Since our "dorm" was the basement of what had been the science building, on the way home we sifted through the remains of a chemistry lab. Two days later we carried our loot to the hospital to help them to get in operation.

The one redeeming feature of this dismal spectacle was that it provided invaluable articles for the kind of life we had now obviously to live. Old desks and benches could become washstands and tables in our bare quarters. Broken chairs could give us something to sit on besides the wet floors. Clearly the same thought had occurred to others; as we walked home, we saw in the dim light, dingy figures groping among the rubble and carting off "choice" bits and pieces. We made up our minds to get started on our own "scrounging" operations first thing in the morning before all this treasure was gone.

Soon after we got back to our room, we were led over to another part of the compound for supper. I saw stretching before me for some seventy yards a line of quiet, grim people standing patiently with bowls and spoons in their hands. Genuinely baffled, I asked our guide—a pleasant man from Tsingtao, with all the comfortable authority of one now quite acclimated to camp life—what on earth they were doing there.

"Oh, queuing up for supper, of course, old boy," said the Englishman cheerfully. "You'll get yours in about forty minutes, actually, if you join the queue now."

Could human patience bear such a long wait three times a day for meals? However, I joined the line, and three-quarters of an hour later, we reached the table where thin soup was being ladled out along with bread. That was supper. Fortunately, there were "seconds" on bread, because we were very hungry after our long train trip without food; I ate five to ten slices to help supplement the tasteless gruel.

Our meal finished, we lined up again to have our bowls and spoons washed by women from Tsingtao. The patterns of chores in the new situation were beginning to come clear. As I went out past the steam-filled kitchen with its great Chinese cauldrons, I saw three men from our Peking group being shown how to use the cooking equipment by the men from Tsingtao, turned into "experts" by their three days of practice. Despite that tasteless meal, I felt content; I was no end proud of my job in housing and looked forward to finding out more about this strange camp and how it worked.

When we walked back to our quarters, it was already getting very cold. The climate in North China is not unlike that of Chicago or Kansas City. Thus in March ice can still form at night, and unless one has dry clothes and some measure of heating, one can freeze. Needless to say, having neither, we felt chilled to the bone as we stamped about in our bare basement room. There was nothing to do but try to go to sleep. People must have some place to *sit* if there is to be a bull session of any sort! And so, still in our clothes, we lay down on our mats. Since each of us had only the things he had been able to bring with him, overcoats became extra blankets and sweaters were pillows. For long I lay there, trying unsuccessfully to find a soft spot in my cement mattress, but sheer fatigue finally overcome even that discomfort, and I fell asleep.

We awoke the next day to a cold drenching rain that had turned the compound into one great mud swamp. In the midst of this downpour, we new arrivals were once more called to the ballfield. Here we were again counted, sworn in, told to be good and, this time, ordered to surrender all our cash. Having been warned by the Tsingtao group that compliance with this order would be a completely unnecessary virtue, we kept back most of our cash, hidden in our shoes and our underwear.

After this, slopping in puddles, wet to the bone, angry but intensely curious, we were guided by a guard to our new "permanent" quarters. These were better by far than the wet basement room of the previous night, but still hardly ideal. In three small 9-by-12-foot rooms, dirty beyond description, we eleven bachelors were crammed into a space comfortable for only four or five people. There were the same bare walls and floors, only our suitcases to sit on and our straw mats to lie on—and no sign of any heating. It was messy, bleak, cold, and wet. Until our beds arrived two weeks later, every place in camp was like that.

The wonder is that flu or pneumonia did not decimate this vulnerable population. Fortunately, I was young and had warm clothes. It certainly never occurred to us to take anything off when we slept on the floor. Thus at the end of two or three days we looked just as bedraggled and unkempt as did the internees we had held in scorn upon our entry into camp.

This existence was of the greatest conceivable contrast to all that had gone before in my life, and the same was true for almost everyone there.

Brought up in the comfort of an upper-middle-class professional home at a large midwestern American university, where my father had been Dean of the Chapel, I had been waited on by maids at home and in the opulence of prewar Harvard College from which I graduated with an A.B. in 1940 just before coming to China to teach English at Yenching. In twenty-four years I had known little else than steam heat, running hot and cold water, a toilet in the next room, good food, clean clothing, plenty of space, and a quiet, academic existence. Only occasionally, when cruising or camping, had these comforts of civilization been absent. These periods, however, were short, voluntary, and such fun that they made no lasting imprint. Life to me, as to most of the camp, *was* civilization. Existence on any other terms was almost inconceivable. But at Weihsien all the vast interconnected services of civilization had vanished, and with them had gone every one of our creature comforts.

If this great crowd of people were to survive, much less to live a passable life, a civilization of some sort would have to be created from scratch. Gradually the nature of the problem facing our community dawned on me. As it did so, everything took on an intensity and excitement I had not known before. Thus for a healthy young man those first weeks of camp were an absorbing experience—physically no worse than army life in the field and yet much more interesting. However, for men and women in their late sixties and seventies in the single dorms, for the sick or the incapacitated, and above all, for the babies and children and their troubled mothers, those first weeks, with no heat and no beds, were a nightmare which I am sure none of them can recall to this day without shuddering.

II ✍ Learning to Live

When the last group arrived in camp about a week later, we numbered almost two thousand people. The implications of such a population figure staggered us, crowded as we were into an area hardly larger than a city block, and quite without visible means of caring for ourselves. What was worse, a closer look at the compound in which we found ourselves only increased the sense of anxiety for our survival. The equipment that was there upon our arrival was in such bad condition that it seemed an almost impossible task to get it started again.

With so many people living in such unsanitary conditions and eating dubious food at best, we expected a disaster in public health any day. The greatest need was for a working hospital. The doctors and the nurses among us grasped this at once, and so began the tremendous job of organizing a hospital more or less from scratch. Perhaps because the mission hospital building had contained the most valuable equipment, it was in a worse state than any of the others. The boilers, beds, and pipes had been ripped from their places and thrown about everywhere. The operating table and the dental chair were finally found at the bottom of a heap at the side of the building. None of the other machinery or surgical equipment was left intact. Under these conditions, considering that there was as yet no organization of labor in the camp, it is astounding that these medics and their volunteers were able to do what they did. Inside of eight days they had the hospital cleaned up and functioning so as to feed and care for patients. In two more days they had achieved a working laboratory. At the end of ten days they were operating with success, and even delivering babies. This was, however, not quite quick enough to save a life. Four days after the last group arrived, a member of the jazz band from Tientsin had an acute attack of appendicitis. Since the hospital was not yet ready for an operation, he was sent to Tsingtao six hours away by train, but unfortunately he died on the way.

Another serious matter was the simple problem of going to the toilet. For a population of about two thousand, there was at first only one latrine for women and three for men—the Japanese had expected a great preponderance of men over women. In each of these latrines there were only five or six toilets, none of them flush toilets. Needless to say, the queues for this unavoidable aspect of life were endless. When the poor internee finally reached his goal after a long and nervous wait in line, he found the toilet so overflowing that often he felt sick and to his despair had to leave unrequited. I recall clearly my relief that a providential case of constipation during the first ten days of camp saved me from having to test the strength of my stomach.

The sole contact the average urban Western man has with human excrement consists of a curious look at what he has produced, a swirl of water, and a refreshing bar of soap. Consequently the thought of wading into a pool of his fellow man's excrement in order to clean up a public john not equipped with flush toilets is literally inconceivable. And so the situation grew progressively worse. It would have continued so had not some Catholic priests and nuns, aided by a few of the Protestant missionaries, tied cloths around their faces, borrowed boots and mops, and tackled this horrendous job.

This doughty crew stayed with it until some of the camp engineers, taking hold in a professional way, freed us all from this daily horror. After huddling long hours over this emergency— unrehearsed at M.I.T. or the Royal College for Engineers—they devised a means of hand-flushing the toilets after each use with a half bucket of water.

But of all the basic needs of life whose resolution had to be organized, the most vital and difficult was the problem of eating. The camp had to keep right on feeding itself while it was learning to do so. In the area of health and sanitation we had trained personnel in the camp, but practically none of our two thousand people knew much about quantity cooking in cauldrons for six or seven hundred, or baking in coal ovens for two thousand. Legend has it that a restaurant owner from Tsingtao taught the raw volunteers in their kitchen how to make soups and stews, and that in our Peking group's kitchen, an ex-marine cook introduced our workers to the finer mysteries of the culinary art. Our food those first two weeks certainly substantiated the latter story!

Meanwhile, the bakery was also struggling to get underway. For the first week we were provided with bread baked in Tsingtao. Since this supply was to stop on a set date, our own bakery operation had to be organized in a hurry, for bread was the only solid food in our life. Our population, luckily, happened to include two aged Persian bakeshop owners from Tientsin. These men spent forty-eight hours straight training two shifts of green recruits to mix, knead, and bake the four hundred daily loaves necessary to feed everyone. Within another week, these amateur bakers had mastered the essentials of their craft. Thereafter, while the good yeast lasted, our camp bakery turned out what we all proudly assumed to be the best bread in China.

Thus it was with all the labor in the camp during those first days. Jobs which had to be done were at first taken in hand by experienced people who alone knew how to handle them, and therefore alone saw the real need. Later, when work was organized and every able person was assigned a task, inexperienced people were trained in the new crafts. Thus bank clerks, professors, salesmen, missionaries, importers, and executives became bakers, stokers, cooks, carpenters, masons, and hospital orderlies. There was also a great deal of heavy unskilled work such as lugging supplies from the gates to the utilities and cleaning up the compound. Work of this sort, while largely voluntary at first, was soon organized so that in a short while everyone had a set job with a routine and regular hours. With such a thoroughgoing organizational plan, the most vital material needs of these two thousand people soon began to be met. The first rude form of our camp's civilization started to appear.

For about the first six months, this sudden dive into the world of manual labor was for the majority of us perhaps the most valuable experience. All manual labor in China, skilled and unskilled, was done by Chinese. Therefore the foreign population in that land included no "working force." The majority of internees were either men accustomed to executive work in offices or women used to the help of innumerable Chinese servants around the house. To be forced to do hard physical labor, often outdoors, was a new experience. We all discovered what it was like to be worn out from work with our muscles and to return black and grimy, our clothing ripped and torn, from a day of hard labor.

In many ways, of course, this regime was good for all concerned, especially for those—and they were many—who had spent the last decade imbibing too many highballs on the club porch. Men with too much fat and sagging jowls soon found themselves lean again, tanned and hardened. At the other end of the scale, a derelict such as Briggs the junkie, lost his green color, put on weight and muscle, and looked a fine figure when he left camp in the repatriation of some Americans in August, 1943. Suddenly we had all become equally workers of the world, and although many of us were not apt to admit it then, most of us enjoyed it. As a Peking student, now a prominent professor of Chinese studies at Yale, said to me, "At least from now on I won't have to wince every time I carry my suitcases in the station!"

A word should be said about how we were housed, although I shall tell about this in greater detail in another chapter. Ironically enough, the spacious houses previously reserved for the foreign missionary staff in a walled-off section of the compound were now "out of bounds" to the Western internees; these were earmarked as the residences of our Oriental captors. The mission compound had, however, possessed three or four classroom buildings and innumerable rows of small rooms for the Chinese students of its boarding school. Here we lived. Families, which made up the bulk of our population, were housed in the 9-by-12-foot rooms; single men and women lived dormitory style in the classrooms and offices of the school buildings.

Since the camp was hopelessly overpopulated for its space, and since the Japanese had made the original housing arrangements hurriedly, our first quarters were nearly impossible. In some of the dorms, men were jammed so closely together that they could hardly turn around. In even the best situation, every one of us in a dorm had only 18 inches between his bed and those on either side, and 3 feet at the end of his bed in which to keep all that he owned. In that little world, 9 feet by 54 inches, each single person had to keep intact all his possessions, and at the same time somehow to maintain his own personal being.

The problem of where to put everything was vexing but seldom insoluble. The cramped space meant that each person

kept his clothes in suitcases under his bed, hauling them out
every time he wanted to change his socks or his shirt. His larger
and more precious belongings he usually put in his one trunk. If
he could, he kept everything else that he owned in a massive
edifice of shelves that rose to precarious heights on the wall above
his head. Beds, like their owners, came in all shapes and sizes:
some majestic and high, some low and cot like. A fellow named
Sas Sloan in our last dorm (we moved three times) had a double
bed despite the Japanese orders. As he told them, it was the only
one he owned; and as he told us, it meant that come what may,
he could have at least that much space to himself. The most
clairvoyant internees had crated their beds before they sent them
down, and so had a ready-made clothes closet or large shelf case
when they stood their crates on end. Add to this the essential
mosquito netting strung in summer high over each bed from four
poles at the corners, and the water-filled tin cans that each bed
leg was carefully placed in to keep out the voracious bedbugs,
and the result was a picturesque sight that greeted any visitor to
the larger men's dorms. Around the walls, beds of all description rocked like full-rigged sailing ships at anchor, and towering
above each one of them, like temples perched on a cliff, rose the
precious tiers of shelves.

Most difficult of all for the dorm resident of the single men's or
women's dorms was the problem of preserving any sense of
personal identity in a society of almost total strangers. While
some were in their teens and twenties, most were in middle
life—from forty to sixty-five; many were even older. The great
majority of these dorm dwellers were middle-class persons accustomed to years of privacy and comfort, and so possessed of
ingrained living habits.

Now suddenly each one found himself or herself thrown into a
large room with strangers, most of whom came from radically
divergent segments of society. For such a single person there was
no hole into which he could crawl, no way to protect his privacy.
Spiritually, and often physically, naked before twenty dorm
mates, he had to live out the most private moments of his life
surrounded by an alien and often prying world. And what was
worse, he or she had to keep trying to adjust his own habits to
the very different ones of his neighbors. To take the most earthy
kind of example: the not unrare need to use a chamber pot at
night within eighteen inches of your next neighbor and within
nine feet of at least six other men, or women, was by no means

easy either on the perpetrator or on those who lay there listening. The adjustment to these trials, not for a week or a month but for years, made tremendous demands on the patience and the nerves of the single people in the dorms. Even if one did not come to hate the people eighteen inches away from his private domain, the loneliness suffered by older persons crowded among diverse strangers and yet isolated from them, was almost worse than their potential enmity.

I recall, for example, as a member of the Quarters Committee, being called in to pacify a dorm of twenty-one single women about a month after camp began.

When I got there the fight was just over. Two groups were huddled at opposite ends of what had been an old classroom, each clustered around their champion and glaring hostilely at the enemy across the dorm. The woman who had greeted me at the door told me that one of them, a missionary from the Iowa farmlands, had roundly bested a rather chic British secretary. The two women were still panting; red, hot, mad, very much ashamed, and each a trifle wounded; they seemed not to know whether to fight, to cry, to apologize—or, as they would both have preferred at the moment, just quietly to die. Somewhat awestruck, I asked what it was all about, and was immediately set upon by ambassadors from each of the groups.

"Those ruddy missionaries," said the representative of the secretaries, "insisted not only on praying aloud at night, but on singing hymns when they awoke each morning, God help them, at six A.M.! We finally got damn well tired of this nonsense, and *that* is the cause of the fight."

"You know perfectly well it isn't," said an outraged British missionary woman. "*They* insisted on chattering endlessly at night in loud whispers when we were trying to sleep, as any normal woman should have been. And not only talking, but talking about all the lurid escapades in their pasts—half of which I'm sure were imagined! [Swipes like that last one, I thought to myself, have not helped the situation!] And *that* started the fight!"

Quite unable to think of anything useful to say in this maelstrom of intense feelings, I looked around the room for some neutrals who might lend me some support. Over against another wall were four women who did not fit either the "capable business secretary" label or that of the pious missionary. Looking closer I recognized two of them as White Russian nightclub

singers a Tientsin friend had pointed out to me a day or so
earlier. The other two, I learned later, were rather well-known
ladies-about-town. Wondering to myself how on earth three such
diverse groups could ever get along inside the same four walls, I
muttered something about the committee taking this matter
under advisement, and fled. We partially solved the problem a
week later by moving the most vociferous of the hymn singers
into a predominantly missionary dorm.

In still another dorm, where the women were more homo-
geneous, I was called in to mark off in chalk on the floor the
exact space belonging to each resident. Their reason: territorial
aggression was occurring! Apparently someone had been moving
trunks and shoving beds an inch at a time, perhaps at night when
the rest were asleep or when the dorm was empty. In any event,
several women eventually realized they had lost some six of their
rightful eighteen inches. Finally one of them had taken a bead
on a line from her bed across her trunk to the window and
thence to a tree outside. When this line was breached one night,
she and four angry mates stormed into our office demanding the
return of their rightful territory. My markings on the floor held
the boundaries firm for about a month. At that time I had to
rechalk them—such was the hostile pressure. For a middle-aged,
unmarried woman to live in such an atmosphere compounded of
loneliness and hostility was as close to hell on earth as I could
imagine. The families in the camp were at least fortunate in that
they lived surrounded by some semblance of affection and concern, whatever their other troubles.

During the first month of camp, explosions occurred continually in the women's dorms. In some cases, single rooms had to be
found for the most difficult individuals, which was indeed unfair,
since everyone in dorms yearned for such privacy. But no one
could live with these two or three temperamental ones, and it
solved none of our housing problems to put an easygoing person
in a room alone. In general, however, the human ability to
adjust is beyond belief. By the end of six months, nearly everyone in the camp had learned to live with almost anybody, and
generally speaking existence in the dorms became in some way
tolerable for all.

Often in those first months we in the quarters office puzzled
about why the explosions were always generated in female rather
than male dorms. Certainly the men complained as much, they
disliked one another as much, and were, if anything, less saintly

than the women. But there never occurred among them this sort of personal conflict, this stark inability to get along with another person or kind of person. Eventually, we concluded that at least two factors were at work here: First, in an objective, impersonal situation, such as a dorm, men feel more at home. Women, many of whom are made very nervous when their most basic relations with people are not organically close and personal, do not adjust so well to this objective environment. Consequently, men are likely to accept and even enjoy any large, male society such as a team, an army, or a dorm, more than women do a similar female society.

Second, it seemed evident that when two men disliked each other, as they often did, they tended to let one another alone. Perhaps this may be because with men the stakes are higher—if they needle an adversary, blows will be sure to follow. This is not the case with women—at least middle-class women. Thus to avoid continual and fruitless warfare, men in conflict in our dorms simply ignored each other. Like ships passing in the night, such men by tacit agreement moved through their lives in close proximity, each unaware of the existence of the other, as if they did not inhabit the same world. By contrast, hostile women could never refrain from continually needling and poking at each other, striking with sarcasm, innuendo, or even just with withering looks. At last one or the other would be unable to bear it longer, and would collapse into hysterics.

At the beginning, the camp gave the impression of an immense crowd of utter strangers. Certain uniquely interesting people, such as the three or four pretty girls who had caught my eye the first day, would stick in the memory. But most of the people I saw seemed no more than parts of an inchoate mass. Gradually, however, over the weeks, these people took on character. In such a small space, in two or three days' time one passed by everyone, and so the unfamiliar became familiar. In a few months, we came to know who everyone was and where he had come from.

It became evident that the whole anti-Axis population of North China, with the exception, of course, of the Chinese themselves, was here. It was as if a great dragnet had swept across the treaty ports of China—those coastal cities where concentrations of Europeans had long resided for commercial purposes and which, since at least World War I, had been ruled by British authorities, British law, and British police. This dragnet in 1943 scooped up all the rich variety of Western humanity that these cities then held—and dumped them in Weihsien camp. If the very sick stayed behind for a bit, when they got well, they came too.

Westerners had been coming to the Orient since, roughly, 1800. They came for every conceivable reason and in every conceivable role: as merchants, evangelists, teachers, tourists, adventurers; as members of an army corps, of an entertainment troupe, of an athletic team. Many of them came to escape something—revolution, bankruptcy, scandal, the police—and to disappear. This total conglomeration, chosen solely on the basis that they were there at the moment in time when Japan attacked Pearl Harbor, constituted the camp population.

We were, in the words of the Britisher, "a ruddy mixed bag." We were almost equally divided in numbers between men and women. We had roughly four hundred who were over sixty years of age, and another four hundred under fifteen. Our oldest citizen, so I discovered, was in his middle nineties; our youngest was the latest baby born in the camp hospital.

We were equally diverse in our national and racial origins. At the start of camp, our population comprised about 800 Britons, 600 Americans, 250 Netherlanders and 250 Belgians (the major portion of the last two groups were Roman Catholic clerics of various sorts). In late August, 1943, however, six months after camp began, about two hundred Americans were repatriated on the Swedish ship *Gripsholm* via Goa in Portugese India. Two weeks later the majority of the Catholic clergy departed as well.

The cosmopolitan character of the camp was still maintained, however. After these departures, and a large British contingent from Cheefoo had arrived, we were 1,490 persons, made up mainly of British (1,000) and Americans (200). Then, in December, 1943, to our great surprise, about one hundred Italians from Shanghai joined us, and were placed in a separate compound. Interspersed throughout were eight Belgian and two Dutch families, four Parsee families, two Cuban families—they had made up a touring jai alai team—a Negro and Hawaiian jazz band, a few Palestinian Jews, an Indian translator and interpreter, and about sixty White Russian women and their children. Most of these women were there because they had married British or American men. Among the British population were many Eurasians, since everyone born in Tientsin was automatically able to receive a British passport if he wished to identify himself with that community.

The most obvious diversity lay in the differences in the social status which each of us had enjoyed in the outside world. As we could see from the first moment, our group ranged up and down the entire social ladder. Our members included some from the well-to-do leaders of Asia's colonial business world and the genteel products of English "public school" life. More were from the Anglo-Saxon middle classes (represented by small-business men, customs officials, engineers, exporters, lawyers, doctors, and shopkeepers), and not a few from among the dopers, barflies, and raffish characters of the port cities. Mingling with this secular *pot pourri* were some four hundred Protestant missionaries. They embraced almost all denominations, theologies, and ways of life. Also, for the first six months, there were the four hundred Roman priests, monks, and nuns.

In taking the camp census for the Quarters Committee, I found, for example, in one row of eight 9-by-12 rooms the following divergent backgrounds. In Room 1, a rough volatile Russian woman and her daughter (she was a widow of a British soldier and so had British papers). In Room 2, the wealthy vice-president of a British mining company, who was slow of wit, honest, and hard-working; also his attractive red-haired wife and their two small children. Room 3 held a Mrs. Johnson and her three children. She was half Portuguese and half Chinese, barely able to speak English. She had married an American army man, and had tried to manage for her children after he abandoned her long before in Tientsin. She told me that the 9-by-12 room in which the four of them lived was the best she'd had since her husband's disappearance. In Room 4 was a well-to-do, elegant, retired British couple with a hyphenated name, the W. T. Roxby-Joneses. He was a wonderful man and cut an extraordinary figure. A kind of tattered and aging William Powell sporting a White Guard's mustache, he was suave, urbane, humorous, cool-headed, and yet very warm. He was also a capable artist and, when he was not on duty managing the bakery, taught painting classes to all of us who were interested. Rooms 5 and 6 contained an orthodox but completely lovable Australian Salvation Army Colonel, his round wife, and their three bright children. In Room 7 was another British business family of four in one room. And finally at the end of the row was an American, formerly of the 15th Infantry, a very tough and bitter character—though a

LEARNING TO LIVE 23

very good softball player—and his rather sullen, slatternly but probably once sensual Russian wife.

In Row No. 47, where some of the single men were first housed, the following trios of bachelors were crowded next to each other in 9-by-12 rooms. In the first were three Britishers in their forties, one a vice-president of a Tientsin bank, another the Lloyd's insurance representative, the third a shipping executive. In the next room came the ballplayer, Karl Bauer, an American dentist, and our friend Briggs the sea-green junkie. Beyond them was Jacob Strauss, the immensely wealthy head of the largest British mining company. Strauss had left two Rolls-Royces and several mansions in Tientsin, and was living in one room with two aging bankers. Next came two jazz musicians (a Polynesian and a negro) housed with a Belgian dope addict; and beyond them were a British banker, an engineer, and the China head of the Asiatic Petroleum Company—and so on down the line for twenty rooms more. It seemed almost as if a ruthless but whimsical fate had sought to bring the mighty of the treaty ports low and to mingle them with those of lesser degree. No one's social ideas could remain the same after living there. All the social grooves of the outside world were here rudely flattened out. People who would have had no contact in normal life found themselves thrown together under conditions of extreme intimacy.

What was revealed there defied the validity of our usual social judgments. The ordinarily accepted symbols of status—money, family, education, sophistication—were totally irrelevant here. Neither blue blood nor advanced education could raise a man above his neighbor. No one had any cash to speak of—nor more than a minimal use for what he did have; money could not buy any fundamental changes in our status.

Since no one could buy new clothes, since everyone had to do his own laundry, and do it with little water and less soap—how I hated that chore—after a few months every tweed looked threadbare, every shirt was equally tattered and dirty. All trousers looked alike, unpressed and baggy. There were some men with girl friends who laundered their shirts and hand-pressed their army shorts. These had an edge over the rest—but such romantic aids knew neither class lines nor old school ties. Everyone was entitled to the same basic rations and the same amount of living space. And above all, everyone was required to do the same sort of work, according to his physical abilities. If a British banker and a Eurasian waiter were weak and sickly, both washed vegetables or were cutters of bread. If an American professor and a cockney were sturdy and able, both had to bake or stoke.

In such a situation, the more basic human virtues suddenly claimed their rightful place. A man's excellence was revealed by his willingness to work, his skill at his job, his fundamental cheerfulness. On a kitchen shift or kneading dough in the bakery, any sane man would rather have next to him an efficient hard worker who could laugh and be warmly tolerant of his fellows, than to have there the most wealthy and sophisticated slacker or grumbler. After working or living beside a man for months, who cared—or even remembered—whether he was Belgian, British, or Parsee? Thus in a very short time people became to us personalities, pleasant or unpleasant, hard working or lazy, rather than the British, Eurasians, or Americans that they were when we first met them.

The three hardest-working and most valuable men in our kitchen were two ex-British seamen—one from a Yorkshire farm and the other a cockney—and an American tobacco-leaf expert raised on a North Carolina farm and, as he used to say of himself, "barely able to read the funnies." Correspondingly, the laziest man on my cooking shift was an executive from a shipping company with "fine blood" and a privileged education. Bored with everything about his life in camp, he was neither cooperative nor charming and so of little use to anyone. Perhaps the greatest value of this experience, as of almost all war experiences, was that we worked our way through the false barriers of the world at large to reach our common humanity. In time, we were able to see our neighbors for what they were rather than for what they had.

At this point, then, we were an uncoordinate mass of humanity. We had to tackle together certain basic problems if we were merely to survive. Such a community, therefore, needed organized leadership as much as it needed anything. But the finding of leaders constitutes the first act of the drama of politics. During our stay there, this problem of politics, of our own self-government and self-direction, remained to me the most subtle, the most frustrating and baffling issue we had to face. It was also the most fascinating, as I discovered very early.

The initial meeting of the "leaders," held that first night we arrived, took place in a large room in the old school building reserved for administrative offices. When Montague and I arrived together, the room was filled with important looking strangers. Most of them seemed to be British businessmen, with some Americans thrown in. There was a scattering of missionaries, and in one corner a small contingent of Catholic priests. Partly by surmise, partly by asking, I found that they were, like ourselves, the temporary representatives of what were clearly the four main groups of the camp: Tientsin, Tsingtao, the Catholics, and the newly arrived Peking contingents. Probably picked hastily and arbitrarily much the way we were, these men represented the informal leadership that had been established in each city before coming to camp. And as each of them sensed, if anybody was to solve these early problems of the camp, it must be these representatives. Hence immediately they agreed to meet there every night in order to plan an organized attack on our difficulties, and to ask the Japanese rulers of the camp to come in to discuss with them whatever needed to be done.

My first sight of how men behave in relation to power came in those sessions when our political structure was being born. What became apparent at once to my fascinated gaze was the serious way in which these Titans of North China's business world began jockeying among themselves for leadership.

With the exception of the priests and a few of us who sat in the back rows, most of those in that large room represented some large European, British, or American business in China fully as much as he did his group in camp. These men were "Stone of Standard Oil," "Robinson of National City," "Jameson of British and American Tobacco," "Campbell of Butterfield and Swire," "Brewster of Lloyd's," "Johns of the Kailon Mining Company," and so on.

In the course of these early stages, each saw himself and the others in terms of the image created by the power of his company, and by the prestige of his own role in that business. Each brought with him, therefore, not only long habits of personal authority, but the expectation—indeed the need—to exercise the same dominating role here that he enjoyed in the treaty ports. As a professor needs recognition when he delivers a paper, or a minister needs gratitude when he has preached a sermon, so these men needed authority—even if realistically it was the paltry power of an official position among a gang of internees in the hinterland of China.

This struggle for leadership made itself evident in many subtle ways. Ostensibly, when each man spoke in those informal meetings, he was concerned that the problem under discussion—whether sanitation, food, or leaky roofs—be solved, and he would carefully address himself to that problem. But it was evident from his tone of voice, his manner, the emphasis of his speech, and above all from the way he handled the alternative suggestions of others, that he was also anxious that his be the germinating mind that provided the resolution, and that his be the voice that ended the discussion.

This struggle for the authoritative voice, for the dominance which others not only respect but give way to in will and opinion, was both evident and fascinating because prior to these meetings no one had such authority. It all had to be generated right then and there and, so to speak, out of the sole materials of human will and brains. There was no camp chairman, no government, not even a chairman of the meeting; all such posts of authority were still "up for grabs." Nor were there any of the outward supports and symbols of personal authority: transparent wealth, support of powerful groups and forces—or guns. The only external authority possessed by anyone was that steadily fading aura of the prestige he had once enjoyed in the world outside. Whatever dominance a man achieved in that group, he gained through inherent personal capacity for power. Such capacity is composed of those intangible but basic qualities that cause the outward signs and symbols of authority to gravitate to and remain with a particular man. These qualities are the ability to think quickly and relevantly, the crucial force of great self-confidence and iron firmness of will, and boundless personal energy. The man who had these inherent qualities, like the man with a rapier among those armed only with clubs, could in a short time stand alone over his fellows.

To those of us who watched this developing political struggle, it was soon evident that by the end of the first week these intangibles had done their work; the men with rapiers were already victorious. The character of the discussions had gradually changed. At the beginning any one of the twenty or so men in the room might have felt he could compete on an equal footing with any other man and, if he thought it prudent, challenge the opinion of even the most potent. This was soon no longer the case.

A hierarchy of power had appeared as a few men attained a subtle but real dominance. Now, before committing themselves

to an opinion, most of the twenty waited to hear what these few
would say; and when these men had made their statements or
suggestions, the others would quickly fall into line. At this point,
only the great dared challenge the great; the rest had given up
the fight. They would rather now be secure on the side of the
winner than reach for the glory of power, only to find themselves
defeated, isolated, and humiliated. So, without any external
force, even without a hint of a ballot, but only by the quiet
processes of self-elimination, the list of contenders had been
reduced to two or three giants who were still able to contend for
the role of Caesar.

In these nightly meetings I also recognized for the first time the
unique character and value of the business mind. The core of its
strength was what I might call the "mentality of decision." One or
two of these men seated around the table had taken part in
academic discussion groups in Peking. There we pondered such
abstract issues as peace, international justice, and the relations of
ethics or theology to the world of affairs. I had noted then how
strangely silent, though observant, polite, and respectful, these
men had been. By contrast, we academicians had fairly flowed
with verbiage. And as hour after hour went by with no comment
from these business types, I thought to myself in some disappointment and not a little disdain, "nice, responsible men, but
hardly bright—surely not able to think."

Here, however, all was different. The minds of these men,
accustomed to practical problems, which called for both know-
how and decisiveness, clamped onto our situation and dealt with
it creatively. What was needed here were concrete answers to
technical and organizational problems. Here general principles
and ultimate ends—their interrelations and connections with
life—could not have been more irrelevant. To be facile in the
area of abstractions or of general truths was of no help when the
oven walls were cracked, when the yeast wouldn't raise the bread
dough, when slightly smelly meat was delivered in hot weather.
Now it was the professional mentality that was proving useless,
and the academic voices that were strangely silent. I could see the
concrete need only after they had pointed it out to the Japanese;
I could recognize the neatness of their solution only after they
had explained it to us.

These political and organizational sessions continued for
about ten days after our arrival. Then, one evening, a Japanese
interrupted our meeting. To everyone's surprise, he announced

that committees to represent the whole camp must be formed within forty-eight hours. There were, he said, to be nine such committees, and he listed them: General Affairs, Discipline, Labor, Education, Supplies, Quarters, Medicine, Engineering, and Finance.

A Japanese would be in charge of each of these departments of camp life; under him would work one internee who would be the chairman of the committee concerned. The internal governing body of the camp, he continued, was to consist of a council of the nine chairmen of these committees. This council, as a body, would represent the camp to the ruling Japanese authorities. For their own reasons, the Japanese did not wish to have to deal with one powerful man in whom could be embodied the will of the camp. At the time we resented this idea as being against our interests. We wanted a strong leader to represent our needs to the Japanese. But long before the end of our sojourn, most of us agreed that the Japanese had been quite right, although for different reasons. No one among us was big enough for that enormous job.

This Japanese order, abruptly laid down without further discussion, tossed into our laps a ticklish political problem: How could the nine-man council be chosen?

An election by the whole camp was out of the question. In the first place, such a complex matter as a democratic election could never be organized within forty-eight hours. Next, the ordinary voter could not at this point have any idea for whom or for what he was voting. Almost no one was as yet known to more than a few of his intimates; and little about the projected political structure would be understood by anyone outside that room.

It was decided that initially, at least, this ruling committee would be formed by appointment. The method was to be as follows: the present informal leaders of each of the four groups (Peking, Tientsin, Tsingtao, Catholic) should nominate a slate of nine men from their outfits—one for each of the nine committees. Each sector of the camp would thus be represented on each committee, the several committees to consist of these four men, one from each group. For example, I was the man chosen by the Peking leaders to be on the Quarters Committee, and so I would presumably join the representatives from Tientsin, Tsingtao, and the Catholics. Then, each of these committees would meet together the next evening to choose one from among the four to be chairman, to sit on the council of nine, and to represent the entire camp to the Japanese in all matters under his jurisdiction. This was a roundabout method at best, but it seemed to make sense considering the situation.

The next night we all met to pick our leaders, and a strange sort of session it was. I felt fairly excited, for I knew that if there had been political pulling and hauling, attack and defense, before in our ordinary sessions, it would be doubled now. The political prizes had now been clarified; and they had been increased in number. The result was that many would-be leaders who had given up the fight to be Caesar could now return to the lists in competition for lesser spots on the ruling council.

As the rest of the men arrived in the committee room, I realized that many new faces had been added to the original twenty or so. Consequently most of us were probably unknown to each other. Then I found myself sent to a corner of the room designated "Quarters," to which three others had been dispatched, a Britisher from Tsingtao, another from Tientsin, and an American Catholic priest. We eyed one another warily for a moment; then we all laughed sheepishly over the fact that we four strangers were to pick from among ourselves a chairman for the camp Quarters Committee.

The first move was made by the priest. He was a quiet, pale, bland, but quite firm American professor of philosophy. He spoke easily but with precise formality.

"It has been settled authoritatively and finally by our presiding bishop that we of the Catholic clergy are not to take any ruling or leading roles in the camp; rather we are to leave the political direction of things entirely in secular or lay hands. Thus, by order as well as preference, I remove myself at once from competition for this post—although I shall be glad to cooperate with the committee in all matters relevant to the housing of our priests and nuns. Thank you."

Thus was exorcized the brief but unreal specter of Catholic rule among us.

I was about to make the same sort of statement, pleading youth and inexperience, when the lively looking Britisher from Tientsin began speaking. He had introduced himself as Shields, "Far East Shipping, you know." He was a handsome man with a small, neat mustache, sprucely dressed for an internee in a tweed jacket and ascot, with matching silk handkerchief in his breast pocket. He had a pleasant, frequent smile and intelligent, alert eyes. But the way in which his remarks seemed to beat one to the gun could signal a lot of ambition—or at least so I thought as I looked at him.

"That seems to me a very wise move on the part of you fathers," he remarked briskly, "I want you to convey to your bishop for me my personal appreciation for it."

He then turned to me, obviously expecting my similar withdrawal from competition. I did not disappoint him, which left the two Britishers to work it out between themselves. At this, the alert Shields grabbed the ball again, and turning to the other Britisher, he asked, "And what sort of experience have *you* had in this kind of work? Robbins—did you say your name was?"

The moment I looked carefully at the man from Tsingtao I realized somewhat sadly that this would be no contest. A genial, portly, middle-aged Englishman, comfortable with his pipe and heavy tweeds, with a round, fleshy, kind face and heavy-rimmed glasses, he was obviously no match for the aggressive Shields.

"Yes, my name is Robbins," he said modestly, "and I'm just an engineer from Tsingtao. I can't say I've had too much experience in housing people—for that has never been my line. I certainly don't want to shirk and will be glad to cooperate with any chap, but actually I can't lay claim to any particular qualifications for this job, you know."

We all turned back to Shields, expecting out of deference for the formalities, if nothing else, much the same modest disclaimer —at least in the first round.

Things had developed so well for him, however, that Shields was not interested in form; he struck while we were all off balance.

"As a matter of fact, chaps," he said, "I happen to have had a good deal of firsthand experience in Tientsin—head of quarters there, you know—and so I'm not altogether ignorant of the sort of problems we'll run into. Actually, in my business I've had to deal quite often with top Japanese, invaluable experience for this sort of job, you know. Also I do speak rather passable Chinese. [Later I found even I could speak the language better than he.] Therefore chaps, since none of you seems to feel like doing this, I suggest that I be appointed, shall we say, temporary chairman. Then when we all get to know one another better, we can choose a permanent one."

We were hardly in a position, since we had all backed out of the door, to prevent his locking it from the inside. So we weakly assented to his proposal, and presto—our chairman had been chosen!

This small political gust over the chairmanship of the Quarters Committee increased into gale force among the four nominees for the General Affairs Committee, considered by all to be the central directing agency of camp life. Ever since we had arrived, the question "Who will run the camp?" had been bruited back and forth by politically minded internees. All the serious candidates for local Caesar had been nominated for the General Affairs Committee: Montague, the British American Tobacco man from Peking; the reigning bishop of the Catholics; Harrison, the leading importer from Tsingtao; and finally Chesterton from Tientsin, the solemn British chairman of the massive Kailon Mining Company. Already everyone knew the real battle would be between Montague and Chesterton, representing as they did the significant social and commercial forces in camp life: American vs. British, Peking vs. Tientsin, tobacco vs. mining. Both men, as had become obvious in our nightly sessions, had the capacities needed for power, however different they were in character.

As I have already hinted, Montague was the American extrovert. Round of face and body but handsome, always clad in a polo coat, he looked among us like a refugee from a country club. He was cheerful, friendly, immensely talkative, quick in repartee, and full of lively stories. He was seldom unkind, never arrogant, and always the embodiment of charm itself—but like most of us, he was never averse to accepting the best room or the favored treatment his importance deserved.

I remember seeing his stout form running down a street the day we were being housed by the Japanese. Out of curiosity as to whither he was bound, I followed. Soon I saw him grab a slight, elegant gentleman by the elbow. Immediately I recognized Dr. Charles Foster, the immensely respected and modest American surgeon. Montague propelled that puzzled but ever dignified gentleman at great speed over to a marvelously private room for two that Montague had just spied. When the Japanese arrived a moment later, Montague assured them that "the overburdened doctor must have quiet and privacy, and has asked me to join him in here." I think he really believed it himself when he said it. But Montague was, more than most of us, lovable as well as sharp, and I never doubted that his heart was in the right place. Certainly he was more than usually intelligent as well as decisive, and when pressed had a very strong sense of responsibility to his community.

Chesterton was as different from Montague as night from day.

A small, thin man with an immensely ugly and sad face, he was as deliberate, both in physical movement and in speech, as Montague was fast. In our meetings, when Montague spoke, he would have the whole room in gales of laughter through his sparkling wit. Chesterton would sit there glumly silent until he was ready to pronounce. Finally, when he did speak, his surprisingly deep voice came out so slowly he was inclined to make me feel impatient and bored in the waits between the carefully deliberated words. And yet, there was no question of his inherent power. Except in those instances when Montague disagreed with him, the men seemed instinctively to follow Chesterton's lead. I observed that the discussion of any subject almost always terminated after one of Chesterton's authoritative pronouncements.

These two very diverse men were evidently those most liberally supplied with whatever it is that produces personal power and the leadership that is its consequence. It was they who gradually came completely to dominate our sessions. Which of the two would ultimately become the more potent figure was endlessly debated among us. Thus, although all of us in that room were immersed in our own little dramas, each of us would look regularly over to the corner where the tussle for General Affairs was proceeding to see who would, in the end, be Caesar.

It turned out to be the sad-faced Englishman who arose and called the meeting to order. Speaking in his leaden-paced drawl, Chesterton announced his own "chairmanship of the internment center," and then apparently felt he must say a few further words on the attitude he intended to manifest as our leader.

"Colleagues in leadership," he began, "I wish to impress upon you how honored and touched I am to be designated for this significant work. I realize that now responsibility for the health and well-being, not to say the lives, of ourselves and our loved ones rests directly upon my shoulders. I shall not disappoint your expectations and hopes; I have shouldered heavy burdens before, and am happy to bear this load for you. And I promise that whatever the temptations that beset a man in high office, I shall rule the camp in strict accordance with our great British tradition of justice and fair play!"

The room rang with muffled "Hear, hears!" as on this solemn (and carefully prepared!) note, our political life began.

As an admirer of Montague's unique abilities to get whatever he wanted in almost any situation, and somewhat shaken by the heavy pomposity of the acceptance oration, I could only conclude as I left that night, that Montague had decided to let Chesterton become top dog because of the preponderance of British in the camp—but of that I will never be sure.

The next morning the first real joke of camp life broke.

When the names were handed in and the Japanese explained further what the duties of each committee would be, it became plain that the General Affairs Committee, far from being the coordinating center for general camp policy, was merely to be caretaker of certain leftover items. As the astonished Japanese said, "This man is not to be 'boss'! He is to rule over such things as sports, the sewing room, the barber shop, the library, and the canteen!"

Poor Chesterton had been wrecked on a semantic reef: "Miscellaneous Affairs" had been mistranslated "General Affairs."

When this coveted prize, over which our giants had fought, turned out to be miniscule, the camp hooted with derisive delight. Chesterton, the victor, was not merely embarrassed but downright sulky about it. He promptly announced his resignation, indicating that now that he understood what the job involved, he saw that it was too small for a man of his stature. At this the camp hooted once more; Chesterton never acquired political prominence again. Needless to say, Montague, holding his sides and weak from laughter, thanked his lucky stars that he had not been tapped for the honor!

Thenceforth the General Affairs Committee was run by another Britisher, a modest, younger vice president of one of the Tientsin banks. The vision of a single political leader of the camp vanished never to appear again.

In this bumbling way, the official camp organization was formed. From that time on, there were nine internee committees, each with a chairman and one or two assistants who negotiated directly with the Japanese. The job of each committee was, on the one hand, to press the Japanese for better equipment and supplies and, on the other, to manage the life of the camp in its area. Thus the needs of the camp began to be dealt with by designated men. The amorphous labor force was organized; the problems of equipment and of sanitation were handled by the engineers; supplies were distributed more fairly and efficiently; the complex problems of housing began to be tackled; and schools were started for our three hundred or more children.

With such centralized organization, our community began to show the first signs of a dawning civilization; it was slowly becoming capable of that degree of coordinated work necessary to supply services essential to life and to provide at least a bearable level of comfort.

By the middle of April, moreover, the camp cleaning force had cleared away all the rubble and debris. Most of the dismal ugliness that had greeted us in March disappeared. At this transformation, the garden-loving British began to spring to action. You could see them everywhere—in front of their dorms or along their row of rooms; around the church or the ballfield, turning up soil wherever they could establish claim to a plot of ground, planting the seeds which they had brought from Peking and Tientsin, and then lovingly watering the first signs of new life. In the same spirit, other families would begin to survey the small plot of ground in front of their rooms, planning patios made of scrounged bricks, and experimenting with awnings fashioned from mats purchased in the canteen—all of this, apparently, spurred on by the prospect of summer "teas." I could feel a new warmth in the wind and see a new brightness in the air wherever I went.

About the same time, evening lecture programs for adults sprouted in every available empty room. These talks touched on a wide variety of subjects, from sailing and woodwork, art and market research to theology and Russian, on which there were unemployed experts both willing and eager to speak. Concurrently, our weekly entertainments began. These took place in the church, starting with simple song fests and amateur vaudeville skits. The culmination of these early forms of "culture" came, surely, when a baseball league (e.g., the Peking Panthers vs. the Tientsin Tigers) started in earnest on the small ballfield, exciting the whole population two or three afternoons a week.

III ✑ Eggs, Guards, and Love

With the advent of spring, a marked change came over the face of the camp. Where there had been rubble and dirt, there were now bright patches of color in the gardens and neat patios. These were only the physical evidences of a change that also occurred on a deeper level. Within a few months this poorly prepared and, indeed, almost desperate group had transformed itself into a coherent civilization, able to cope with its basic material problems and day by day raising the level of its life on all fronts. The food was almost palatable, the baseball league enthralled everyone; and the evenings were now warm enough for a stroll with a girl friend. The camp was almost becoming a pleasant place in which to live.

Not the least among the elements contributing to this general state of well-being were the sources of "extra" supplies. Of course there was always the camp canteen: a small store supplied by the Japanese and manned by a Tientsin department store owner and an elderly importer. In it such necessities of our life could be purchased as cigarettes, soap, peanut oil, toilet paper, and mats— for which goods in great demand ration cards were issued. Also on rare occasions such items as dried fruits, spices, and ginger could be found there. There were never any fresh fruits or sweets available there or in the kitchens during the two and one-half years we were in camp.

It was, however, the black market that added the most to our life during the first six months. Although I enjoyed its fruits as much as the next man, I was never involved in the operation of this flourishing industry. Even the most ingenuous, however, could not long remain unaware of its existence. He had only to saunter past any row of rooms or dorm of a morning to smell eggs frying on a newly made brick stove, or to have a friend casually press upon him some succulent jam for his bread. When he stopped by a neighbor's room, he was likely to be offered a little bacon or chocolate, *By-gar* (Chinese whisky) or wine.

It was no time at all until the members of our group, too, were buying eggs, jam, and sweets from "those who knew." There were, as I found, a considerable number of the latter. When I inquired whom one might contact for some of this marvelous manna, friends suggested the following: some of the tough ex-army men at the end of our row; several businessmen over near the wall in Block 54; two bachelors in Dorm 49; and so on. But the majority replied: "If you want to get eggs and jam cheap, and in great quantity, see the Catholic fathers."

During the middle of that first summer, at least two-thirds of the internees had an egg to fry each morning. At one point in fact, when the black market was at its height, we had so many that an extra hot plate in the Peking kitchen had to be constructed to handle the long line queued up for a stove. This meant that an average of about 1,300 eggs a day were coming over or through the wall; an equivalent amount of jam, peanuts, and sugar was there for the buying if one knew whom to see. Wherever there was a sheltered spot in the wall, goods seemed to pour over. The Chinese farmers were eager for cash and in summer they had plenty of produce to sell. Many a time I strolled into the Bertram Carters' room in Block 3 to find jam, sugar, and eggs all over the bed, and one or the other of them scurrying to get these goods into boxes before a guard appeared. I remember once our horror when, without warning, a live chicken was tossed over the wall. It got loose from Bertram's clutches, squawking and flapping about over a large part of the block before we managed to retrieve and silence it. As Bertram said with an eloquent sigh after its neck had been wrung, "Not an easy item to explain to a passing guard, what?"

As it was apparent that the fathers were the major source, I decided to find out how they worked it. The three hundred or so priests and monks lived under horribly crowded conditions in the upper floors of the hospital building and one or two adjacent small blocks. This was an area which was next to the wall, and at the beginning quite out of sight of the guardhouses. Each time I had been in their neighborhood, I had felt a slight shock, for I was not used to this monastic world. Early in the morning or late in the afternoon, I found that the yard around the hospital resembled a medieval courtyard. A hundred or so priests in black and monks in brown were there slowly pacing up and down near the wall saying their prayers.

I learned from one Passionist father that the black market began at the hour of evening devotionals a couple of weeks after camp started. Quite without warning, a covey of cabbages flew over the wall into the midst of these praying priests. Immediately, so my friend noted with great amusement, all purely religious concerns receded. The priests closed their prayer books, scooped up the cabbages, and hoisted one another up high enough to talk over the wall to the Chinese beyond it. Regular rendezvous spots and hours were fixed, and if one of them did not work, they tried another.

The most successful and certainly the most intriguing of the clerical egg runners was a small, bespectacled Trappist monk named Father Darby. The strict rules of his order against speaking at any time were temporarily lifted so that these monks could work with the rest of us. Thus Father Darby was able to tell us a good deal about his life as a Trappist. He explained to us that he had been in the same monastery for twenty-five years. For that quarter century prior to coming to camp, he had not spoken more than three or four words to any living soul. A charming, friendly little man, while he was with us he more than made up for lost time. He would talk by the hour with anyone who would listen to him. I am sure he was a devout Trappist, but one summer evening I came to realize he had many other facets to his personality. Passing by one of the camp's more elegant patios, I saw a group sampling *By-gar*. In their midst was Father Darby, dressed in a "secular" white summer formal,—replete with white jacket, black tie and black trousers—and regaling that fashionable audience with his Irish stories!

Father Darby had a seemingly foolproof method of receiving eggs undetected. In an obscure corner of the wall about a foot above the ground, he had pried loose a few bricks. He would kneel down at this spot and pull the eggs through the hole as a Chinese farmer pushed them from the other side. If a guard happened along, two Trappist friends down the line would begin a Gregorian chant.

At this signal, Darby would quickly cover the eggs with his long monk's robe and, already on his knees, be deep in prayer by the time the guard reached him. He kept up this practice for two or three months without being caught. Some of the guards were apparently more than a little afraid of these "holy men" with their massive beards and long robes. But finally one day a guard lifted Father Darby's robe as he knelt by the wall. To his surprise and the monk's embarrassment, he found one hundred and fifty eggs nestling there. Whatever the guards may have thought of the occult powers of Western holy men, they certainly never gave them credit for being able to lay eggs!

Father Darby was whisked off to the guardhouse. The first trial of camp life began. The camp awaited the outcome of the trial with bated breath; we were all fearful that the charming Trappist might be shot or at best tortured. For two days, the chief of police reviewed all the evidence on the charge of black marketeering, which was, to say the least, conclusive.

At the end of the elaborate trial, the chief announced his stern verdict. First, he said that because he was determined to stamp out the black market, he would have to make an example of Father Darby—adding parenthetically that it pained him "to punish a man of the cloth." The camp heard this pronouncement with a shudder. And so, said the chief, he was going to sentence Father Darby to one and one-half months of solitary confinement! The Japanese looked baffled when the camp greeted this news with a howl of delight, and shook their heads wonderingly as the little Trappist monk was led off to his new cell joyously singing.

From that time on, the black market had a strange and uneven history. During the fall of 1943, the Japanese reduced the flow of goods to a trickle. They managed to catch some more of the internee leaders and put them in "solitary." Since they were not Trappists, that was bad enough. But then they caught two Chinese farmers. To the horror of the internees, they stood the Chinese up before a firing squad within earshot of the camp.

In May, 1944, moreover, a new chief arrived. A man of force, he apparently succeeded in stopping the illegal commerce altogether. So it was with sinking hearts that we looked out over the walls one day to see Chinese laborers at work. They were digging a deep trench and rearing a high embankment fifty yards beyond the walls, and then building wire fences on the farther side. We knew that no Chinese could approach the wall without the greatest risk, and so we sadly contemplated the remainder of the war—eggless, peanutless, and dry.

I can still remember my amazement when, about July of that same year, a friend rushed into our dorm with some raw bacon. Since by no stretch of the imagination was anyone keeping pigs in camp, I knew that the black market must have started up again. In high excitement, we asked where he had got it. Our astonishment doubled, however, when he told us that it came from a friend who had obtained it through the Japanese guards. Short of cash themselves, these guards had agreed to take valuables owned by internees, such as old watches, clothes, jewelry, etc., and to trade them to Chinese merchants in exchange for goods or money. Needless to say the guards, as middlemen, were pocketing a goodly portion of the transactions. They were not interested in carrying on much of what we might call the "grocery trade," that is, the great quantities of eggs and peanuts that had been our earlier delight. They had to confine themselves to small, yet lucrative items, and so it was jam, sugar, Chinese whisky, and above all Chinese money that they brought into camp and sold to the internees.

It was hard during those last years to get any extra food, and whenever we did manage to get a batch of eggs, it had to last a long time indeed. I remember one two-dozen load that I got in early February, 1944. Being without the luxury of an icebox, I kept them in a basin under my bed. Because the room was generally chilly (50 to 55 degrees), the eggs remained edible a surprisingly long time. Since I ate one for breakfast about once every four days, they began to run out sometime in early April. I usually took them to the kitchen to boil them in one of the many huge cauldrons. On this particular occasion, after the customary three or four minutes, I hauled my egg out of the water and, looking forward to a hearty breakfast, sat down at a table full of kitchen workers. Announcing that this was almost my last egg, I hit it a sharp crack on the edge of my bowl—and then jumped at the explosion that occurred.

The table around me was in chaos. Some men were wiping their faces to get the spattered egg off and cursing me. Others were jamming their handkerchiefs to their noses and pushing themselves away from the table to escape the awful stench. I sat there in utter amazement. My hand was still frozen over my bowl. I gradually became aware that not one piece of shell remained in my fingers! We never found any part of that egg—except for the thin film that had to be scraped off faces, wall, and table! This experience somewhat dampened my enthusiasm for hoarding black-market eggs.

Illegal money was the most important black-market commodity during the latter years of the war. As time wore on, such money became vital to our existence in camp. From a camp canteen stocked by the Japanese, we had to buy many of the necessities of our life: soap, toilet paper, cigarettes, peanuts (for peanut butter), mats used for awnings or for rugs, and peanut oil for any home cooking and for our lamps at night (the electricity failed to work about one-third of the time). For this purpose "comfort money" was provided in Chinese dollars to each of us every month. This was a small sum sent through the Swiss government by our own government, changed by the Swiss into local currency, and brought into camp each month by the local representative of the Swiss state.

While we were at Weihsien camp, a fierce inflation of the Chinese currency had developed. When we came to camp, the Chinese dollar was worth about five cents, or one American dollar bought about twenty Chinese dollars. Accordingly, on the amazingly low scale of Chinese prices, a ration of ten packs of native-brand cigarettes had cost eight Chinese dollars when we went to camp. But in May, 1945—two years later—the same ration cost over five hundred Chinese dollars; which meant a rise of over 6,000 per cent.

Every other price rose proportionally, and the rate of inflationary increase seemed to accelerate all the time. Naturally the amount of "comfort money" given us each month could never keep pace with this galloping inflation, since every increase had to be negotiated between Washington and Tokyo via Geneva. More money than was legally provided was therefore essential for us, if we were to buy such necessities as toilet paper, soap, and cigarettes. From this situation stemmed the real significance of the Japanese black market.

After this commerce began, the amount of illegal money that entered the camp at any one time was enormous. For example, the total "comfort money" received legally in one month's period for one group of fifteen persons in mid-1944 was three thousand Chinese dollars ($200 per head). I learned later from the canteen director that the same group had spent in one week at the canteen over thirty thousand Chinese dollars. At that point in camp, then, each person in this group was receiving illegally on the average about eight thousand Chinese dollars monthly.

Naturally it required an efficient organization, including both important Japanese and reputable internees, to handle all these financial transactions. As I discovered when I went searching for extra cash, there was on the internee side a formal council or syndicate who acted as middlemen between the ordinary internees and the Japanese. To no one's surprise, this financial council was made up mostly of former bankers and stockbrokers.

It worked thus: An internee who wanted more cash might have a gold watch or a piece of jewelry to sell. Naturally, in an inflationary spiral, he would not wish to find himself suddenly loaded down with all the Chinese currency that such a valuable item would bring, amounting, say, to $200,000. Thus he would approach the syndicate, and negotiate with them until a price was agreed upon. The syndicate would sell his valuable to the Japanese, receiving from them in currency the $200,000. Having given the original owner whatever immediate cash he needed, the syndicate would then "sell" the remainder of the $200,000 to other internees in return for promissory notes in American currency. These notes would then be turned over to the seller. Such notes had to be doubly guaranteed, once by the syndicate itself and once by the corporation or concern for which the creditor internee had worked. On several occasions I borrowed about six thousand Chinese dollars on the credit of Yenching University where I had been teaching. By such means, cash was spread around the camp to all those who either had personal possessions which they could sell, or who could guarantee payment after the war. So almost all of us could—and did—avail ourselves of this service.

We were continually amused by the strangeness of this situation—with our captors subverting their own order. One day I swung around the corner near the kitchen and saw two of the guards going at each other angrily until one finally laid the other out cold with a large club. When a man who saw the incident asked another guard what had been the cause of the quarrel, the latter replied in effect: "Oh, they were just arguing about the black market. One of them had muscled in on the other's customers. It happens all the time!"

Shortly after this, I heard that a guard had been in Dormitory 49 consummating a private deal with an internee. When he had finished his business, he said calmly to his client, "Would you look out the door for me to see if there are any guards about? We are not supposed to be caught doing this work for our bosses!"

It had now become clear why the new chief had so firmly and quickly stopped the old black market when he came into camp. He wanted to get this lucrative business into his own—or at least into Japanese—hands.

I was continually surprised at the relatively minor role our Japanese rulers played in our lives. We were, of course, always conscious that they were there. Military guards strolled through the compound at regular intervals to take up their positions on the walls. Any young man, out with his girl friend after 10 P.M.

when the lights were turned off, had to dodge guards on his way home in the dark. Men in committee work had daily to deal with the Japanese civilian officials, for all our supplies and equipment came from them, and most of our major decisions had to be discussed with them. But on the whole, they left us alone to do our work and solve our problems in our own way. Except for the 7 A.M. roll call, and later on, one in the afternoon as well, the average internee, unless he were a black marketeer, seldom had any contact with the Japanese.

We were fortunate also in the kind of officials and soldiers who had charge of our camp. Strictly speaking, we were neither in Japan nor in "enemy" territory—we were in that part of China which was an occupied or "puppet" territory, held by the Japanese since 1937, and so maintaining at least nominal diplomatic relations with Japan. Thus we were under the Consular Service rather than the army or the military police. As a result, civilian diplomatic officials were in charge of us. Our guards were a part of the consular guard rather than soldiers in the regular army. These guards were men who for one reason or another had been given this "easy duty" far from the front, so that most of them were quite happy with their assignment. While we were, of course, enemies to them, they had not captured us in hard combat nor had they seen us shoot down their mates. Our situation was, therefore, quite different from that of captured folk in the Philippines, the East Indies, or Singapore, where internee camps were maintained by an army in the field and where inmates were brutally treated by soldiers against whom they had just fought. With the exception of a few cases where black marketeers were beaten up, generally decorum and good discipline marked their relations with us. Some of the guards were gruff or cruel, arrogant or mean. But no one was tortured or killed in our camp. Indeed many of the guards were courteous and kind to us.

For this reason, my own experience of five years under varied Japanese rule fails to substantiate the sweeping statements often made about the Japanese by others. I do not and cannot doubt the truth of their reports of endless and brutal atrocities—all I can say is that for whatever reason this was not my experience with them.

When the war first started in December, 1941, the faculty at Yenching University was imprisoned in one of the residential compounds on the campus. We were guarded by the dread Hsien Ping Twei, the military police. Knowing their reputation for cruelty to prisoners, we were wary of any contact with them as they marched up and down the small compound.

It was, therefore, with great apprehension that we saw one afternoon at teatime one of their soldiers, loaded down with every kind of portable weapon, approach a house where, among others, an American family with a baby were housed. I was the only male present at the time. Gingerly I opened the door at the guard's brisk knock. He bowed, and sucked air in sharply through his teeth. Then, unloading his extensive armor, to my utter amazement he opened his great coat and pulled out a small bottle of milk.

"Please," said he haltingly, "take for baby." After we had recovered from our surprise sufficiently to invite him to come in, we asked whether there was anything we could do for him in return.

"May I hear classical records?" he asked. Again, we gasped and said, "Who *are* you?" He answered, "I second flutist in Tokyo orchestra—miss good music!"

During the first few months of camp, I was on the Quarters Committee with Shields, the aggressive Englishman whom I have already mentioned and with whom I had now become good friends. He and I came to know quite well the Japanese official in charge of housing and engineering, since we shared an office with him. His name was Izu; he was an intelligent, courteous man who never lost his decorum even when he became angry with us.

We must have put his Oriental aplomb to the ultimate test with our camp census. In the beginning, the Japanese government apparently had no more notion than we did how many persons the camp was supposed to contain or what their names were. The first order that Izu gave to the Quarters Committee was to take a census. Such a measure would be very helpful to us, too, for what we needed to do first was to find out where the worst conditions of housing were and then determine where we might find any extra space. Almost as soon as our committee was formed, a house-to-house count began. Gradually we filled in with names and numbers the great map of the compound that hung in the office.

All went well until we came to the hospital. There on the upper floors lived about 250 Dutch and Belgian monks. To our dismay, we discovered that apparently not even the Catholic leaders had any idea how many monks lived there or who they were. They were so jammed into each dorm that no man in a given room knew how many it held. Thus we almost had to buttonhole them one by one in order to make our list.

A census of monks, moreover, presents endless difficulties because each monk has two names. One is his given family name which is on his passport and all official lists; the other is his "religious name" acquired at ordination or induction into his order and identifying him to all his Catholic brethren. No Catholic leader would necessarily know that a certain American priest had been Michael O'Malley, nor would any Japanese list indicate that O'Malley was, indeed, now Father Paulinus. Sorting out accurately these two kinds of names was bad enough. If one were to add that these monks all looked more or less alike to a lay observer because of their identical robes and great flowing beards, and that few of the Dutch or Belgian fathers spoke English, one can understand how impossible it was to make a reliable count. For days on end we could not get those lists to check. Finally, after a great deal of checking and rechecking, we were satisfied that our census was reasonably accurate, and so we handed it in one morning to Izu at the quarters office. At once he asked us with the greatest seriousness, "Is your count correct?"

Not realizing the importance of his question, and sick to death of the whole business, we replied, "Sure, as good as makes no matter."

He nodded and scurried out of the office to cable his report to some "higher up."

We thought little more of this matter until two days later when a leader among the nuns—a most attractive American sister—appeared in our office. Deeply apologetic, she confessed that the day before she had come upon two elderly Dutch sisters buried somewhere in their dorms. She had had no idea of their existence when she gave us her list. We assured her that this slip was not fatal and told Izu, when he came into the office, to raise the camp total by two.

The reaction of this invariably calm gentlemen took us completely by surprise. He blanched snow white, began to tremble, and even uttered a few rasping oaths at us in Japanese. He so far forgot himself as to slam the table in front of him and to lift his hand as if to strike us. But he lowered it—and tore from the room, clearly in even greater terror than anger. We went into the supplies office next door to ask Brown, the chairman there, to find out from his "boss" Koga what on earth had gone wrong with Izu. Koga was a tall Japanese who had been reared in

California. A victim of discrimination in college, Koga as a result
was a dedicated hater of everything and everyone Western. Half
an hour later he returned and said angrily, "You damn fools, Izu
had sent that figure off to Tokyo as an official report and signed
it. Now you've forced him to send another cable saying a mistake
has been made. Heaven knows what will happen to him!"

The terror with which a Japanese in that era regarded those
sacred beings in authority over him was plainly manifest, not
alone in Izu's stricken flight from our office, but in Koga's awestruck recital of his friend's predicament.

By a stroke of good fortune—for we did not want the courteous Mr. Izu to lose his head through our error—a leader among
the priests came around the next morning and said apologeti-
cally that they had made a mistake in his dorm of seventy-five
Dutch fathers. Two men had appeared twice on the list! Sadly he
realized that through his mistake we would have to reduce our
total count by two!

Almost before the words were out of his mouth, we split up
and went looking for Izu to prevent his sending off the fatal
second cable. Happily he had procrastinated out of fear and was
telling himself, as he admitted later, that he would send it that
afternoon. When we told him the good news, he almost fainted
from relief. He laughed nervously, sucked his breath through his
teeth, and bowed very low to each of us—signs, as we well knew,
of intense Japanese pleasure.

For the next six months, until we left quarters work, we got
along remarkably well with Izu. He seemed to trust us in the
management of camp housing, and we found we could trust him.
On two occasions we had to appeal to him to deal firmly with
uncooperative internees. He not only promised to do nothing to
them without consulting us, but did, in fact, only what we had
recommended to him.

There were always, of course, three or four Japanese in the
camp who were roundly disliked by all. The usual causes for this
seemed to me to be twofold. First, some Japanese often showed
an almost compulsive need to assert their dominance and authority. They would rant and bark, slap and kick, as if the person in
front of them were a hideous spider that had sent them into a
panic and must be crushed. Second, anyone under their authority apparently inspired in them a streak of meanness, the
desire to prevent another from doing whatever appeared fun,
and on the contrary, to make him do what was unpleasant.

I am sure that in their own way all people illustrate these same unlovely traits, and most of us probably repress them only with difficulty in our daily contacts with others. It also seems plain that these particular urges are strongest in those people long humiliated by more powerful competitors. When they are finally able to strike back, they do so in this fanatical manner. Add to this the unfortunate but inescapable difference in size between, say, the average Japanese soldier and a towering Scot, German, or American—and there is additional reason for this bluster and feigned arrogance. Thus I would seek to understand it when some Japanese guard or official would suddenly break into almost mad ravings, stamp his feet, kick at the available furniture, flail his arms threateningly—all for no apparent reason.

One petty officer, who was for a period in charge of the guards, seemed to us perfectly to incarnate these unlovely traits. Short, powerful, with a square head and a heavily whiskered chin, he was the Japanese equivalent of the classic Western drill sergeant. Seemingly every time anyone in camp was doing something that looked as if it might be fun, like sunning himself in a bathing suit or holding some lady's hand, this officer would appear on the scene and bellow out the familiar Chinese words, *"Bo-shing-de,"* which means "You can't do it!" "It isn't allowed!" or *"Verboten!"*

The result was that everyone came to call this pompous little man "Sergeant Bo-shing-de." Often you could see his squat form strutting along a camp street, surrounded, like a horse with gnats, by a dancing throng of small children. They would hop up and down and yell at the top of their lungs, "Sergeant Bo-shing-de, Sergeant Bo-shing-de!" Needless to say, he did not appreciate this regular reception, and so apparently, in what must have been an interesting scene, he asked the commandant to do something about it. But how does one get children to stop yelling a name—short of shooting them? And how can the soldier concerned be identified to the public if none of them knows his real name? I can well imagine the head office spending tedious hours pondering those puzzles! Apparently deciding there was no other way out of this thicket, the commandant put up the following notice on the camp bulletin boards:

HENCEFORTH IN THE WEIHSIEN INTERNMENT CENTER, BY SPECIAL ORDER OF HIS IMPERIAL MAJESTY, THE EMPEROR OF JAPAN, "SERGEANT BO-SHING-DE" IS NOT TO BE KNOWN AS SERGEANT BO-SHING-DE BUT AS SERGEANT YOMIARA.

That notice in the classical military style almost carried our sagging spirits through the last winter!

Another incident, however, cast an entirely different light on Bo-shing-de's character. My bunkmate and friend, Lawrence Turner of Yenching University, at sixty-five, was scholar, hard worker, and iron-muscled athlete. Lawrence had come to know some of the guards very well. He had asked for and received permission to sleep outdoors in his camp cot, as was his wont at home. There, dressed in his Chinese gown and sipping his tea, he frequently chatted with the guards as they made their evening and predawn rounds. Also Lawrence liked, as he always had, to run his daily mile around the inside of the camp wall early in the morning. This feat so much impressed the age-venerating Japanese that they frequently told others they respected him more than they did any other internee.

Much to his surprise, Lawrence was invited to have tea one day in Bo-shing-de's quarters, a large bedroom in one of the old mission houses in the walled-off section of the compound. When he entered this drill sergeant's room, Lawrence could hardly believe his eyes.

Decorated by the sergeant himself, it was furnished in the most artistic Japanese taste, illustrating utter simplicity, a remarkable sense of the harmonious use of space, and a painstaking attention to detail. At the focal point of the room, complemented by a pair of classical flower arrangements, was an exquisite little home shrine to the sergeant's samurai war god. It was true, Lawrence remarked later, that this diety, with his grimacing face and bow-legged stance, was hardly a thing of beauty. Yet the harmonious and artistic effect was in such striking contrast to the American soldier's gallery of mother, assorted pin-ups, and model airplanes, that the sight of it made Lawrence gasp.

The horrible war god, expressing all the barbaric cruelty of one side of Japanese culture, yet honored in the delicate, sensitive taste of this cruel soldier, seemed a perfect symbol for the mystery of the Japanese character as I knew it during the war.

We had not been long in camp before it seemed an ordinary thing to wake up in a room with twenty men, to hear Joe Jones talking to Maitland about his lumbago, or Sas Sloan griping at the extra long line at the hot-water boiler where we took turns to get our shaving water in a pail. Then we would stand yawning and sleepy for a half hour to an hour waiting for roll call, talking together about our girl friends, the dance coming up next week, or the baseball game that afternoon. And soon I would go to the kitchen for breakfast and hear another man saying, "The old lady was sick last night, but a spot of hot tea fixed her up," or another complaining that, "It's always those people next door that give us the *most* trouble." And when I would arrive at the quarters office about 9 A.M., I might hear Shields sighing as he came in, clean shaven for the day and natty in his army khakis, "If only this bloody weather would stop and the sun would come out again, I would feel a hundred per cent better about life— God, did we have a bunch of lousy hands at bridge last night!"

I remember thinking with a laugh as I went out on a quarters job that morning, that you could have heard these same remarks in Manchester or Chicago. It was obvious that the interests of the people in the camp were really very much like those of people everywhere: their health, where and how they lived, the weather, their work, the neighbors, the inconveniences of life and, of course, sex. And I suddenly stopped short wondering at this strange fact. How quickly man makes his life—whatever its character may be—into what he can call "normal." What would have seemed a fantastic deprivation to a man comfortable, well fed, and serene in an easy chair at home, had by the end of a few short months become just "life" for us.

We recognized Weihsien as the accepted framework of our existence, and so the familiar context *within* which we reacted emotionally to things. It no longer represented a new horror *against* which we reacted. We would now gripe if a queue was slow, but not at the fact of the queue—for this aspect of life was "normal" to us now. Yet realistically, here we were, crowded into a ridiculously small space, shut off from the outside world, living a most uncomfortable life, and one that was radically insecure. What possible certainty did we have that the relative well-being of this moment in camp would continue; that it would not be replaced by a turn to brutality, by starvation, or even by extermination? And soberly I had to admit that when I looked facts in the face, there was no ground for certainty here—these things might easily happen to us. To be sure, we talked about such things now and then, but the threat of them remained unreal to us and we did not *feel* insecure. Usually we got quickly back to familiar gripes, to girls, and to food we liked. No, I concluded, camp life was now normal to us; we have accepted it and accustomed our emotions to it, and as always, we humans expect the normal to continue to be the case.

Musing further on this tendency of man to "normalize" whatever may come his way, I decided this was, after all, a fortunate trait. How much better that we were able to accept emotionally what would have horrified us three months ago; to forget most of the conveniences that we now lacked; and above all, to pretend that this life which we had learned to bear was certain to continue! Only thus, I decided, can mankind live with any serenity amid so much social misery, through such unsettled periods in history in which wars have been far from abnormal. Only thus can he stand the stark insecurity that the next moment may bring to any vulnerable creature!*

Altogether, then, the normal interests of life were uppermost in our consciousness. Thus, as in the ordinary life of man, personal relations took the center of the stage. Man is primarily a sexual and communal being, and he can exist sanely and happily only in and through the various sorts of relationships he has with his fellow men and women.

Immediately after we arrived in camp, those of us younger men from Peking—and there were several—were delighted to notice attractive girls of our own age here and there in the crowds. It did not take long for us to get to know one another. We ran into each other at the small informal dances in the Tientsin kitchen where the jazz band played, at the early baseball games between the groups, or organizing some weekend entertainment.

The latter was the way I met Alice, the British girl with whom I spent some of the best hours in camp. Her good company did more than I can say to make camp life not only bearable but often gay and pleasant.

Soon we began excitedly to pair off more or less permanently. Few of these relations were real "love affairs," and only one or two resulted in marriages either in the camp or later. Most of our younger group were still too much adrift in the world to consider marriage, and many had deeper obligations to persons outside the camp.

For this reason many of us, brought up to believe that any form of sexuality is immoral unless it leads to marriage, felt guilty about these relationships, however dependent we were on the affection, the loving, and the security they brought to us. But looking back, I find them very natural and good, bringing to us

---

* These meandering thoughts in camp received confirmation when I heard later of Reinhold Niebuhr's famous prayer: "Oh Lord, help us to accept those things we cannot change, to be dissatisfied with what we can change, and to be able to discern the difference."

in a rather dreary and uncertain life at least hints and brushes of the deep joys of loving and being loved, which are surely primary among the basic values of life.

It was not always easy, however, to carry on a relation of whatever sort with a girl in camp. Single people all lived in dorms so that opportunities for love-making were minimal, and the lack of modern contraceptives made intercourse too risky for most of the unmarrieds. The only chances for any modicum of privacy came in the spring, summer, and early fall when it was warm enough to walk in the open parts of the compound in the evening. Even then those sections were usually so teeming with people taking the night air that, as in a park in Manhattan on a warm night, it was not easy to get more than twenty feet from anyone else. Only after the lights were turned out at the 10 P.M. curfew could the "dating" at Weihsien begin. Each of us who were young came to know all the available secluded corners of our small space, how to be quiet when a guard came by, and above all how to tiptoe back to our dorm at the end of the evening so as not to be caught.

As a young man in my middle twenties, it literally never occurred to me that "old folks" in their late thirties and forties had the same urges I felt so strongly. Thus I never even wondered how that great crowd of single men in the dorms, men between thirty-five and fifty-five, most of whom had been married for years, not to mention the equal number of single women, resolved the problem of their sexual life. We assumed that young people alone had such problems, and went about finding our own solutions. All I knew, as a relative expert on who was and who was not out dating after curfew, was that none of these older persons in the dorms were to be encountered there.

The most significant changes in our love life came with the changes in our dorms. At the end of the first six months the camp became much less crowded, owing to the repatriation of some two hundred Americans, and many single people were moved out of inadequate dorms into the upper floors of the hospital. Our group from Yenching University fell heir to a gorgeous room on the top floor. We could look out across the flat, dry farmland to two small Chinese villages a few miles away, and watch the donkey carts, peddlers, and old women with their bundles plodding their way past the camp to Weihsien city. Best of all, for my roommate Arthur Howell and me, was the fact that on the floor below, our girl friends had a room with two other British girls their own age. Joined by another American boy and a Britisher, we would go down there after work. The eight of us would laugh and talk on the room's four beds until curfew time, and then later sneak upstairs in our stocking feet.

This arrangement, idyllic alike for housing and for young love, came to a rude end in June, 1944. Two young men managed to escape from the camp to join the guerrillas in the hills nearby. As a reprisal, or perhaps to prevent contact with the outside from the upper floors of the hospital, the Japanese moved all of us who had been their roommates into large dorms in the center of the camp. In the same move, the girls were put in a similar room in the women's building, Block 24. The cheery evenings we four couples had so enjoyed vanished. We had again sadly to content ourselves in the summer with late walks around the camp, and in winter with intermittent evenings together baby-sitting in some friends' family room.

The much more serious consequence of this escape was that roll call was henceforth a serious matter. Instead of being a perfunctory check in our rooms in the early morning, as it was before the escape, it was now held both morning and afternoon. The camp was divided into four "roll call groups," and twice a day each group had to line up on its designated parade ground. Since each mustering required from forty minutes to an hour of patient standing while the entire camp was counted, roll call became a crushing bore for us younger folk and a source of real discomfort for the families and the elderly.

One other personal relationship was perhaps the warmest and closest of all for me. This was with Matthew and Edith Read, British Methodist missionaries from Tientsin. Matt was a most unusual man. Lean and handsome, humorous, intelligent and warm, he had the rare gift of getting on with all sorts of people, and was regularly elected to the Labor Committee. He loved to ponder and analyze the complexities and humors of our life by the hour, holding his pipe carefully in his hand—and Edith had many of the same gifts. Thus we were all delighted to find that invaluable addition to a quiet life: conversational partners with whom one's experiences can be shared and enriched. For through such conversations not only was I able to learn my own mind by talking out my thoughts; even more it was possible for me to see things anew through the wiser eyes of that unusual couple.

Soon I found myself going there frequently, two and even three times a week, and thrashing out with them all the issues that our life was bringing to us: the development of the war outside, the future complexion of British and American politics, our own internal problems of organization and morals, the latest crisis or scandal in the camp, and so on indefinitely. By the end of our sojourn, I was eating most of my suppers there and every Sunday breakfast. Their warm hearts made me a member of their family, along with their lively little girl, and the difference that that made for my life in Weihsien cannot be imagined.

IV ✍ Medicines and Recipes, or How to Outwit Circumstances

The other interest, besides our personal relationships, that fills our human days whether we be in a city, on a farm, or in a camp, is work. Work and life have a strange reciprocal relationship: only if man works can he live, but only if the work he does seems productive and meaningful can he bear the life that his work makes possible. The work in the camp was, then, central to each of us. All of this coordinated activity kept us alive by providing the services and goods necessary for our existence. And however dull it seemed, it gave a focus of interest and energy to a life that otherwise by its confinement and great limitations would have been overwhelmed by boredom. Perhaps the best way to describe what our work was like is to tell my own experience of it.

After six months spent in the wearing and bruising conflicts of the Quarters Committee, both Shields and I felt that we and the camp needed a change, and so in September, 1943, I chose to do manual rather than office work. For a time I was the assistant to the camp mason. He was an American technician from Tientsin —tough, cool, and capable. Masoning was good for the muscles, but in the end I found mixing mortar for this good man boring, and so I applied for a job in the kitchen.

Kitchen III, the one serving the Peking group, was the ideal place to be introduced to camp cooking. This had been the liveliest of the three kitchens. Serving only three hundred people, this kitchen was small enough for its cooks to be teams of women. They were able, for example, to make and fry small hamburgers, a process that was then inconceivable in a kitchen serving eight hundred. Above all, filled as it was by the educational and missionary personnel who had been centered in Peking, this community had a cooperative spirit which was unmatched elsewhere. The cooking teams were thus able to call on ten or fifteen more women to help them when there was extra work to do, and so to pioneer in experimental ways with our strange Chinese equipment. When the American evacuation of August, 1943, took place, however, and most of the Catholic fathers went as well, this community's food standards dropped noticeably, and a British pall seemed to settle over our menus.

It was at this point that I became an assistant cook, hardly knowing then how to boil an egg. My boss was a gay and talented bachelor named Edwin Parker. With graying hair and a round face, he had been a curio and art dealer from Peking. Edwin knew how to cook, but he hated to boss anybody or to organize his meals too carefully. As a result, our life was filled with confusion and laughter, but also with frequent culinary triumphs. My job was to keep the pans and cauldrons clean, to cut up meat, stir soups and stews, fry leeks, and braise meat—in other words, all the routine chores, while Edwin, as chef, planned, directed, and seasoned the menu.

Since we both wanted to live on as good food as possible, we worked hard. Although we were not the best of the three cooking teams in our kitchen (each one worked every third day), ours came to have a growing favorable reputation among our ordinarily disgruntled diners. As the first winter closed in, I liked to come to work before dawn, to watch our stoker (an insurance man from Peking) coax the fires into life under the cauldrons, to start cooking the cereal in the large *guo* (caldron), and to fry people's black-market eggs on our improvised hot plate. Then, after spending the rest of the day preparing lunch and supper, I would return in the dark to the hospital and an evening with Alice, tired but full of the satisfaction of one who has worked with his muscles all day.

It was, therefore, a severe blow when word came from the

Japanese that on January first (1944) we would have to move out of Kitchen III into one of the other two large kitchens. Each of these was filled with what seemed to us to be immense crowds of unfamiliar people, and from all reports, enjoyed a notoriously bad spirit and worse food. But since the Japanese insisted—they intended to house the newly arriving Italians in that section of the camp—we had no choice but to leave Kitchen III.

As luck would have it, my first day of duty in the new place, Kitchen I, came on New Year's morning. I had never been inside the place—so much vaster than our intimate kitchen with two small *guos* and a team made up of only two cooks—and so I hardly knew my way around its vast interior. What made matters worse was that the night before there had been a very gay dance in the Tientsin kitchen (Kitchen II) to which Alice and I had gone and, reasonably enough, we had not got in until about 4 A.M.

So, sleepy, headachy, and angry, I groped my way, about 6 A.M., into the unknown recesses of Kitchen I. It was a cold, damp morning; the newly made fires created such thick steam that I could only dimly discern the long line of huge *guos* with many strange figures bending over them. Gradually, as the steam cleared, I became aware that the voice giving sharp orders belonged to the boss cook, and the feet I kept seeing under the rising steam to the six helpers on the cooking team; also I realized that I was helping to cook cereal and that others were beginning the preparation for lunchtime stew.

It took little longer to grasp that no one there was much concerned about the quality of the food we made, and no one was eager to work more than absolutely necessary. McDaniel, the boss, was a nice enough guy in a rough, indifferent, and lazy way; but we knew that his sharp-tongued wife told him what to cook. He used to run home in the middle of most afternoons because he had forgotten what she had told him about supper! Beyond carrying out these orders, he knew little and cared less about cooking. For my first two months there, I felt frustrated about the job we were doing. There must be some way, thought I, of pepping things up and turning out better food. And so I began to look around for others who might feel the same way, but who, unlike myself, knew how to cook.

Gradually as I worked in that kitchen and learned to know it, its strangeness and size diminished. I even found myself enjoying my hours every third day on duty. There was a sunny courtyard just off the main kitchen, and on good days, when we could prepare the food for stews out there and eat our lunch at the big table, there was an atmosphere of rough, ribald fun that I heartily enjoyed. As this sense of at-homeness grew, I found that the functioning of the kitchen as a complex of coordinated activities came to interest me—for it really was a remarkable organization.

This organization began outside the kitchen when food supplies were brought into camp on carts by Chinese. They were distributed by the Supplies Committee proportionally to each of the two main kitchens. Then the supplies gang carried them in wooden crates to the kitchens—vegetables to the vegetable room and meat to the butchery. At this point the two cooks for the following day looked glumly over the meager supplies they had been given for their eight hundred customers, racked their brains for some new ideas for a menu, and then told the vegetable captains and the butchers what they wanted in the raw preparation of these supplies.

That same afternoon and into the next morning, the two butchers sliced, cubed, or ground the meat (this would be the winter procedure; they boiled it in summer in order to ensure its keeping at least over night without refrigeration). Teams of some fifteen to twenty women diced carrots, peeled potatoes, and chopped cabbage, while middle-aged men helped them by carrying the vegetable baskets around and by cleaning the produce in a pair of old bathtubs taken from the residences in the "out of bounds" section of the compound.

The next day the two cooks and five helpers came on duty about 5 A.M. They prepared breakfast cereal if there was any, and then lunch and supper for that day. A pan washer on my shift (actually a scholar of Chinese literature, and now a professor at Cornell University) washed the containers we used in preparing the food and from which we ladled out the dinner. Then women servers distributed the food to the waiting lines collecting food for our eight hundred people. They were checked and watched over by elderly men counters who made sure no one came in twice, and kept tabs on how fast the food was running out.

Girls then passed tea—if there was any—around the tables in the dining room. Men tea servers poured it into flasks for the majority who, being families, preferred to collect their food in covered containers and to eat it *en famille* in their rooms. Near the serving tables was the bread room where five or six older men sliced two hundred loaves of bread daily and distributed to each his ration. And finally, two teams of women dishwashers cleaned up the dishes after the meal of those who ate in the dining hall. All of these groups got time off depending on the hours and heaviness of their work.

Cooking food and boiling water, however, required heat. For this purpose, coal and wood were brought to the kitchen yard from the supply house in carts. In our yard two men were always chopping wood while others molded bricks out of the coal dust that made up most of our usual coal issue. Two stokers got up the fires and tended them, one in the cooking area and the other where water was boiled for drinking. Stoking was a job which called for great skill since the coal was poor and the cooks extremely demanding about the level of heat they had to have under their precious stews.

To keep this intricate organization running smoothly, there was at first only an informal structure, headed by the manager of the kitchen, who seemed to do everything, and two women storekeepers. The latter kept an eye on our small stores of sugar and oil; also they purchased raw ginger, spices, and dried fruits when they were available in the canteen; and generally functioned as advisers of the manager on his many problems.

One morning my career as a kitchen helper was rudely interrupted by a fairly serious accident. It was a raw February day in 1944. Since there was nothing much to do in the cooking line, some of us, spurred on by the complaints of our more sensitive diners, decided to clean up the south kitchen where water was boiled for drinking. Our kitchens were terribly dirty; soot from the fires covered ceiling and walls; grease was inevitably added to this layer on the cauldron tops; and the floor combined all this with its own tracked-in mud. Cleaning meant trying, with brooms and cloths, to get as much of this dirt and soot off the walls, ceiling, and pipes as possible.

Along the wall above the top of the cauldrons was a chimney ledge that protruded about five inches. Thinking that it was wide enough to stand on, I clambered up. I had not been there twenty seconds when I felt myself losing my balance, and instinctively I stepped back—into a cauldron of boiling water. "Boy, that's hot," I half-said to myself, and in the same instant I was across the room. I can recall no conscious mental command telling me to jump as I found myself leaping out of that cauldron. In fact, I catapulted out so fast that my working mate only saw me crashing into the wall opposite and thought, he admitted later, that I had simply gone mad. Next I found myself hopping up and down as fast as I could. Then I sat down and eased off my shoes and socks to see what had happened to my feet.

I had no idea I was badly burned until, taking the sock off my right ankle and foot, I found the skin coming off with it. By that time the boss cook had come over from the north kitchen. With one look at my now skinless ankles, he gave quick orders to take me to the hospital immediately. Two burly fellows on the shift made a chair with their arms and trundled me off. It was not until we got out in the air that I became conscious of real pain. To be sure, when I was hopping up and down, my feet stung; but this was worse. From that time on for about five hours, my burns hurt a lot.

The doctors in the hospital did a wonderful job. A British doctor for the Kailon Mining Company put picric acid on the bandages and did not take them off for about ten days. Due to the sulphanilamide that was smuggled into camp through the guerrillas, I was able to avoid infection. When the bandages finally came off, new skin had grown almost everywhere. Within three weeks, I was hobbling around. In six months all that was left to show of the burn was a rather grim abstract color effect of yellow and magenta.

I learned through my experience that ours was a remarkable hospital. Devoid of running water or central heating, it managed to be not only efficient but personal. It seemed to me a far better place in which to be sick than many "modern" hospitals, equipped with the latest gadgets but run on impersonal terms. It is this negation of the individual person, this sense of being "the bladder case in Room 304," or "that terminal heart case down the hall"—not its food or even its service—that makes many an American hospital, despite its vast efficiency, a dreaded place in which to be sick.

The nurses and doctors, who formed the backbone of the staff of our hospital, had, of course, to work for long hours since no one could replace them at their tasks. But as I soon came to realize, a lot more than their skill was needed. Among the essential services provided were a pharmacy where medicines (bought with a camp fund derived from a tax on comfort money) were given out, and a lab where urinalyses, blood and other tests could be performed. There was also a diet kitchen with its own staff of cooks and vegetable preparers (all women), a butcher, a supplies gang, a stoker, and a wood chopper. The hospital also had a hand laundry; there five women and one man washed the many sheets, towels, and bandages that were needed for the thirty or so in-patients. To keep the building itself clean, a crew of moppers, dusters, and window cleaners daily made the rounds of the rooms and wards. And finally, there was a staff of men orderlies and girl servers who helped the nurses to wash the patients and make them comfortable.

What made this small hospital unique in my experience was the unusual relationship between staff and patients, and among the patients themselves. The workers who came every day to the wards, sweeping under a patient's bed or bringing him tea, were not strangers moving impersonally in and out of his area. Rather, they were friends or, at least, acquaintances who entered the patient's life and communicated with him there. They had known him as a person in camp before he became a case in the hospital, and thus, greeted by them as a person, the patient never felt himself to be merely a rundown organism whose end might well be the disposal in the basement.

And, of course, the patients in the ward knew each other, too. For example, when old Watkins in the bed at the far end reached the "crisis" of his serious case of pneumonia, we were all aware of it, and waited in concern for him to ride it out. When the ex-marine bartender, the foreman of a "go-down" in Tientsin, and the Anglican priest—all of whom were the orderlies in the ward I was in—made up our beds and carried out our slops, they would find time to ask me about my feet, kidding me for thinking I could walk on water. Thus, quite unconsciously, because this was so normal among friends, they created a sense of personal community that for the sick is one of the few real guards against inner emptiness and despair. I left the hospital refreshed and sorry to return to normal internment life.

One of the hospital's greatest trials was keeping up its stock of medicine. We had each brought into camp quantities of medicines in our trunks, as our doctors had directed, but this supply ran out before the end of 1943. The Japanese supplied only a fraction of the medicines we needed. The Swiss representative in Tsingtao, who came to camp once a month with the comfort money, was able to buy for us in local pharmacies only the most commonplace drugs. What in the end saved our health was the happy collaboration between American logistics and the Swiss consul's ingenuity. The solution of this problem, when finally found, was so unusual we came to regard it as one of the best stories in the camp.

The two men who escaped from camp in June, 1944, were able to report via radio to Chungking that we were in desperate need of medicines. In answer, the American Air Force "dropped" a quantity of the latest sulfa drugs to the nationalist guerrillas in our immediate neighborhood. But how were these supplies, obviously of Allied origin, to be smuggled into the camp past the Japanese guards?

The only man from the outside world permitted access was the Swiss consul in Tsingtao. During a war, while other nations draft civilians into their armies, Switzerland, the perennial neutral, drafts civilians into its diplomatic corps—and with equally strange results. I remember, for example, dear old Duval, whom we had known as the nearsighted, brilliant, charming, ever courteous, but utterly unorganized, professor of history at Yenching University. Duval was a man with great popping eyes, a large, bald dome of a head, and an enormous black mustache. To our surprise and mild dismay we found that he had been made the assistant Swiss consul in Peking charged with extracting concessions for us from the Japanese military police! No man at the university was more respected and loved. But it was hardly for his practical competence, his wily ingenuity, or his crushing dominance of will that we held him in such high esteem.

An even more unlikely selection—if possible—was Laubscher of Tsingtao, the temporary Swiss consul for Shantung Province. Laubscher was, therefore, the man slated by the vagaries of fate to visit us regularly at Weihsien camp and to represent us and our governments to the Japanese. According to those who knew him in Tsingtao, he had formerly been a small importer. He seemed formal, stiff, and somewhat reticent in his old-world ways, and certainly he was red-nosed and rheumy of eye—probably, so the report ran, from years of silent sipping while he sat on the club porch or while playing a quiet game of bridge in the men's bar.

To look at Laubscher was to know that he would be quite incapable of pounding a table, even if he dared to, without hurting his hand. He seemed far too vacant of eye and unreal of being, too much inclined to try hard for a time but to effect nothing in the end. To be sure, we did not expect him to free us with a wave of his umbrella or even to force anything out of the Japanese against their wishes. We were, however, aware that a firm will, steady and unrelenting pressure, and an ability to appear loudly outraged and genuinely angry while keeping a cool head could work wonders. No one gave Laubscher the slightest chance of producing these traits out of his seemingly flabby ego. We waited, without much hope, to see what he could do for us.

What he did in fact accomplish, he explained to a group of us shortly before the end of the war.

"You see, friends," said he in his soft, old-world voice, "it all started when a Chinese dressed like a coolie rang the Swiss consulate bell in Tsingtao late one night and asked for me. Since he would allow no one else in the room when he spoke to me—he said he did not trust my servants!—I was a trifle nervous. However, I tried—ahem!—to keep a walking stick near me!"

A small chuckle went round his group of listeners at the picture of the 120-pound Laubscher defending himself in single combat!

"He told me," Laubscher continued, "he had sneaked into town that night from the guerrilla band in the hills. The day before the American Air Force from West China had made one of its usual 'drops' to the guerrillas. Among the packages were four large crates. It said in an attached letter—fortunately, friends, the Yanks had enough sense not to mark the crates!— these were designated for the camp at Weihsien. The letter also said the crates were full of medicines. The next night, said the coolie, four of their band would come to the consulate at two A.M. to give the crates to me. I was to receive them quite alone and to tell no one. It was up to me to get those crates into the camp to the internees.

"With these abrupt words the coolie left me. I must admit, friends, I was dazed and worried by all this. Not only was it risky; it was baffling—how could *I* carry off the role of fearless and omnicompetent secret agent? For the first, but not the last, time during this episode, I allowed myself a little drink to calm my nerves!

"Sure enough, the next night at two, the bell rang at the gate. Having cleared the residence of servants, I opened the gates myself. Without a word four coolies marched in, each with a large wooden crate on his shoulder. At my order they piled them in my private office—I had planned to stow them away myself afterward in the consulate strong room adjoining it. Then they left.

"I stared at this treasure: four boxes of medicines! How wonderful for the camp, I said to myself—but then I stopped dead, paralyzed by my next thought. How the hell—pardon me!—was I going to get those crates into the camp? The Japanese knew well that bicarb and aspirin were the principal medications I could buy in Tsingtao. Where would I have run across all of this? For three hours I sat there on one of the crates almost in despair, trying to think of an answer—and again friends, I cheered myself a very great deal with a nip now and then!

"I kept asking myself: 'What will I say when I try to get approval for this list at the consular police office here in Tsingtao?' Discouraged there, I would then ask, 'What can I tell the Japanese at the camp one hundred miles away when I arrive with all of these crates?' And friends, it came like a flash! Suddenly my brain focused on the distinction between these two authorities, one in Tsingtao and the other at Weihsien, and my plan began to form.

"The next morning I told my Swiss secretary—I could, I decided, trust her—to type me out a list of all the drugs I could buy in Tsingtao. There were about twenty-five to thirty such items, I should think. Most important, I told her, she was to leave four spaces in her list between each item. Puzzled, but obedient to my command—ahem!—she did this and gave me a list about four pages long.

"Then I rushed with this list to the office of the Japanese consular police for their approval—everything I bring into camp must, you know, be okayed first by them. I must admit that the official looked at the open spaces on my list with some amazement; then he looked at me curiously, as if to ask, 'What the hell is this little fool up to?' I tried not to notice his look or to seem nervous, so I hummed a little tune to myself, tapped my umbrella impatiently on the floor, and gazed out the window. Hopefully, so I told myself, this official cannot figure out anything wrong or dangerous about all those spaces. How could he, I thought, even form a sensible question to me about it? If I wanted to use up the consulate stationery in such a scandalously wasteful way, then that was my funeral! I almost chuckled at this thought, as I stared out the window. At last, with a skeptical sigh, the Japanese reached in his drawer, pulled out his little seal, and gave the list his official chop.

"Elated I sped back to the consulate. I told my secretary to use the same typewriter and now to fill in the vacant spaces on the list with the names of all the drugs in the crates. I must say, gentlemen, she *did* look at me then with new eyes!

"The next day I caught the early morning train to Weihsien, and was at the camp gates with the crates by midafternoon. Again the Japanese officials were puzzled. Where had this little foreign fool gotten all these drugs? Had a shipment come from Japan that they didn't know about? Again they looked curiously first at my list and then at me—and again I hummed my little tune and gazed in the other direction. Apparently they decided it must be all right since there was no doubt about the consular chop at the bottom of the list. The official said, 'Okay'; at last the gates swung open; and my cart filled with the crates rolled into camp and up to the hospital door. I shall never forget the look on the faces of you doctors when I took you out to show you the crates and then gave you that list with their contents!

"Again, friends, I must tell you that I had myself quite a nightcap when I got home again to Tsingtao!"

When Laubscher had finished and stepped down, everyone looked at him with as much amazement and curiosity as had the Japanese officials he had so completely outwitted. From then on he was greeted whenever he came to camp with a new affection and certainly a new respect. I often thought that he deserved at the least a small statue placed somewhere near the hospital, complete with battered homburg, rolled umbrella, stiff collar, and rheumy—but cagey—eye!

When I returned to the kitchen after my stay in the hospital, I found that there had been some changes. McDaniel had quit his cooking job; and I, being for various reasons the only one available, was asked to take his place as boss cook.

I was totally inexperienced in the real art of cooking. But the ablest of the helpers on the shift promised that I could ask him to check the amount of seasoning to be used, the timing of foods, and other matters. So I agreed to boss a shift, and that remained my job until the winter following. I had been grumbling a good deal that no one wanted to make the food better, and that nothing more was needed than a little energy and ingenuity. Now I had the chance to show what I could do.

Things got underway when Taffy Griffiths joined us about a month later. Taffy was a handsome, bony, blond Welshman, an executive for Kailon, with plenty of energy and brains, and a wild temper. No cooking project, however grandiose or complicated, daunted him. No plan involved too much work.

As the youngest of seven in his family, he had been responsible for helping his mother in the kitchen in Aberdare. There, as he often said, he learned a great deal about cooking; he had a feeling for what would work and how to fashion a dish so that it would taste good. Taffy became the brains of our team. I tried to maintain diplomatic relations with the helpers, the management, and the public, which was no simple task, for Taffy would go right through the roof if any stupid, lazy, or irrational person got too near him! Later we were joined by another inventive person, Laura Holcomb, an American from the Y.W.C.A. These two were largely responsible for the virtual revolution in camp cooking that took place during that spring and summer.

Weihsien food was not only meager and lacking in nutrition; it suffered from being monotonously liquid. All we seemed able to cook—given our great cauldrons and the numbers to be served—were soups, stews and, for an occasional dessert, a rather sloppy vanilla or caramel custard.

A cook's greatest challenge, then, was to prepare the small issue of beef and potatoes, our basic foods, so that they could be served "dry"—that is, put on a plate rather than in a bowl. Our first effort was to braise the cubed meat, fry the potatoes—no easy task in a great iron cauldron over a temperamental fire—and serve them on the side with a separate gravy. This sort of dry stew with its elements separated involved a lot more work, but it delighted everyone.

A considerable variety of dishes followed this first "break-through." We began to use the bakery ovens after the bread was finished. Soon we were turning out shepherd's pies (meat pies with a biscuit-dough crust) or *peroshki* (large dough balls with meat fillings) made by the Russian women. Such undertakings involved a large crowd of women volunteers working with us, filling the two hundred bread tins while we carted them to and from the bakery. Sometimes when we had a sufficient supply of cooking oil, we could fry in deep fat; once in a great while, when we received an unusually large issue of meat, we could roast the pieces of meat in the ovens and serve them sliced. This was luxury indeed.

Perhaps we were proudest of our very occasional desserts. Desserts, such as cakes and tarts, were not easy to make in the large quantities we required even when we had saved up the needed supplies. But with Laura's help, we developed a way of making them that involved a kind of assembly line along which several large bowls were passed successively. One woman would work in the oil and sugar; another would add the flour to each bowl; a third the flavoring and soda, and the last one the water. After eight or nine bowls had thus passed down the line, there would be a batter for one hundred cakes, a shortbread dough for eight hundred pieces, or even—when we could buy dried fruit in the canteen—individual tarts for everyone. In such cases, the bakers would volunteer their help. Not a little of our shift's ability to cook extras came from the help of an American veterinarian from Tientsin. Unable to practice his profession in the camp, he became the camp's master baker. He would turn out two hundred tins of shortbread in touchy and often uncontrollable ovens without scorching a single piece.

Looking back at it I am sure that this sort of development of new and better techniques—at first slow but gradually gaining momentum—took place in every area of camp work. I was a part of it in the kitchen and I found it very exciting. I hated, therefore, to give up being a cook. But during the last winter of the war (1944–1945) our able manager tired of his thankless job, and persuaded me to run for the office in his place. Since I had the backing of most of the kitchen staff and, thanks entirely to Taffy and Laura, a reputation as a cook, I was elected. For the last nine months of camp, therefore, as manager I was not so much involved in the creative problems of how to devise new dishes as I was in the political and organizational crises that such a large institution as a kitchen for eight hundred diners inevitably generated.

There were many other sorts of heavy work besides kitchen cooking and stoking. But once in the kitchen I was never seriously tempted by them. Our most serious rival—that is, work for which men were apt to leave the kitchen—was the bakery. This seemed at first strange to me because baking was almost the hardest physical labor we had, and in summer certainly the most unpleasant. There men had to set, knead, shape, and bake four hundred loaves a day in a crude, hot bakery.

Apparently, however, the job held satisfaction all its own and one peculiarly male. Baking required of each man a regular routine of exacting hard physical labor as a member of a closely coordinated team. In this effort there was no "boss" forever giving directions; rather each exercised his own well-learned skill in oft-rehearsed coordination with the others. At the end of his day, a baker felt he had worked both hard and productively; he had never been bothered by the complaints of a howling public;

and he had done this demanding yet serene work in a tight and very familiar community of his fellows.

By contrast, kitchen work, while equally a team operation, was always varied and hence always had to be directed by the boss cook who alone knew what was planned and how he meant to produce it. Thus the "helper" was no more than that, a skilled man but one working always under someone else's direction. If the stew was tasteless or ran short, the public let a man know quickly enough that his shift had "done a lousy job that day." Whereas if the bread turned out poorly, the public commiserated with the bakers over their poor yeast!

Besides stoking at the ovens, working in the kitchens, tending the boilers, pumping water into the water towers at kitchens and showers, and hauling supplies to and fro, the other heavy work was carried on in the carpenter and fitter's shop. Surprisingly, a crew of some thirty men was kept busy continually, repairing utensils, supply crates, rooms, windows, etc., which hard usage had rendered unusable. The men in the shop also rebuilt much of the hospital, one of the kitchens, and redid the boilers that gave us hot water. They did this work wholly with materials "scrounged" here and there in the compound, and refashioned for this new use. The equipment with which the camp was originally furnished consisted of next to nothing.

Besides kitchens, bakery, hospital, and shop—what we called our "utilities"—there were many other forms of work necessary for our common life. There was the leisurely, comradely, but otherwise unappealing task of keeping the three men's latrines clean. The two-man crew in charge of the one near our dorm consisted of a middle-aged American missionary and a retired British banker. The casual naturalness with which they went about their job showed the radical changes camp life had wrought in attitudes. Instead of being horrified at their work, these men made the most of its friendly, social possibilities. They laughed and joked with each client—and everyone was their client!

Often that retired banker with his white mustache and twinkling eyes would complain to me that we cooks had given them more business than they really wanted that day—or to the baker that the bread had been unusually heavy. As a result, he and his partner had seen no one at all after breakfast—and "How the hell am I to get the news of the world if no one comes in?"

Interestingly enough, for whatever reason, no women in camp

would take on as a steady job the cleaning of their latrines. All the able-bodied ones had to take it in turn, therefore, each one doing her bit of cleaning about one week during the year. Although it was admittedly an unpleasant enough job, most of the men suspected they relished its opportunity for conspicuous martyrdom, for without fail, one could always tell who was on that week.

And the gayer ones had a fine time with it. Clad in long boots and carrying a large mop—symbols of their trade—they would greet every male they met with a cheery wave and ask, "Guess what job I've got this week! Why not come along and give me a hand with the heavy work?"

Most fascinating of all about these strange (to men) female arrangements was the fact that the only women in camp who deliberately avoided this latrine duty were two Russian women married, respectively, to a wealthy American and a wealthy Briton.

The point certainly was not that they were Russian. They hired other Russian women to do these chores for them, paying them in coffee sent in to them by relatives in Tientsin. And it was a wonderful Russian woman, married to the British Professor of English at Yenching, who voluntarily took on the odorous and bruising task of running this cleanup crew for the women's latrines.

Obviously the cause of their refusal was that they were both hoping to move up socially into colonial society and out of the nothingness of refugee society. They had, one could not but guess, married these well-to-do men for their wealth and their prestige. They did not intend to lose all this newly gained social status by falling back into the kind of life they had left behind them. For them, if there was any one symbol of that old life, it was the job of taking care of women's conveniences!

The irony of this was intensified by the fact that the socially prominent wives of high-ranking British business officials would never have dreamed of refusing to do this work, once it became a recognized form of community service. While the two women who aspired to grandeur were too proud and too insecure to do it, the British possessors of status were too proud and too secure to refuse.

The mind of the refugee Russian woman, working her way up, was dominated by precisely those values lacking in the social milieu she had just quitted. Refugee society in the Orient was dismal: abysmally poor and protected by no government of their own, they were the most vulnerable of any foreign group to every economic or political upheaval. They had been badly misused by the Japanese, who had forced them into all sorts of unwelcome labor. Anyone with energy would do almost anything to leave that society.

Among the values idolized by this group were, therefore, material security, personal cleanliness, escape from lower-class life and its humiliating chores, and so on. To do this work of cleaning toilets was to repudiate every value of one's new existence. A woman dare not do it for fear of falling back and so losing her one hope of being a lady. In her own mind, she was still a poor refugee. Work like this, so perfectly fitting her inward assessment of her status, frightened her.

To the secure British woman of the colonial upper class, on the other hand, who had been placed at the top by birth and breeding, this job held no social threat at all. Even in dirty, refuse-covered boots, she felt and knew herself to be a "lady." This job was merely a role adopted for the moment; it did not fit either her inward assessment of herself or the way she thought others would assess her and so it held no terrors. Moreover, she was also conforming to the subtler standards and requirements of that upper class, namely to be a sport, to do your share, to co-operate willingly even though it was distasteful. These standards she dare not ignore, however uncomfortable the job might prove to be to her. Only such a person well within an upper-class group would even be *aware* of those standards—not someone looking longingly up from below. The Russian women had no idea at all that they had broken those rules. In this situation, a lack of "breeding" did seem to hurt, but it did hurt only those women desperately wanting to be considered well born, and in their very desperation proving to all and sundry that they had not been.

There were innumerable other jobs, although none of them so unusual. One of them was in the shoe repair shop. No new shoes were available in Weihsien. Since many people had arrived with only the well-worn pairs bought on the last trip home years before, four men were kept continually busy rescuing dilapidated shoes from nonexistence. Finally, next door to the watch repair and barber shops, was the sewing room where a crew of women tried to patch together the tattered garments of the camp's bachelors.

One pair of undershorts of mine brewed up quite a metaphysical storm in our dormitory. Since the shorts were so covered with patches that only the band around the middle contained some of the original cloth, a nice philosophical point was raised: was it now the same old pair of shorts, and if not, at what point had it become another pair?

Day in and day out, the camp was a small hive of activity, most of it manual and vigorous. Everyone became more efficient in dealing with the practical problems of life than he had been when he came in. Men who had never used a hammer put up shelves on their walls. Others who had never seen a mason's trowel built clever brick stoves in their rooms; these stoves had an oven inside so that they not only heated the room, but also baked a modest cake or cookies. In summer everyone constructed elaborate awnings of mats bought in the canteen, and thus provided pleasant shade for the patio in front of their room.

After we had been there a year or so, an exhibit was held of the artifacts that ingenious people from all professions had made. They were almost unbelievable to one not blessed with technical or inventive gifts. They included the fanciest of brick stoves, sliding screen doors and windows, homemade cooling systems, elegantly fitted cabinets, and beautifully wrought oil lamps. Most fascinating to me was an intricate and finely balanced system of shelves that would, at the mere touch of a finger, disappear on ropes to the ceiling and thus free half the floor space of a small room.

The display drove home to me the truth that no practical situation, however unwieldy or difficult, was too much for human ingenuity. This group of humans had been faced with the total lack of all the comforts to which they had been accustomed, and for once they were unable to purchase gadgets ready made. Thus all the intense technical creativity that resides in any group of men became active. Each in his own way embarked with energy and skill on the task of raising ever higher our level of material comfort.

We came to realize, however, that a community of people needs more to keep them going than the bare necessities. We all felt this as early as the first dreary week, when we crowded into the church on Saturday night and sang our throats out, as a talented monk and a Salvation Army captain led us in familiar songs. Encouraged by this visceral response to even the simplest form of entertainment, some of us from Yenching University started to work up a few topical skits.

The missionary and educational community in North China, happily, on the whole, as long on brains and talent as on piety, had for many years been putting on an annual summer revue at their common vacation spot at Peitaiho. Almost all of them were accustomed to writing or to singing silly lyrics to old songs, and to cavorting in kilts, togas, or what have you about a stage while some elderly professor solemnly intoned "Lochinvar" or "Hia-watha."

We began to write, plan, and practice a small revue. We were sure *we* liked this kind of nonsense. But would this conglomerate community find it funny?

We were a somewhat apprehensive foursome as we strode to the front of the stage, dressed in camp working clothes and looking as grimy as possible. Then we pantomimed and sang a song about camp labor to the tune of "Solomon Levi." To our relief and delight, the audience shook the building with their roars, and stamped for us to return and sing it again and again. The reason, of course, was not that either song or singers were good, but that after that trying first month, this was the best— almost the only—laugh the internees had had.

For the first time, they were able to get out of their miserable selves and to rise for the moment above their troubles by laughing at them and at themselves—a kind of reverse "cathar-sis" in which the tragedy in an audience's real life is relieved by an analogous comedy on stage.

This was the beginning. From that point on, it was just a matter of time until the large number who were interested in drama and music went to work and eventually developed our Saturday night entertainments in the church to a high level. Later that spring we were treated to our first real theater. This took the form of two one-act plays; I had a part in the second, a very funny thing by A. P. Herbert. There was no attempt to make sets for these; one or two simple articles of furniture sufficed.

By summer, full-length plays began to appear, each developing its dramatic art and its sets to a little higher point than the last. Among the dozen or so plays produced, I recall having small parts in Noel Coward's *Hayfever* and James Barrie's *Mr. Pim Passes By,* and enjoying thoroughly a hair-raising production of *Night Must Fall* and a most hilarious *Private Lives.* Two British couples in their thirties took the four roles in that latter play and did not need, it might be noted, too much coaching for those parts. These couples were our most talented dramatists, and were able to write and produce two very funny comedy-and-song revues of their own. After the rather heavy dose of Barrie, this more earthy sort of humor in which they excelled came as a great relief. The culmination of this dramatic development was reached in June, 1945, when a full-scale performance of Shaw's *Androcles and the Lion* was staged with three complete stage sets, a full-sized lion made of cloth and cardboard, and armor and helmets for ten Roman guards soldered together out of tin cans from the Red Cross parcels.

We had musicians among us as well as actors, so two musical Saturday evenings were provided during each "season." There was a choral society which sang Handel's *Messiah,* Stainer's *The Crucifixion,* Mendelssohn's *Elijah,* and others. The camp boasted a more than passable symphonette of some twenty-two pieces, whose last concert included a full performance (minus bass violins and tuba) of Mozart's Concerto in D Minor. Unlike the other instruments, most of which had been brought from Peking or Tientsin in a trunk or by hand, the piano had been found in a most dilapidated state in the church basement. It had been banged up by the soldiers quartered there, but it was speedily renovated by camp musicians and used to great effect in all our concerts.

Except in the worst heat of summer and cold of winter when the church was not habitable, there was a remarkably good entertainment each weekend: a play, a revue, a choral program— all calculated to take the edge off our otherwise monotonous life. As we often said to one another, when one is immersed in a play or listening to a symphony, the mind is most easily transported beyond the walls of the camp. For two hours each week that rather ragged group of people were enabled to make a brief return to London's West End or to an off-Broadway haunt. Hence every person in camp, many old hands and many who had never been to a play or a concert before, jammed into our entertainments; for the last year and a half we had to run shows on both Friday and Saturday nights to accommodate the crowds.

A person could not live through this vivid experience of the dynamic and progressive development of a small civilization without having his ideas profoundly affected—and I found my own changing right before my eyes, so to speak. First of all, I was deeply impressed not only by the courage and tenacity of my fellow humans but also by their inventiveness. However strange the world in which they may be set down, they will adapt themselves to it bravely, I was finding. Then gradually their ingenuity will find means to improve their situation. No problem of sanitation, cooking, or drama was so difficult that some means can not be devised to cope with it. Soon that means itself will be improved, and so on in a progressive spiral of development.

I rapidly concluded that the capacity of men to develop the technical aspects of civilization—know-how—is limitless. I knew I would never again despair of man's ability to progress in both knowledge and practical techniques.

Along with this new faith in man's inherent capabilities to make himself increasingly comfortable and secure, I gained a fresh appreciation of the basic character of these material problems. As I became involved in the day-to-day crises of housing, toilets, and food production, I could not deny, whatever my philosophy or my faith seemed to tell me, that these were the problems that must be solved first of all. I felt this because they are the essential base on which the rest of life might be built later. Our concerts, lectures, and library were, to be sure, important to our life. But whatever else happened, we had to eat, to be warm, to be dry.

Given sufficient food and water by a well-oiled civilization, those of us of the so-called intelligentsia are apt to undervalue the importance of material values in favor of the life of the mind. Consequently they come to regard the world's producers of food, shoes, blankets, or medicines as somehow less worthy, less meritorious, than the artist, the philosopher, the poet, and the preacher, all of whom may feed men's souls.

This view is possible, I discovered, only when material needs are so completely satisfied that they can be safely forgotten. I found that whenever this satisfaction was endangered, the importance of physical needs immediately became apparent to everyone. In the beginning, the men who made our camp civilization possible were the practical men who could learn quickly and efficiently to cook and bake our food, to repair our equipment, and to cleanse our latrines.

When the full impact of this important truth bore in on me, I found myself facing a crisis in belief. In my own life I had already experienced some profound changes with respect to religion and its place. I had been brought up in a tolerant but strongly dedicated liberal religious home. I had early imbibed its ethical idealism and its de-emphasis of the material and sensual sides of life. Then, as a college philosophy major, seduced by the beguilements of Santayana, I had found the religion of my youthful environment uninteresting, naïve, and somewhat sentimental. Because of this I took from my early environment only its ethical emphasis and left the religion aside. "Why," I asked myself, "add religious frills to the ethical commitments any unbelieving naturalist can easily avow? Cannot the modern agnostic intellectual be capable by himself of leading a creative and upright life devoted to the moral absolutes of peace in the world and justice in society?"

One might call this a collegiate idealism, resting uneasily on a naturalistic base. It "came a cropper" under the hammer blows of the years 1939 and 1940. Hitler's rise to power revealed such naturalistic idealism to be itself not only naïve but ineffectual. To support justice in that time was to relinquish peace, for Hitler could be overcome only with force. On the other hand, to support peace through noninvolvement was to acquiesce in the injustice of a Nazi-dominated world. It seemed that if a man were to devote himself to either of the two great ideals and work wholeheartedly for peace or for justice, he had to be unrealistic about the real world. While if he tried to be realistic, and saw the ambiguity of the true historical situation, inevitably he became cynical about the relevance of these great ideals to practical life. An ethical existence based on devotion to ideals seemed to have run aground.

Like most of my college generation, I sat miserable and confused as France fell, unable to take a stand anywhere. Should we enter the war and disrupt our peace? Should we remain in neutrality and so allow a tyranny to rule the rest of the world? I knew in this experience that loyalty to something deeper than these now conflicting moral ideals would be necessary if I were going to live creatively in the real world.

This deeper framework for life came to me rather suddenly, as to many in those years, through the speaking and writing of Reinhold Niebuhr. Here was a searching realism that was willing to face all the ambiguity and squalor of any human social situation. At the same time, it was intensely moral, for it had a deep commitment to human good. The difference was that this commitment was not based either on a belief in the overriding goodness of men or even on the possibility of establishing ideal solutions in social history—both of which seemed contradicted by the obvious facts. It was based on faith in God, and it resulted in a call to serve one's fellows however ambiguous the situation in which man might find himself. It was now possible for me to face the war with a realism that was not cynical and an idealism that was not naïve.

I was intensely interested in this new "realistic theology" when, just out of college, I went out in 1940 to China to teach English at Yenching. Although I had had no seminary training, I devoured theological tomes every moment of my free time from then until I went to camp in 1943. By that time my whole orientation had changed: from the naturalistic humanist of my college days, I became what I felt to be a "convinced Christian." My new faith, however, was not so much the result of any personal religious experience as it was the intellectual conviction that only in terms of the Christian view of things could I make sense out of the social history in which we live and the ethical decisions we humans have to make. And so to camp I went, replete with theological jargon, many secondhand concepts, and a conviction that mine was the only way in which to view life.

For a person thus encumbered, those first months of camp raised the most urgent and devastating of questions: What's so important anyway about the way a person looks at life? Isn't this a typically intellectualist way of looking at our crises? Are these "big problems of life" really problems at all? Surely the issues of our existence are not these intellectual points of naturalism vs. Christian faith, or even of idealism vs. psychoanalysis. Such are all right for the philosophically minded collegian; but are they basic? The real issues of life are surely material and political: how we can eat and keep warm, be clothed and protected from the weather, and organize our common efforts. These matters are resolved by practical experience and by techniques, not by this or that philosophy or religious faith, however convincing an expression of that faith may be to the cool observer of the scene.

It was not that I thought religion wrong; I simply thought it irrelevant. What real function in actual life does it perform under conditions where basic problems are dealt with by techniques and organizational skill?

I was quite willing to admit that there are people who are interested in the nature of man and the universe; and that apparently there are others who enjoy religion and going to church. But, unlike food and sanitation which one must have in order to live, is not religion merely a matter of personal taste, of temperament, essential only if someone wants it but useless if one does not happen to be the type that likes it? Is there any "secular" use for religion; does it have any value for the common life of mankind? Or is it there useless, because secularity with its techniques, its courage, and its idealism is quite able to create a full human life without religion? As I asked myself these questions over and over throughout those first months of camp, I became what we might call "secular." That is, I was a man convinced that while religion might help those who liked it, it was a waste of time for others. Certainly "the others" now included myself.

Wherever I turned, everything I saw reinforced this view. Of what use to our life were the vocations of teaching philosophy or preaching Christianity? Those of us who had performed these tasks in the outside world now carried our weight of camp work, yes—but not in *those* roles. We were useful only insofar as teacher or evangelist became able stoker or competent baker.

No one on the Labor Committee ever ventured to suggest that philosophizing or preaching be regarded as valid camp jobs. That fact alone appeared to me to be an adequate commentary on their social usefulness. Apparently our intellectual, and especially our "religious," vocations were so unrelated to the real needs of life that they had to become "avocations." They were relegated to the categories of leisure-time and Sunday activities. The engineer, the doctor, the laborer, the producer, on the other hand, were asked to modulate, but not to abandon, their vocations when they entered our community. Each of their callings proved its worth by the necessity for it in the support of our material existence, and by the fact that those of us in "spiritual" vocations had to learn other skills if we were to take part in the daily work.

For these reasons, after I arrived at camp, I quickly lost my former interest both in religious activities and in theological reflection. The missionaries were, it is true, achieving a unity and accord hitherto unknown, both among the various groups of Protestants and between the Protestants as a whole and the Catholics. Numerous joint enterprises consisting of lectures, services, and the like were planned and initiated. In all of this I took only the mildest interest, and soon found myself dropping out altogether.

My feelings found full expression one Sunday when, rushing by the church bent on some errand for the Housing Committee, I heard a familiar hymn ringing out through the open windows. I asked myself irritably, "What for—when there are so many important things to be done?" And shaking my head in disbelieving wonder, I went on about my business.

V ✍ A Place of One's Own

By the end of the first month of camp, my view of life was being altered. I went back to the confident humanism so characteristic of the liberal academic circles in America I had recently quitted. As I looked around me during those early weeks, I felt convinced that man's ingenuity in dealing with difficult problems was unlimited, making irrelevant those so-called "deeper issues" of his spiritual life with which religion and philosophy pretended to deal.

Gradually, however, as I encountered more and more unexpected problems in my work in housing, I began to realize that this confident attitude toward things simply did not fit the realities of camp life. It was not that our material crises seemed any less urgent, or that our minds were any less capable of dealing with them. Rather, new sorts of problems kept arising that improved know-how could not resolve. For over and over what we can only call "moral" or "spiritual" difficulties continually cropped up. Crises occurred that involved not a breakdown in techniques, but a breakdown in character, showing the need for more moral integrity and self-sacrifice. The trouble with my new humanism, I found myself deciding, was not its confidence in human science and technology. It was rather its naïve and unrealistic faith in the rationality and goodness of the men who wielded these instruments. If the courage and ingenuity of man were evidenced in every facet of camp life, equally apparent was the intense difficulty all of us experienced in being fair-minded, not to say just or generous, under the hard pressure of our rough and trying existence.

But most important of all, what became increasingly plain was that these crises of the soul were not of such a character as to disturb merely the prim and the straight-laced in our midst. On a critical level equal to an outbreak of dysentery or a stoppage of our bread supply, these moral breakdowns were so serious that they threatened the very existence of our community. It became increasingly evident to me that unless these inward crises could be resolved, the entire microcosmic civilization which we had so painstakingly established to feed and care for us would not live much longer. I began to see that without moral health, a community is as helpless and lost as it is without material supplies and services.

This was the deepest lesson I learned from this experience. Since that time, both in studies and in observation generally, it has seemed to me to be a truth validated over and over in the life of every human society, great or small.

The first inkling I had of the approach of these crises of a deeper sort—caused by what we can only call the essential intractability of the human animal—came shortly after we on the Housing Committee had made the camp census. Shields and I knew that great sections of the camp were terribly overcrowded. We also knew that our next task was to try to provide these people with more room. The difficulty, of course, was that nowhere in camp did anyone have any more space than he needed. Thus, if any extra space for our unfortunates was to be won at all, it had to be snatched from the person barely able to make himself comfortable and so, fair game. One or two brushes with the public had shown the difficulty of our task, and with both apprehension and excitement we began to talk about what we would do.

While we were pondering our first steps, a deputation of three single men appeared in the quarters office. When asked what they wanted, they replied a trifle aggressively, I thought: "Fair treatment from the Housing Committee."

Somewhat taken aback by this, I nevertheless said confidently, "Sure, and that's what you'll get! What's up, and how can we help you?"

"Our case is quite simple," said the elderly head of the group, an ex-soldier lamed by World War I and formerly the proprietor of a small bookshop in Tientsin. "We three," and he looked at the other two, a young American tobacco man and a British schoolmaster, "live in a dormitory room in Block 49. There are eleven men in our small room, and we have barely space to turn around, much less to stow our stuff in any comfort. Across the hall is a room exactly the same size—isn't it, chaps?"

The other two nodded in agreement. Apparently two of them had measured it while the third held its unsuspecting inmates in conversation.

"In that room there are only nine men—and in ours eleven. Now we suggest that you rectify this obvious injustice by moving one of our men in with them. Surely that's fair enough, isn't it, chaps?" The other two mumbled in grim agreement.

I must admit I felt elated. Here at last was a perfectly clear-cut case. Surely the injustice in this situation was, if it ever was in life, clear and distinct: since the rooms were next to each other, anyone who could (like Descartes) count and measure could see the inequity involved.

The solution was so easy: if we did move one man, then each room would have ten persons. "Are not people rational and moral?" I asked myself. "Does this not mean—if it means any-thing—that the average man, when faced with a clear case of injustice which his mind can distinctly perceive, will at the least agree to rectify that injustice—even if he himself suffers from that rectification? And besides, isn't it true that people are more apt to share with each other when they are in some common difficulty, like on a raft at sea, than they are in the humdrum pursuits of normal life?" So I argued to myself as I confidently accompanied the delegates to Block 49.

Justice is, however, one thing in theory and another in actu-ality. In the realm of theory, justice brings with it few liabilities, but in life, being reasonable and fair may mean the loss of precious inches of living space!

When I entered the dorm and said that I was from the Housing Committee, at once I could feel the inmates becoming wary. Their suspicions, I noted, did not decrease when they saw the three-man deputation from the next room behind me. Then, when I began to talk about the problem that had brought me there, their hostility came out into the open. One rather hard British engineer summed up the sentiments of the men standing there sullenly silent: "Sure we're sorry for those chaps over there. But what has that got to do with us? We're plenty crowded here as it is, and their worries are their tough luck. Listen, old boy, we're not crowding up for you or for anyone!"

In response, I argued with a good deal of passion the logic of this situation. I stressed as strongly as I could the sheer irrationality of nine men in one room and eleven in the other when both were the same size, and so the evident fairness of their taking in another man.

"That may be, friend. But let me tell you a thing or two. Fair or not fair, if you put one of them in here, we are merely heaving him out again. And if you come back here about this, we are heaving you out, too!"

Some of the others standing there wanted to be reasonable rather than emotional or threatening. So they argued the whole matter with me, expressing their doubts as to the wisdom of this particular course, or asking me, "Why do you pick on this particular dorm?"

In rebuttal, I found myself defending all the actions of the committee to date, explaining the present housing situation of the entire camp, and most of our future plans—and slowly realizing that these rational arguments were futile and would lead nowhere. Clearly the driving force behind the reaction of these men was not their intellectual doubts as to the justice of our proposal but, on the contrary, the intense desire to hang onto their space.

This desire was at the root of the matter. It determined not only their emotional reactions but, to my wide-eyed surprise, it seemed even to determine the way they approached the issue in their minds. Thus, to try as I did merely to move their minds by rational or moral persuasion was to leave quite unaffected the fundamental dynamic force in the situation, namely the fear that if another man came in, each of them would be that much the more crowded. I almost laughed aloud when a queer thought struck me: Why *should* a man wish to be reasonable or moral if he thereby lost precious space? Do men *really* value their own moral excellence more than they value their own comfort and security? I seemed to be staring suddenly into a new abyss of complexity and trouble in human affairs. If men really cared less about being "rational" and "good" than they did about their comfort, where did that leave my belief in men's basic goodness?

I came home that night confused and shaken. Everything that I had believed about "our sorts of people," about the ordinary civilized man, had said to me that his behavior would be fair and generous once he understood a situation. Most of our philosophers, educators, social scientists, and social psychologists had assumed this. For did not most of our modern culture hold that scientific knowledge and technical advance *did* lead to social progress? And did this not imply that the men who used this knowledge would be rational and just when they understood things clearly through organized inquiry?

But in Block 49 men understood—they understood fully. They understood that a "reform" meant their own loss, and so they fought that reform, whatever its rationality and justice, as if it were a plague, a poisonous thing. Self-interest seemed almost omnipotent next to the weak claims of logic and fair play.

Ironically, in this first and most logically clear of all our many cases, our committee, if justice were to be done, finally had to appeal to the least rational of all principles: the authority of force. We asked Mr. Izu to tell this recalcitrant dorm to take one more man, which they did readily enough—and we heard no more from Block 49.

Discouragingly enough, this was the consistent pattern of all the scores of cases with which we dealt in the following weeks. Only in one case in six months of quarters work did I manage to convince anyone that a change for the worse was the just and fair thing to do, and persuade them to do it.

A young boy of thirteen or so had been put by the Japanese in one 9-by-12 room with his mother and stepfather, a small trades-manlike couple in their middle forties. Crowding into such a small space would have been hard going for a family made up of any three persons, but in the case of these particular three, it was impossible. The two parents were temperamental and irritable in any event, and the intense pressures built up in this small room caused them to fight endlessly, driving all of them, and especially the boy and his stepfather, to mutual hatred and despair.

We had to get that boy out of there into some dorm where, in his presently vulnerable state, he would not be hurt overmuch. But where to send him? Most of the dorms were overcrowded, and their rather sullen atmosphere would surely have become even more hostile against an added inmate. Then I had an idea, and hurried around to one exceptionally crowded dorm. This dorm held an unusual group made up of missionary doctors, preachers, teachers, engineers, and architects who were in China to perform their diverse professional services for the various mission boards. When I explained to them the nature of the problem and its extreme urgency for the boy's future, they recognized its seriousness at once. One middle-aged architect for the Presbyterian Board, named Leighton, looking at the narrow spaces between the beds, queried, "I can see why you need to get that boy out of his room all right. But why do you ask *us* to do this? We are already more crowded than most dorms."

I decided that with these men only direct speaking would work. "Because," I said, "you are the only group of men who might care about this problem enough to be willing to squeeze up for the boy."

No more was said. Leighton, a wonderfully gentle man, assured me as I left the room that they would make the boy feel at home. They did, and the boy, and his parents, made out surprisingly well from then on.

Of the other cases that came before us, the reaction in every one was the same as in Block 49. Not only would people fail to see the fairness of any action which threatened their welfare; often they would refuse even to consider the issue. It seemed as if the person's entire being or self, mind and emotions alike, would resist and struggle against the loss of space. It was impossible to penetrate that resistance by logic, pleading, or argument. Something about the loss of space touched a "vital nerve." When that happened, objectivity and reasonableness seemed automatically to vanish.

The importance of space to the well-being, nay the existence, of a person came as a surprise to me. I am sure it was partly because I had never lacked space before. I used to think about this situation a lot, especially after seeing mature people battling to maintain their small plots, or even, as in the case of the women's dorm, sneaking precious inches from their neighbors at night. Somehow each self needs a "place" in order to be a self, in order to feel on a deep level that it really exists. We are, apparently, rootless beings at bottom. Unless we can establish roots somewhere in a place where we are at home, which we possess to ourselves and where our things are, we feel that we float, that we are barely there at all. For to exist with no place is to fail to exist altogether.

Perhaps the greatest anxiety that dormitory life created was the feeling of not belonging anywhere, of existing so to speak in the free and faceless air. Everyone, having lost his "place" in his home and club porch in the treaty ports, and thrown into cramped quarters with insufficient room to establish himself, felt less than real until he had made some small corner of space his own.

Needless to say, this problem of space is confined neither to a camp nor to the problem of physical area. All of us need a space that is ours in every environment in which we exist, whether it is in the physical world, in the social world of family, friends, and community in which we identify ourselves as persons, or in the vocational world where we function professionally. In many cases, one of these levels of space can replace another level, so that a man can put up with having no physical space of his own if he has a creative and definite place among friends or in his work. But no man can bear rootlessness on all levels at once.

Thus lonely and isolated people in our dorms would cling to every inch of space as if it were the very foundation of their being—as indeed it was. They would lavish on it and its sacred dimensions the same fanatical love that a nation will lavish on the boundaries of its territory. And in the wider world, each of us, driven by this fear of never "being" at all, is eager to "make a place for himself" by almost any method available. And it is for that reason that we will defend our present status with all our ferocity if we should feel it threatened.

The clearest illustration of the relation of space to human intractability came with the problem of families of four in one room. Apparently when they housed the camp at the beginning, the Japanese treated the families with two children in two very different ways. They gave two rooms to the twenty-four families with two teen-aged children. But to the twenty or so families with smaller children they gave only one room. For the latter, therefore, life was intolerable. It meant that in a space only 9 by 12 feet—about the size of a dining room rug—two adults, used to a large house, had to live with their entire family. There they had to find room for two more bunks or beds for the children, and provide space for them to play during the long, wet, cold months of North China's winter—not to mention doing the extra cooking and washing that any mother must do for infants. As one of these mothers bitterly accused us in the Housing Committee office shortly after the camp began: "By doing nothing, you are making us bear the main burden of the war!" We could only agree. Something had to be done.

When we began searching for extra space into which these crowded families might overflow, we naturally eyed the twenty-four families of four who had two rooms. Here, obviously, was the only real "Gold Coast" living in the camp, for in each of these twenty-four cases, two teen-agers shared one entire room. Clearly our best hope involved getting these teen-agers to squeeze up a little in some way in order that the embattled mothers of two infants might have a little more space. And as always, I was hopeful of not too difficult a time. When Shields and I looked over the list of twenty-four families with two rooms, I felt optimistic.

"They seem a good lot of folks," I said. "Look here, they are mostly either business or professional types. Here is Roberts the Tientsin doctor, Schmidt the missionary, Ramsbottom-Thomas and Robinson the Tsingtao lawyers. None of them is a trouble-maker or uneducated. Why, they're all respectable middle-class citizens and as moral as they come; just the kind that would support any good cause in their communities at home. Come on, this won't be so bad. With a little persuasion, they'll understand the need and cooperate straight off. You'll see."

We did see. The moment we began to talk with the people on this list about ways of giving the crowded families more space, trouble erupted. No one on this roster of eminently reputable British and Americans would cooperate. Some slammed their doors in our faces; some received us only to argue it out. But one and all were balky.

Our days from then on were filled with endless conflicts. On a typical morning, two or three of the unhappy mothers, acting on the totally correct assumption that the "squeaky axle gets the grease," would storm into our office with the bitter query, "Why don't you men *do* something for us?"

Impelled by an instinct of self-protection as well as by our sense of justice, we would then return to our discussion with the families who had two rooms. "Why is this an issue for us?" they would ask. "We feel sorry for them, sure. But why do you bother us with this business? Good day!"

I remember coming back to the office on one such morning feeling very much beleaguered.

"My God," I said to myself, "their real argument is with each other—not with us. Gee, I'd like to see Mrs. Watts try to remain so aloof in her two rooms if Mrs. Wyndham-Smith got after her! I'll bet they'd soften up fast enough if they heard about the crowding, not from us, but straight from the other mothers themselves."

In the midst of these mutterings I stopped abruptly. An idea had at last dawned. Why not round up all forty-four families and bring them together to discuss the matter? This would relieve us of the onus of blame from each side. What was more important, out of the discussion might come some sort of real compromise or solution. On hearing the moans of the crowded, the other mothers might relent. When I told the idea to Shields, he thought it a capital notion. We asked the camp doctors to be present on the theory that if there were any arguments between the two groups as to which had more need of extra space, the doctors might be able to illuminate the issue with their informed and unbiased judgment.

So we looked forward to the meeting with great expectancy: here would be the rational discussion so desperately needed if the injustice was to be corrected. As soon as the meeting began, however, irrationality took over. As chairman, I could not fail to realize that no discussion whatever was taking place. The two groups of parents sat glumly on opposite sides of the room, their jaws set, their arms crossed in irritation, and their eyes on the floor. They refused to speak to one another on this topic. As one said to me later, "We knew we couldn't change their stubborn minds on the issue, and we knew they were wrong—so why get into a fight about it?"

Representatives from each group rose and argued their respective cases. The other side, like a high school debating team, listened only for some clue to a flaw in their opponent's presentation. If we had hoped by this means to escape the common wrath—and resentment at us was the only theme on which everyone agreed—we were sadly mistaken. The families with crowded rooms continued to tell the committee that we were weaklings and fools to allow mere teen-agers to hang onto all that space. The others berated us for threatening their meager comfort.

By this time I was resigned to the fact that no resolution of the central question of the meeting—"Which sort of family, those with teen-agers or those with infants, needs the most space?"—would be forthcoming.

The arguments were long, intricate, and bitter. When they were ended, not one parent thought the other group had any case at all. Those with small children pointed to potties, to tantrums, to room needed for play, and to the space-consuming chores of washing and cooking for infants. They scoffed at the plight of the teen-agers, "They come home only to sleep," they said, "*if* they do that!" The others argued that the mere physical size of older children crowded a small room unbearably. They also maintained that teen-agers' maturity created real sexual difficulties, because of the crowding, both for the youngsters themselves and for their parents.

Finally, I asked the panel of three doctors if they might not give us some judgment on the merits of each side's case. To my astonished disappointment, these doctors, while undoubtedly lion-hearted as healers, turned out to be cowards politically. They refused to commit themselves, possibly fearing they would lose the respect of one half of the families, and wanting, as one explained to me later, to remain professionally aloof from the battle. (Apparently, like most of us, only when their own professional interests are directly threatened, is this profession—or at least its professional association—willing to give "professional opinions" in the political realm.) In any case, when both sides had "spoken their piece," they all went home agreeing on one point only—that the meeting had been a total waste of time.

We, however, of the Housing Committee were deeply impressed by the weight of argument on both sides: "After all this," I thought, "I don't know which group needs space the more!" And as I walked home that night, I felt depressed.

"Out of those forty-four families, everyone saw *only* the logic of his own case," I reflected. "If that is at all typical of human affairs, then what sort of reality *is* there to the concept of 'impartial reason'? For when it is needed most desperately, that is, when the stakes are high for both parties and they begin to be overwrought, then impartial reason is sadly conspicuous by its absence! Does it fly away every time it is needed, to return only when harmony reigns, when the conflict is over? If that is so, then surely reason is more a symptom or effect of social harmony than it is a cause—and if *that* is so, from whence can we expect social health to come?"

A week or so later, to our delight, we found that owing to the skillful work of the carpenters and engineers, two small dorms, which had hitherto been considered unsalvageable, could now be used for housing. Here was what looked like a heaven-sent solution. Why not form two supervised dorms, one for teen-aged boys and one for the girls? By so doing, we would provide the extra rooms needed to help the crowded families. Two good-hearted missionaries in the camp, both of whom happened to be immensely popular with the teen-agers, volunteered to "proctor" the dorms.

At last we seemed to have found a solution. To make matters even easier, the carpenters had just developed a kind of double-decker bunk which they could install in any room where the occupants requested them. Because of this development, we were able to provide the twenty-four families with an alternative to sending their kids to a dorm, namely, combining forces with another family also with teenagers, and thus save one room between them. But we had not counted on the old Adam. If the children went to a dorm, or even if they moved in with other teen-agers in one room, then the family as a whole was cutting its living space exactly in half. And that was no easy sacrifice for any group of harried humans to contemplate.

At this stage, three unforgettable cases occurred, all of them revealing what we might call variations on the common theme of intractability.

One had to do with a prominent American missionary family. The head of the house, although then middle-aged, was a handsome, intelligent, sophisticated Ivy League graduate. With graying hair, ruddy complexion, and clean-cut features, albeit now a little rotund, he cut a suave figure in gatherings of either business or religious leaders. His wife was a capable, respectable, motherly woman, wedded to innumerable social causes, a born hostess, at once elegant and gracious. They represented almost the model of the American professional couple: educated, liberal, kind-hearted, epitomizing good will and Christian concern. They had two sons, one sixteen and one thirteen, one or both of whom might, therefore, move into a dorm. Since one of the over-crowded families of four lived right next door, I knew these good people were by no means ignorant of the problem. When I knocked at their room, I expected a relatively easy time.

Mrs. White greeted me, as I anticipated, with courtesy and graciousness. As I warmed to my subject, she expressed concern for the plight of these unfortunate people, and assured me that she and her husband were only too willing to do what they could to help solve this problem. Considerably encouraged, I unfolded our plan for a dorm for boys. I told her of the "fine Christian schoolteacher" who would proctor it, and how much I hoped they might agree to help us effect this resolution. At this point in our conversation, Mrs. White, if anything, grew even more polite. But she also grew more vague—I noticed a certain hesitancy. It became harder and harder to get back to the practical details. Finally I suggested that perhaps they would like to have time to think it over and that I would come back the next day for her answer.

"Why, thank you so much" she said with her soft smile, "This will give my husband and me a chance to think and pray about it tonight." On that encouraging note, I left.

When I returned the next day, she seemed both more definite and more sure of herself. I was mildly elated. Here at last, I thought, is someone who will take the lead, not in opposing us but in helping us. I listened eagerly as she began graciously to approach the subject.

"We have had our evening of thought and prayer about the problem you shared with us," she said, smiling at me, "and we have reached our decision. We cannot allow our young sons to go into the dorm."

"But they will be only fifty yards away, Mrs. White!" I exclaimed. "Surely you don't think anything will happen to them there under Eric Ridley's care!"

"Oh no, it's just that Paul is only sixteen and subject to so many influences right now. I don't want to say anything about those other boys, but you know how they are! And besides, the heating and drafts here are very unusual, and I know that, with the little he gets to eat, unless someone watches over him, he will always be getting colds and flu. And it is quite out of the question for Johnny at thirteen to leave us."

"Okay, fair enough"—though I was very disappointed—"Let's look at another alternative then. How about your youngest moving into this room with you, and Paul moving in with the two Jones boys in the next block?"

"Oh no. We talked about that, too, and have made up our minds. We believe in keeping a nice home for our boys to come to, and *that* would be impossible with three in one room. As we talked last night, all this became clearer and clearer: home and family are so important in a place like this. We decided that our first moral responsibility in the camp is to keep a real American home for our two boys."

I could see that in her gracious but determined way, she was feeling more comfortable now that she had found a clear moral principle to back her up. Brought up all her life in a "moral" atmosphere, which assumed that anyone fully human would be morally responsible and cooperative, she could not react to anything except in a morally responsible way—even when actually she was fiercely defending the interests of her own family against those of others in the community. And so I knew it would be hard to pierce this armor of righteousness. By now, I was somewhat nettled.

"Granted that home and family are important to everyone,

Mrs. White," I retorted with some force. "How about the 'real American home' of the couple next door to you, the ones living with two boys in their one room?"

At this reminder, Mrs. White's Christian concern overflowed. She flushed with indignation and pity. Then, as she nodded her head in complete agreement, she said, "I know—aren't those Japanese just too wicked for words?"

And so it went. I could see no possibility of sending Paul to the dorm. As I walked home, angry and disappointed, I thought to myself, "If the Whites won't cooperate with us, who on earth can we turn to? Isn't there any good will anywhere among us?" And then I almost had to laugh aloud.

A picture of our theological discussion groups in Peking came to my mind. I remembered how the Rev. Mr. White, an extremely "liberal" minister theologically, had maintained with some fervor that the older theological doctrines of the Fall and of an inherent selfishness in mankind were "so much tommyrot" and that "the moral good will of ordinary people, if only mobilized and directed by the gospel, would lead us without any use of force to justice at home and peace in the world."

The second case could hardly have been more different. A prominent British businessman from Tientsin, Pickering was tall, nervous, and cadaverous looking. He possessed a wide reputation for a fierce temper. One felt that he would not be too much worried about finding moral grounds for whatever course of action he chose to take.

When I knocked at the door and told him that I was from the Housing Committee, his normal air of hospitable courtesy vanished at once. Pushing on to take up my business with him, I explained that some new dorms were being formed. His daughter, age nineteen, would be able to go into one, and his son, age fifteen, into the other. At that point he quite lost his control and ordered me off "his property."

"Your committee has no authority whatsoever over my home and its arrangements," he rumbled. "It cannot take one inch from me. I refuse to discuss this matter with you further. The problems of the overcrowded masses are not my problems. Good day, sir."

With that he slammed the door. I persisted, however, shouting against the closed door that it might be hard for him to show the British title to his room in the camp and that our committee did have some official jurisdiction in these matters, after all. At that remark, he opened the door again just far enough to threaten quite seriously to sue me after the war for deliberate persecution.

At this I must admit my own temper cooled and I laughed. I asked him what court he thought might have jurisdiction over this case of a British subject against an American citizen in a Japanese camp on the Chinese mainland? But he was too furious to debate this interesting legal question, and slammed the door shut for good.

The third case was the most interesting of the three. It concerned this time an American missionary family named Schmidt, who had two teen-age daughters. The father was a fairly pious sort who seemed to equate Christian love with a ready smile and a gush of friendliness. He could never allow himself to get angry, to curse or threaten us, as we had come to expect from the more forthright businessmen. When presented with our alternatives, therefore, all he would do was to smile unhappily, apparently thinking that all he as a Christian could do was be tolerant of the fact that we had put him in so difficult a position as to force him to refuse. But he still managed quite effectively to argue, stall, and balk.

With the saintliest sort of smile and the friendliest manner, he said, "You know, Gilkey, I write lots of sermons here. I am asked a good bit by the other missionaries to preach in our church services. It is for their sakes, and for that of the camp as a whole, that we need a little extra space in which I can have quiet to think out these sermons."

Reviewing these cases in my mind as I walked back, I felt that somehow I preferred the irascible Pickering. He hid behind no pretense of Christian virtue but went "all out" for his own interests. On the contrary, Schmidt would block with all his considerable force a move to help others which might hurt him. He would maintain in a righteous voice that he was "dissatisfied with the committee's attitude in this matter"—and then the next day with Christian concern and a wide smile ask you about the state of your soul.

In one way or another, all the other families shared this general reaction. Over and over we would call on them, argue with them, cajole them, and urge them to make up their minds before summer's heat overtook these crowded rooms. Finally we learned that two families—the Pickerings and another British family named St. George—had stated to the others that they were categorically refusing to have anything to do with the matter, and would never give up a room. "It is our home," they said. And that was that.

We knew that if these two families got away with their refusal, none of the others would ever agree to giving up space, and so all were delaying until the cases of the Pickerings and the St. Georges were settled.

Thus we on the committee had to tackle these families hard. The authority of our governing body to deal justly with camp life depended upon our success. So, for a second time we went to our Japanese boss of housing. We explained the whole situation and asked him how we could force these people to obey the injunction. Straightway he sent for them, asked them their side of the matter, thought their answers over carefully, and then ordered each of them to evacuate one of their two rooms. To our amazement, they meekly agreed. It seemed psychologically much easier for them to give in to enemy authority than to their own peers. But before they left the office, both men solemnly reiterated their promise to sue us after the war.

Once these two families were compelled to cooperate by Japanese order, the others quickly fell into line. We established a successful dorm for teen-age boys; and other families combined comfortably enough. Thus, the overcrowded families were able to expand somewhat so that the summer heat was not unbearable when it came.

The final solution to this, as to most of our other housing problems, came only when the evacuation of Catholics and Americans in August and September, 1943, reduced the total number in the camp from about 2,000 to 1,450. At that point, the first thing we did was to give to every family of four, two rooms apiece. We hardly deserved anyone's thanks for this, but the continuing complaint from those families that "for six whole months the committee had done nothing" seems a fitting word on which to close this episode.

Such experiences with ordinary human cussedness naturally stimulated me to do a good deal of thinking in such time as I had to myself. My ideas as to what people were like and as to what motivated their actions were undergoing a radical revision. People generally—and I knew I could not exclude myself— seemed to be much less rational and much more selfish than I had ever guessed, not at all the "nice folk" I had always thought them to be. They did not decide to do things because it would be reasonable and moral to act in that way; but because that course of action suited their self-interest. Afterward, they would find rational and moral reasons for what they had already determined to do.

Once I had seen this condition through these episodes, I wondered how I had ever missed it. "Even more," I asked myself, "why has our whole culture, especially its academic life, remained so determinedly unaware of what almost all the evidence clearly indicates?"

Surely our everyday life, founded on common sense and what we might call the "wisdom of the household budget," rather than on philosophical and academic principles, assumes the abiding self-interest of mankind. Do we not all recognize that most men have to be brought to court if a claim against them is to be made good? Do we not know that most people will vote the way their economic, social, or religious interests impel them? Do we not agree that no group or class ever relinquishes power or privileges simply because it is just and reasonable, but only because they have in one way or another been forced to do so? Do we not assume in democracy that every form of power must be checked by other forms of power if tyranny is to be avoided?

Men in business (especially its sales and advertising aspects), in politics, and in the law are perfectly cognizant of this self-interest of the public, and plan all their activities accordingly. Our mechanisms of government and of law—from the courts, through national defense, to the regulatory and legislative agencies— assume this self-interest in each of their provisions and powers. None of these social structures would make the slightest sense without this assumption. With our social institutions and habits based, therefore, on the assumption of the dominant self-interest and even of the selfishness of men in communal life, why was it, I pondered over and over, that our culture and so I myself, as one of its products, regarded man's rationality and morality with such fond optimism?

As I thought about this question, lying on my back staring at the ceiling in our dorm, I had to admit that there had been little in the ordinary social contacts of my past life to challenge such an optimistic estimate of mankind. In the upper-middle-class society to which I was accustomed, where everyone is comfortable and goods are plentiful, it is easy to gain the impression that people (at least in one's own group) are, on the whole, fair-minded and generous. In every home where I visited in a college community, in a suburb, or at the shore, I found the host glad to offer me a guest room and to share with me his cake. Why not? There was, in that social class, always an extra bedroom and plenty of flour, eggs, and sugar still in the cupboard.

I now understood that beneath this surface harmony lay the reality I had just discovered. But only the ruthless competition in the offices of the business world, the bitter economic and political clashes of our wider community life—where the fundamental conflicts of career, race, class, or nation are waged—manifest to those of us who live in comfort the ugly specters of human hostility, self-interest, and prejudice. The ordinary social relations fostered in college or country club seemed continually to validate the modern liberal estimate of man as rational and moral, able to see what is right and willing to pursue it for the common good.

Certainly this is the way we all like to think of ourselves. Unless some crisis explodes in our family or in our secure communities, there is little on the polite surface of things to contradict this opinion. In this padded environment of friendliness, good cheer, and generosity, at least one thing seems as sure to everyone as it was to the liberal Rev. Mr. White: the old pessimism about a "fallen existence," about "original sin," or about a fundamental selfishness in man is either antiquated monastic gloom or the twisted view of modern novelists and playwrights. Are not most of our colleagues at the office, our acquaintances on the university faculty, or our friends in the country club "lovely people"? And do you mean to say that the generous people of good will who support our church are "sinners"?

The revelatory value of life at Weihsien camp, I decided, was that this false estimate, based on the surface pretensions of a secure society, was cut down to size. In an internment camp there is no more flour and sugar in the cupboard; there is no guest room with an extra bath. There is only the absolute minimum of everything. Each of us had barely enough food and space to make living possible and bearable. In such a situation, the virtues of fair-mindedness and generosity completely changed their complexion.

To be fair and rational required the sacrifice of some precious good needed for one's own existence. Hence here to be just or generous is by no means easy or natural. Rather, since they require self-sacrifice, these "virtues" tend to make one's own security and comfort more vulnerable, and this no man really wishes to do. In such circumstances no one feigns virtue any longer, and few aspire to it, for it hurts rather than pays to be good. Consequently, here virtue—as the wise men have always insisted—is rare indeed. The camp was an excellent place in which to observe the inner secrets of our own human selves— especially when there were no extras to fall back on and when the thin polish of easy morality and of just dealing was worn off.

Strangely enough, I still kept expecting the opposite. For one of the peculiar conceits of modern optimism, a conceit which I had fully shared, is the belief that in time of crisis the goodness of men comes forward. For some reason we think that when there is little food or space among a community of people, they will be more, rather than less, apt to share with one another than in the ordinary well-fed existence. Nothing indicates so clearly the fixed belief in the innate goodness of humans as does this confidence that when the chips are down, and we are revealed for what we "really are," we will all be good to each other. Nothing could be so totally in error.

What is unique about human existence "on the margin" is not that people's characters change for better or for worse, for they do not. It is that the importance and so the "emotional voltage" of every issue is increased greatly. Now much more vulnerable than before, we are more inclined to be aware of our own interests, more frightened if they are threatened, and thus much more determined to protect them. A marginal existence neither improves men nor makes them wicked; it places a premium on every action, and in doing so reveals the actual inward character that every man has always possessed.

To be sure, people at Weihsien did not continually snarl at each other, nor were they obviously brutal or continually selfish. As a matter of fact, they remained surprisingly cheerful. We found that a sense of humor, incidentally, is the most pervasive and most welcome of men's better qualities. Good will did manifest itself in many features of our life. People showed a genuine consideration for others in many ways: helping their fellows to fix up their rooms with useful gadgets; making a stove for a person too old to do for himself; helping an invalid to make his coal bricks or to do his laundry; standing in line for one another. On this level, common trouble *did* bring out an admirable generosity.

When, however, the point at issue was not an hour's work but a basic condition of life—such as the space a man lived in or the amount of food he had to eat—then this good will tended to recede and in most cases to disappear. This is why in our larger society the same people who, like many of my suburban hosts in college, appear to be extremely generous in their personal relations, can become intractable, prejudiced, and even vicious on the deep social issues of national security, economic privilege, housing restrictions, or racial justice. Here the basic conditions of life become involved, fundamental securities are threatened, and we are all much more touchy and skittish than when merely an extra piece of pie, a church benevolence, or the donation of some of our time is at stake. For this reason among others, I am sure that Christian moralists ought to be as much concerned with the character of our social structures as with the problems of "personal goodness." In the realm of social structure, the fundamental conditions of men's lives are determined; here is precisely where we find it most intensely difficult to be just and generous.

As I was forced continually to notice, in any situation of tension and anxiety, when the being or security of the self is threatened, the mind simply ceases to be the objective instrument it pictures itself as. It does not weigh the rational arguments on both sides of an issue and coolly direct a submissive ego to adopt the "just and wise solution."

Such a picture of the mind of man is a myth of the academics, accustomed to dealing with theoretical problems in the study or the laboratory rather than existential problems of life as it is lived. In life, man is a total self, interested above all in his own well-being. His mind, like his emotions, is an instrument of that self, using its intelligence to defend his status when that is threatened and to increase his security when opportunity arises.

It was a rare person indeed in our camp whose mind could rise beyond that involvement of the self in crucial issues to view them dispassionately. Rational behavior in communal action is primarily a moral and not an intellectual achievement, possible only to a person who is morally capable of self-sacrifice. In a real sense, I came to believe, moral selflessness is a *prerequisite* for the life of reason—not its consequence, as so many philosophers contend.

One of the queer things about the modern liberal academic

culture is that the social scientist, when he considers man as the *object* of his study, adopts this "realistic" view. He assumes, as does the politician, the advertising man, the lawyer, and the policeman, that men are determined by social and economic forces which lure, compel, or elicit their self-interest, voting as their pocketbooks or their social position dictate. Here man's reason is by no means assumed to transcend his self-concern; for unless the rational powers of men were determined by their self-interest, human action in the aggregate could not be as regular and predictable as the "laws" of the social sciences presuppose.

When, however, the social scientist speaks of man's destiny, of the possibilities for man's life which his new knowledge can bring him, he looks to another side of man for his evidence. Here he expresses not what he has found out as an investigator, but what he hopes for and believes as a man. In the personal philosophy of the social scientist the model for man is provided not by other men as they act out their lives in the community, but by man as inquirer, "the man in the white coat" using the instruments of modern technology to discover the objective truth.

The social scientist is at this point taking himself—not the population in general—as his model of man. So, as with all of us, he gazes more sympathetically on this personal model than he does on the behavior of others. For man, as each of us sees him embodied in ourselves, and as the scientist surely sees him in himself, is a rational being. He is, therefore, here pictured as one unmoved by prejudice or emotion, concerned only with the discovery of the truth and with the welfare of the mankind he studies and seeks to direct. Such an objective, rational, and moral man would be, of course, a valid object of our hope and faith. In *his* hands widening scientific knowledge and technological advance promise us a bright future indeed.

This picture of man as directed only by reason and good will, and so able impartially to direct his own destiny into the unknown future, is, however, not only diametrically opposed to their own evidence—on the face of it, it passes all credence. It was precisely the picture I found getting in my way as I sought to comprehend my experience in camp. Like many a wise man before him, the white-gowned scientist and technologist has revealed very much to us about nature and about ourselves. But when he comes to tell us how we really behave in life, his own flattering image of himself has led him into a delusion—and the most unschooled ward politician can tell us more of what man is than can he.

With the background of these thoughts about the academic culture that I had imbibed in college, I realized that technology had, for all its blessings to our camp life, now taken me in, too. At the outset, our very success at Weihsien in dealing with the material problems we faced had given me the wrong image. This was the image of man as technological inquirer, inventor, and so conqueror of natural difficulties. I was beginning to realize that a more helpful and accurate image of man was as an existing and competing self in a community of selves and, as such, exposed to the continual and difficult pressure of moral and political decisions for or against his own interest.

For Western society to form an image of man as basically inquirer and knower was almost inevitable during a period of great scientific advance. Present-day culture had been imbued with the thrill of recent empirical and technological discoveries, and fascinated with the conquest of space, time, weight, cold, heat, and disease that such discoveries make possible. Thus society could easily mistake these accomplishments for the solution to the deepest of human problems and man as "knower" for the crucial image with which to think with enlightenment about themselves and their destiny. With this image before it, such a culture could easily reach a belief in the perfectability of man, that is, it could have faith in the rationality and objectivity with which he attacks social and political problems since he had demonstrated these virtues as scientist and engineer.

With our traditional religious faith already on the wane, moreover, the temptation was overwhelming to center our hopes about our destiny now solely on the human virtues that this image seemed to imply—and this image did imply vast hopes for man. Technological advance, let us note, spells "progress" only if men are in fact rational and good. A man motivated only by self-interest, a man subject to brutal or vicious prejudices and passions, one who can kill and maim with ease if his security is threatened, is no technologist in whom to have confidence. Scientific weapons in the hands of such a man may mean retardation if not extinction for the race. If man is viewed in this darker light, a new and deeper insecurity rather than progress seems to face man, as the literature from *Brave New World* through *1984* to *Dr. Strangelove* has so cogently indicated. Thus a realistic view of man tends to undermine the confidence a technological culture has in its own progress. Since we all want to believe in something, our secularized culture has tended to adopt an idealistic view of man as innately rational and good, as able to handle himself and his own history with the relative ease with which he dealt with nature. Consequently, the scientist rather than the politician, the knower rather than the moralist, has seemed to us to be the guarantor of security and peace, the harbinger of a better world.

As I learned in camp, this vision is a false dream: the things we long for—peace, prosperity, and a long life—depend to a far greater degree on the achievement of harmony and justice among men than they do on the latest inventions from our laboratories, valuable as the latter may be. That achievement of harmony and justice confronts us as a race, not with problems of technological know-how or scientific knowledge so much as with the problems of political and moral decisions. There is little comfort to be derived, however, from this undoubted truth; for the political and moral capacities of man are so much more ambiguous than are his intellectual endowments. As I asked in camp, and as many have asked elsewhere and at other times: If we can't believe in man as we once did, in what or whom *can* we believe?

VI ✍ A Mixed Blessing

Next to space, food was the necessity in very short supply. We never reached the point of starvation, but supplies were meager at best and hunger was always with us. In the last year of the war, our rations steadily diminished. This was reasonable enough, we kept telling ourselves, because one can't very well expect to win a war and at the same time be well fed by the enemy. Such logic may have reassured our minds and cheered our spirits. It did not soothe our empty stomachs.

When we came into camp our supplies, although they had seemed dismal enough to us then, had actually been remarkably plentiful when measured by later standards. All through our first year we were issued breakfast cereal. Though hardly as smooth as Wheatena, often being *gao-liang,* the roughest of Chinese grains, or *lu-dou,* a coarse and *"explosive"* sort of bean, nevertheless it provided a kind of solid substance to our diet that felt good on cold days. Also we were issued more flour than was needed for baking the camp bread. This excess enabled us to make various helpful fillers such as noodles and dumplings.

Moreover, during those early days a cook could count on having not only an adequate supply of meat per day, but also potatoes and two vegetables. From one of the latter he at least had the makings of a soup at night as well as a nutritious stew for lunch. Since bread was unrationed in the early days, every internee knew that he could eat all the bread he wished. Once we got used to our rough diet, we were neither painfully hungry nor did we worry too much about our food situation.

As 1944 developed, however, these supplies decreased steadily and at an alarming rate. Throughout that summer, when the cereal and tea ceased entirely, we were left with only two slices of bread and a cup of hot water for breakfast. All through the fall and winter, there were progressive cuts in our basic supplies: meat, flour, and oil issues were halved, leaving us no possibility of those fillers that had kept hunger away. The quantity and quality of the vegetables steadily worsened. Instead of two different vegetables a day, the cook often had, in addition to a small issue of half-spoiled meat and gnarled potatoes, only a stalky, leafless sort of spinach that defied softening and had an impossibly bitter taste or some rotting eggplant.

Such cuts in food supply were announced by the Japanese authorities at their regular monthly meetings with the Supplies Committee and the kitchen managers. In that last winter, we came to dread these meetings, knowing that they could only mean bad news. We could also be sure that we would be blamed by the internees for "not standing up to the authorities and refusing to accept the cuts."

As a result of these steady cuts, in the last winter of camp, 1944–1945, our bread was rigidly rationed to six slices a day; we drank only boiled water; and on an average day, we received only a bowl of stew for lunch and a cup of thin soup for supper. Our doctors estimated that this meant approximately 1,200 calories per day—not so low a diet as many people managed to subsist on throughout the war. Nevertheless, as a community of normally well-fed Westerners, we lived always with pangs of hunger and the specter of future starvation. It must be borne in mind that we had no idea how long we would have to be there, or how much worse conditions might become before it was all over.

To our mixed amusement and dismay we found that our stomachs, like implacable slave masters, completely supervised our powers of thought. A conversation might begin with religion, politics, or sex, but it was sure to end with culinary fantasies. As we would warm to the topic, soon we would again be describing in intricate detail and tasting in our excited imaginations long forgotten dishes in restaurants visited in some dim past. My one silly ambition, which obsessed me day and night, was to walk once again into a Howard Johnson restaurant and to savor their hamburger and chocolate milkshake.

The organic basis for the spirit of man was never so evident to me as in those fated conversations about food. It was a subject from which our thoughts could not stray for long without fatigue and to which they would eagerly return as fledgling birds to their familiar nest.

Where there had been excess weight before, there were lean shanks and flapping dewlaps now. Some who had been grossly overweight lost as much as 100 pounds. I myself, having weighed 170 pounds when I came in, dropped to 125. Few signs of dangerous ill health manifested themselves from this cause, although the number of fainting and low blood pressure cases began to mount alarmingly, threatening the ability of men over forty to do heavy labor. Since the war, many more have experienced the ill effects of those three years of malnutrition in failing eyesight and various internal afflictions. As we were always slightly hungry, I suppose the one thing we all longed for most—next to our freedom—was more to eat.

There did come a time when this unremitting hunger of the last year and one-half was partially appeased for some of us. At the time the exchange of evacuated American internees had taken place at Goa, India, via the *Gripsholm* in the fall of 1943, hundreds of American Red Cross parcels had been handed to the Japanese for delivery to those Americans still in prison in the Far East. Nine months later, in July, 1944, two hundred of these parcels arrived at Weihsien, addressed by covering letter to the two hundred Americans remaining in the camp.

None of the Americans will ever forget the day we first saw

those parcels. We had heard that they were large and that their contents surpassed all belief. Still we were not prepared.

We were waiting in line outside the General Affairs office. Brown was at the head of the line—he was at the head of every line, whatever was being given out. We could hardly believe it when we saw him stagger out with what seemed to be a gigantic box in his arms.

"Is that *one* parcel?" a still rather stout woman next to me called out. "In that case I'm ready to get fat all over again," she cooed in sheer delight. All of us felt the same way when at last we, too, stared down at the immense boxful that was *ours* to eat. Happily we found ourselves barely able to tote the box home to explore its magic contents.

These were indeed magnificent parcels. About three feet long, a foot wide, and eighteen inches high, they contained a seemingly inexhaustible supply of unbelievably wonderful things. In them was all that a hungry internee had longed for and had thought he would never see again.

Each parcel had four sections. Each section contained a pound of powdered milk, four packs of cigarettes, four tins of butter, three of Spam or Prem, one pound of cheese, chocolate, sugar, and odd cans of powdered coffee, jams, salmon, liver paté, and a one-pound package of dried prunes or raisins. After a diet made up largely of bread, low on meats and oils, and lacking in sweets of all sorts—in fact, without real taste—fifty pounds of this sort of rich, fat-laden, and tasteful food was manna from heaven.

Since that time I've heard many complaints from G.I.'s about the army canned food. But in our hungry camp, Spam, butter, Nescafé, and raisins seemed to us the last word in gustatory delight.

These packages, moreover, represented more than the mere pleasures of unfamiliar taste. As I looked down at this mass of stuff on my bed, and thought of it in terms of the new future it would bring me, I grasped the idea that this parcel meant, above all, security, safety from hunger for an amazingly long period of time. For as my friends and I found out, if a hungry man disciplined himself and ate only a little each day, his parcel could be stretched to supplement the daily diet for almost four months, and keep its owner from being really hungry.

To each of us, therefore, this parcel was real wealth, in a more basic sense than are most of the symbols of wealth in civilized life. No amount of stocks or bonds, no Cadillacs or country estates, could possibly equal the actual wealth represented by this pile of food—for that food could prevent *hunger* for four months. A Red Cross parcel made its possessor an astoundingly rich man—as each of us knew the minute we looked up from that lovely pile on our bed into the hungry eyes of our dorm mates who had received none.

Accompanying this food was also a considerable complement of men's clothing. Again, since this was consigned to the Americans, every American man was given one article of each type: an overcoat, a pair of shoes, heavy underwear, a flannel shirt, a sweater, a cap, socks, gloves, and a set of durable coveralls.

I shall never forget the Greek-American barber in the camp looking with some disgust at this pile of new clothes and saying with deep pathos: "Where de hell are de pants?" Why none had been included was the topic for some amusing theories among the British in our dorm, one of whom remarked, "Doesn't *anyone* wear the pants in your country, old boy?"

Fortunately there was much more of this clothing—especially overcoats and coveralls—than there were American men. Therefore the rest was distributed to other nationals. This fact and the fact that almost without exception the Americans were most generous about giving their non-American friends food from their parcels, made the whole affair the source of a good deal of international good will, as well as of better-filled stomachs and better-warmed backs. British friends told me they thought there was hardly a person in camp who had not received something from these parcels. Obviously, they were impressed with American generosity.

By the beginning of the winter of 1944–1945, food from the parcels had long since vanished, and the cuts in our supplies were growing ever more drastic. Winter on the plains of North China is biting cold—such as one might expect in Detroit or Chicago. We were issued very little coal dust with which to heat our rooms. Morale in the camp was at its all-time low. The future stretched on as endless and dreary as the snow-covered flatlands beyond the barbed wire on the walls of the compound.

Then suddenly, without warning, one cold January day the most wonderful thing imaginable happened. Some internees who happened to be near the great front gate saw it swing open as usual. The familiar donkey carts that carried our supplies came plodding in through the snow. But what they saw in those carts, they found hard to believe. Piled high, box on box, were seemingly endless numbers of Red Cross parcels! Word spread swiftly around the camp. In a twinkling, a huge crowd had gathered. Everyone was laughing and crying at once. We all looked on in disbelief as cartload after cartload kept coming through the gate. In utter amazement, tears streaming down our faces, we counted fourteen of those carts, each one carrying well over a hundred parcels!

"Why, they're the same parcels!" someone said. "See there's the label—AMERICAN RED CROSS—but there are many, many more than before!"

"I just heard from a committeeman that there's no covering letter for these parcels, no indication as to who is to get them."

"Then *who* are they for?"

This question, "Who is to get them?" ran like wildfire among us. Quite naturally, the first reactions had been generally that the Americans were in luck again. But, when more and more carts kept coming in the gate, notions as to who would be given them became confused. The Americans, counting the carts as they went by, began to speculate happily on this windfall.

"My God," exclaimed one in a loud voice, "I figure there must be at least fifteen hundred parcels there—wow! Why, that's seven to eight parcels for each American! I don't even know where I'll put all that stuff!"

But other thoughts were going through other minds as the significance of the quantity struck home: "Why, fifteen hundred is just about the number of people in the camp! Could it be that we British are going to get a parcel, too? Could they be for *everybody* this time?"

As this question swept through the assembled crowd—which, by now, was comprised of the entire camp—it collided head-on with the exultation of the Americans. Frowns replaced looks of amazed wonder, angry mutterings succeeded the early shouts of joy.

"Damn it, you limey," one outraged Yankee voice cried out, "that's American stuff, and you lousy spongers aren't going to get a bit of it. Why doesn't *your* Red Cross take care of *you?*"

The answer was a snort of disgust.

"Well, you Americans *are* a bunch of bloody buggers! You want everything for yourselves, don't you? If it's your property, no one else is to have a look in, is that the idea?"

And so it went. The parcels were piled up in a great heap in the church building awaiting word from *some* authority as to how all this wonderful wealth was to be distributed. A heavy guard was posted to watch over them. Every row of rooms and every dorm where Americans lived with other nationals began to stew in bitter disputes. In those where no Americans lived, there was general gloomy agreement that while Americans might be rich, they were certainly neither very human nor very trustworthy; for when the chips were down, they wanted to be sure they got theirs—and who cared about the other fellow.

Two days later the Japanese authorities posted a notice which seemed to settle the issue to everyone's apparent satisfaction. The commandant, after stating that he was acting according to official instructions, proclaimed that the parcels were to be distributed to the entire camp the next day at 10 A.M. Every American was to receive one and one-half parcels; every other internee, one parcel. This ingenious distribution was possible because there were 1,550 parcels for a camp of 1,450 persons, 200 of whom were Americans.

I was elated. I regarded this as a master stroke of statesmanship in a touchy situation. It looked as though the whole camp would be well fed by this arrangement. At the same time, the super patriots among the Americans would be appeased because they were getting substantially more than did the "damn furriners."

It is impossible to set down the joy and excitement that gripped the camp that night. It was as though everyone were living through every Christmas Eve of his lifetime all rolled into one.

What a heaven of goodies awaited each child with a parcel of his own! What blessed security was promised to every father and mother with three, possibly four, parcels for their family, enough surely to last through the spring, whatever might happen to our camp supplies! The dreary remnant of winter and the stark uncertainty of the days ahead seemed no longer impossible to contemplate as each internee savored the prospect of rich food and tried vainly to quiet his excited children who were already pleading to get in line for the great distribution.

Universal good will flooded the camp; enthusiasm for American generosity was expressed on every hand. Our morale and our sense of community had climbed swiftly from an all-time low to an all-time high. As Bruce, the sardonic Scotsman in our dorm, said, "I almost feel tonight that I might be able to love other people—and *that* for me, brother, is a very rare feeling indeed!"

The next morning, long before the appointed hour, the camp in festive mood lined up for the parcels. Then suddenly the bottom dropped out of everything. Just before ten, a guard strode past and hammered up an official-looking notice on the board.

Those at the head of the line crowded around at once to see what the announcement said. They came away looking black as thunder. I made my way up to the bulletin board, peering over the heads of the crowd to read the words. As I approached, an Englishman was turning away. "The bloody bastards!" I heard him say. "What the bloody hell am I going to tell my kids?" An awful heart-sinking prescience told me what the notice said—and I wasn't wrong.

The notice contained one short but pregnant sentence:

DUE TO PROTESTS FROM THE AMERICAN COMMUNITY, THE PARCELS WILL NOT BE DISTRIBUTED TODAY AS ANNOUNCED.
THE COMMANDANT

When we tried to find out what had happened, we were told that seven young Americans had gone to see the commandant about the matter. They had demanded that he produce his authorization to distribute American Red Cross parcels to internees who were not American citizens. Since there was no such proof, the seven insisted that these parcels be turned over at once to the American community, the rightful owners, for them to do with as they saw fit.

One may, I think, legitimately surmise that the Japanese official was caught completely off guard by this strong and reasoned appeal to what is a peculiarly Western sense of ownership. From his own cultural background he could conjure up no ready defense against it. The commandant had apparently acted solely on the basis of his own moral judgment in announcing the distribution to all internees, and had no higher authority with which to back up this judgment. In this case, surely, it would have been better for all concerned had he used some of the customary military inflexibility. Had he merely told the delegation to get out, the camp would have been spared much bitterness and the Americans much later humiliation. But he wavered, promising he would refer the whole question to the arbitration of Tokyo. Then he canceled the distribution.

Through the action of these seven men, the American community found itself in the unenviable position of preventing the distribution of life-giving parcels to their hungry fellows. Apparently we were content to let them go hungry so long as we got our seven and one-half parcels.

The inevitable result was that all the bitter arguments of the two days previous broke out more strongly than before. Men who, like the Englishman I overheard, had to explain to the expectant children that "the Americans had taken away Santa," were not inclined to feel lightly about this. The Americans, finding themselves bitterly accused of a selfishness and greed which they had not explicitly encouraged, were not inclined to admit their own fault nor that of their countrymen, especially to enraged foreigners. With that pathetic but automatic defense mechanism almost every man develops with nationals of another country, Americans hotly defended whatever their countrymen had done long before they found out either what it was or what they themselves really thought about it.

There followed about ten days of delay, while we all waited for word from Tokyo. This hiatus provided the opportunity for all the hostility, jealousy, and national pride of 1,450 hungry, exasperated, and anxious people to accumulate and to boil over. Where there had been only arguments before, now there were fist fights. In one row, an American boy and a British boy got in a scuffle over the matter. When the fathers discovered this battle between erstwhile best friends, they at first chastised the youths. But when they learned what the fight was about, they themselves came to blows. Others had to step in and separate this pathetic but furious pair who had been neighbors and friends for a year and a half.

It was the same story all over. A community where everyone had long forgotten whether a man was American or British, white, Negro, Jew, Parsee, or Indian, had suddenly disintegrated into a brawling, bitterly divided collection of hostile national groups. Ironically, our wondrous Christmas gift had brought in its wake the exact opposite of peace on earth. The massive mounds of life-giving parcels lay inert in the center of the camp, while gusts of human conflict and ill will swirled turbulently around them.

For the first time, I felt fundamentally humiliated at being an American. The British in our dorm were too courteous to be openly nasty—they knew how most of our group there deplored this—but their silence spoke volumes.

The experience of the Red Cross parcels vividly revealed to me aspects of human communal life of which I had been formerly unaware. A day or so later as I was staring moodily at that heap of magnificent parcels, pondering the irony of our suddenly brawling society, I came to see that wealth is by no means an unmitigated blessing to its community. It does not, as may often be supposed, serve to feed and comfort those who are lucky enough to possess it, while leaving unaffected and unconcerned others in the community who are not so fortunate. Wealth is a dynamic force that can too easily become demonic—for if it does not do great good, it can do great harm.

The arrival of those parcels represented for our camp an accretion of sheer wealth almost of incomprehensible scope. It was as if, I thought, our small community had been whisked overnight from the living standard of a thirteenth-century village to that of modern affluent industrial society. Now we had food to keep us all from hunger through the spring.

And yet, the introduction of this wealth—the central factor in material progress—was in fact the occasion for an increase in bitterness and conflict such as we had never known before. Staring at those symbols of our material advance, I suddenly realized that Western culture's dream of material progress as the answer to every ill was no more than a dream. Here was evidence before my eyes that wealth and progress can have demonic consequences if misused.

Had this food simply been used for the good of the whole community, it would have been an unmitigated blessing in the life of every one of us. But the moment it threatened to become the hoarded property of a select few, it became at once destructive rather than creative, dividing us from one another and destroying every vestige of communal unity and morale.

I realized that this was no mere matter of angry words and irate looks. It was just the kind of issue which men were willing to fight over. Seeing the guards now patrolling the streets, I was glad they were there. Had there been no Japanese guns guaranteeing order in the camp, we might easily have faced real civil strife. Thus might our community have destroyed itself over this issue.

I suddenly saw, as never so clearly before, the really dynamic factors in social conflict: how wealth compounded with greed and injustice leads inevitably to strife, and how such strife can threaten to kill the social organism. Correspondingly, it became evident that the only answer was not less wealth or material goods, but the development of moral character that might lead to sharing and so provide the sole foundation for social peace. It is the moral or immoral use of wealth, not its mere accumulation, it seemed to me, that determines whether it will play a creative or destructive role in any society. The American claim for all the parcels, and its devastating effects on our social fabric, had taught me at last the true significance of moral character in any human community, and I would never forget it.

In the world today, Western culture as a whole is learning that material progress and the wealth that it creates are no unmixed blessings. The present possession of security and goods in a world where the majority are hungry and insecure puts the Western world in much the same position as those Americans in the camp, hugging to themselves their seven and one-half parcels. If the material gains of modern Western society can be spread over the world with some evenness, this new wealth may create a fuller life for us all. But if we hoard it for ourselves alone, it will surely become a demonic possession creating bitterness and jealousy all around us, and ultimately threatening our very existence. Wealthy classes and wealthy nations are unmindful of the destructive effects of their wealth, isolated as they are by the comforts and perquisites of their possessions. Those outside the charmed circle of privilege, however, remember, and no lasting community can be formed in the midst of the bitter resentment that inequality and selfishness inevitably engender. Thus the creation of a viable community is as dependent on the moral ability and willingness to share what we have with our neighbor who is in want as it is on the technical ability to produce and accumulate wealth.

Should the democratic culture of the West go down before an alien Communist world, its demise can probably be traced more directly to its failure to learn and to enact this moral truth than to any other source. The forces now arrayed against this culture have been created precisely by this sort of resentment at the unwillingness of the predominantly white West to share its privileges.

Marxism itself is the direct result of the unwillingness of propertied classes of the past to share their economic privileges with the peasant and the working classes. It has a continuing potent appeal mainly because of this resentment. The openness of many former colonial peoples in Africa and Asia to a Communist influence, if not alliance, is likewise the clear effect of the past unwillingness of Western nations to share their political privileges with peoples then subject to Western imperialism. The resentment against the West on the part of the whole nonwhite world is mainly the consequence of the white man's refusal to share his social privileges with men of another color. "Moral" actions undertaken solely to save one's own skin can hardly claim to be fully moral. Nevertheless, it is demonstrably true that a desperate attempt to hang onto wealth and privilege can destroy the community in which all, rich and poor, may live, and so can bring the mansions of the wealthy toppling down about their ears.

Some of us in the American community were understandably troubled by the action of our countrymen that resulted in canceling the distribution of the parcels. As always, it was with optimism that we embarked upon our program of rectification. As I said to my bunkmate Stanley Morris, close friend and colleague in this program, "This *can't* express the will of the American community. Surely the majority want the whole camp to get the damn parcels."

So we got together with a number of others who felt the same way. We decided that each of us should talk with certain "representative" Americans to find out what our community's sentiments really were. If it turned out that the American community did seem to favor the universal distribution of the parcels, then we would call a meeting and take a vote repudiating the action of the seven. Thus in effect we would guarantee the distribution as well as express a needed sense of solidarity with our "foreign" mates in the camp.

The talks were fascinating, although shattering to the remaining shreds of my old liberal optimism. They revealed to me with stark clarity the subtlety and infinite depth of the human moral problem, and the strange behavior of which we are all capable when we are under pressure.

The first man I approached I had suspected would be tough. His name was Rickey Kolcheck. He was a hard, slightly pushy, defensive, sardonic, completely unsentimental small businessman from Chicago. Rickey had never been known to take the lead in any "good works" for the community, and he successfully managed to preserve the air of a cynical, humorous, "hard guy." One never knows, however, what lies under such a Runyonesque surface, and Rickey was generally regarded by the worldly as a "good guy" because of his ready humor and tolerant ways. I had no idea what sort of response I would elicit, when I approached him on the subject of sharing the parcels with the camp as a whole.

Rickey never really understood what I was saying. These were his sandwiches, and he was hungry—it was as simple as that. It might be tough luck for the ones who'd brought no sandwiches, but that wasn't *his* problem. Looking at me with his hard blue eyes, he said bluntly, "These parcels are mine because I'm an American, and I'm going to see I get every last one that's coming to me. I'm sorry for these other guys, sure—but this stuff is ours. Why don't their own governments take care of *them?* No lousy foreigner is going to get what belongs to me!"

As I listened to Rickey, I knew he spoke for many Americans, who had lived and worked next to these "foreigners" for two difficult years. For them any sense of a bond with their neighbors and so of any obligation to them, vanished when the security of the self was at stake.

The next man I talked to would have found such a direct attack fairly crude. He was an American lawyer from Tientsin. He began by saying he liked to look at these things from the legal point of view.

"Don't misunderstand me," he remarked emphatically. "I'm not worried about the parcels—about how many I or the other Americans may get. I couldn't care less. With me it's the legal principle that counts.

"This is American property—simple, isn't it? You can't question *that!* You see, this property can only be administered by Americans and not by the enemy. We've got to make sure in this hellhole, whatever price we have to pay in popularity, that the rights of American property are preserved and respected. Come to think of it, we've also got to be faithful executors to the American Red Cross donors who sent these here for our use. But mind you, I speak as a professional lawyer. For myself, I don't really care how many parcels I get."

"Sure, sure," I thought. I marveled at the ways by which we can fool ourselves. We don some professional or moral costume so as to hide even from ourselves our real desires and wants. Then we present to the world a façade of objectivity and rectitude instead of the self-concern we really feel. It was the Quarters Committee all over again. As in those cases, I found myself entangled with this man in endless legal arguments about property rights and their relation to the Red Cross, to the Geneva Convention, and to the principle of nationality. Yet I knew these arguments were meaningless because they did not deal with the real factors in the situation: hunger, anxiety and self-concern. Surely it was ironic that the Red Cross, established by the

voluntary donations of countless good souls to feed the needy—
whoever and wherever they might be—should have its magnificent gifts claimed entirely by a small group on the principle of
the absolute right of property!

It was my next interlocutor, however, who presented the
strangest posture so far. He was a kindly, elderly, conservative
missionary named Grant. Grant had a Chinese wife and four
small children about whom he was naturally much concerned.
But surprisingly, he did not bring up this point as his main
concern at all. Rather, it was the "moral" side of the issue that
exercised him.

He said to me, "I always look at things, Gilkey, from the moral
point of view." Fascinated, I heard him out.

"You understand, of course, that I am not at all interested
personally in the parcels, even for my family. I only want to be
sure that there be a moral quality to the use we make of these
fine American goods. Now as you are well aware, Gilkey, there is
no virtue whatever in being *forced* to share. We Americans
should be given the parcels, all right. Then each of us should be
left to exercise his own moral judgment in deciding what to do
with them. We will share, but not on order from the enemy, for
then it would not be moral."

Thinking of Rickey and my lawyer friend, I asked, "How
many parcels do you really suppose the Americans will share with
others?"

"Why," said Grant with satisfaction, "I'm sure that most of
them will give away at least two of their packages."

At this answer I quickly phrased my rejoinder:

"That would mean that each non-American would get, on the
most optimistic guess, less than one-fourth of a parcel instead of
one parcel apiece. Would that be moral sharing when all of us
are equally hungry and in need?"

Grant looked at me in bafflement. This was not at all what he
meant by "moral."

"I don't understand you," he said. "If the Japanese share it *for*
us, no one is doing a good act, and so there's no morality in it
anywhere."

I was incredulous as I listened to this argument. I was hearing
from the mouth of Grant a widely held but surely by now
discredited view of morality. It was, namely, that moral action is
to be understood as the means by which an individual becomes
"good." Thus human actions, however creative their conse-

quences for the people around, that are not the results of the free acts of individuals—actions, for example, by a government—cannot be "moral." Who then becomes holier by means of them? Grant would ask. Correspondingly, actions at the expense of the well-being of one's neighbors can be moral if the individual has done them freely and in order to be good.

To Grant, moral actions are to be conceived only in reference to the individual who performs them: good actions add to his virtue, bad ones detract from it. In such a view an act that is compelled by some authority, even if it results in good for all, has no moral implications whatsoever. No wonder, I thought, that men like Grant can never see any connection between the actions of government and the morality of that government's citizens, and, no wonder they find it impossible to relate morality to the problems of politics!

Such a theory of moral action as a means merely to personal holiness completely ignores the fact that moral action has to do primarily with the relations between persons in a community. Thus in reality moral actions are those in which the needs of the neighbor are given an equality with one's own needs; immoral acts are those in which the neighbor is forgotten for the sake of the self. Moral action, then, certainly if it is to be called "Christian," expresses in the outward form of an act a concern for the neighbor's welfare, which concern is, if anything is, the substance of inner virtue.

In such a view all actions which help to feed the hungry neighbor are moral, even if the final instrument of that sharing is an impersonal arm of government. Thus, as I argued to Grant, efforts designed to bring about a universal sharing were moral, efforts to block such a sharing, immoral.

But Grant, for all his piety, would not listen. He did not really care how well the hunger of his neighbors was appeased, so long as the Americans were given a sporting chance to become "holy." Further, his view of moral action was one which envisioned merits for the individual self, established by credit in some heavenly bank account. It thus fitted in very well with the self-interest of each of us, as the Protestant reformers continually argued in their struggle with the medieval merit system. How ironic, then, that the rabid, if peaceable anti-Papist Grant should espouse this view!

The advantage of Grant's view was that on its terms, "being moral" allowed us both to eat our cake and have it too. For as was plain from his argument, if I were good and shared two of my parcels with our British neighbors, I would not only gain moral credit (and also, incidentally, be humbly thanked by the British for my generosity) but even more, I would be able to keep five whole parcels for myself!

I could not help being reminded of similar arguments at home with regard to helping "the poor." Is it not more moral to care for the needy solely through private acts of benevolence, so the reasoning went, rather than through impersonal law? And is it not more fun, too, since we can, by doing so, ease our consciences while retaining our wealth virtually untouched?

After a day of such heated discussions, I came back to my room struck with the intense difficulty that each of us has in being truly humane to our fellows, and the infinitely subtle ways in which we are able to avoid facing up to this difficulty. The pressures of self-interest in this case were, of course, immense. This was especially true in the case of those men and women responsible for hungry children.

When one is hungry, and when the threat of worse hunger to come nags continually at the subconscious, then even seven and one-half immense parcels hardly seem enough. We begin to picture to ourselves the dread time when even those seven will be gone. So the prospect of losing any one of them to our neighbors—of having only three or four instead of six or seven—creates as much anxiety of spirit as had been there before the parcels came.

In the possession of material goods, there is no such thing as satiety. One seems never able to accumulate enough to be a safeguard against the unpredictable future, and so the requirements of full security remain in principle unlimited. Thus, men who otherwise appeared quite normal and respectable were goaded by their insistent fears about the future into claiming all they could for themselves and their own. And concurrently, the needs of the neighbor receded into the dim background. Men in such a situation seemed hardly free to do the generous thing, but only free enough to act in their own self-interest.

As Brecht puts it in the *Threepenny Opera:*

> For even saintly folk will act like sinners
> Unless they have their customary dinners.

And his other observation:

> What keeps a man alive? He lives on others,
> And forgets that they were supposed to be his brothers.

This was the reality of all of us. Not many of us, however, can stand to admit that this is the truth about ourselves. Something in us, some strange desire to remain "moral," is offended by this self-concern; refusing to acknowledge it, we become hypocritical. These examples indicated that rarely does self-interest display itself frankly as selfishness. More often it hides behind the very moral idealism it is denying in action; a legal, moral, or even religious argument is likely to be given for what is at base a selfish action. And what is more, the moral disguise usually deceives even the self who has donned it. For no one is more surprised and outraged than that self when someone else questions the validity of his moral concern.

For this reason, as I saw for the first time, idealistic intentions are not enough; nor is a man's idealistic fervor the final yardstick of the quality of his character. We commit most of our serious sins against our neighbor—and these *are* the serious sins—for what we regard as a "moral principle." Most of us, in spite of whatever harm we may be doing to others, have long since convinced ourselves that the cause for which we do what we do is just and right. Thus teaching high ideals to men will not in itself produce better men and women. It may merely provide the taught with new ways of justifying their devotion to their own security.

This truth is manifested in every political struggle for power and security in the wider world. Classes, nations, and races, like individuals, seldom either defend their own interests or grasp for their own advantage without first finding a legal or moral reason for doing so. Marx called this tendency "an ideology" and Freud a "rationalization."

The experience of camp life, and the lessons of history generally, established to my satisfaction that men act generally in an "immoral" way when their interests are at stake. With equal force, however, they showed me that men remain at least moral enough to be hypocritical, to wish to *seem* good—even if it is beyond their capacities to attain it.

A day later we gathered once again in a friend's room to pool our findings and to decide on our next move. I came feeling discouraged, for I had found few who agreed with our position. I was still hopeful that the others would come in with more favorable reports. When the others began to speak, however, it became clear that their experiences roughly paralleled my own.

On a wide variety of grounds, the majority of those interviewed favored supporting the protest of the seven men and keeping the parcels in American hands. Greatly disappointed and frustrated, therefore, we concluded we dared not take a vote. For the American community officially to indicate by vote its calloused unconcern for the other internees would merely have aggravated an already unhappy situation.

As we parted morosely that night, I thought to myself, "That certainly settles it. If ordinary men were as rational and good as they like to believe, we would have won that vote by a huge majority—but we didn't dare even take the vote!"

Several days later, the final decision arrived from Tokyo. It was at once announced to the camp. Every internee was to get one parcel—"the one hundred extra parcels," so the announcement said curtly, "previously assigned to the Americans, are to be sent to other camps."

The irony of this was not lost on the gleeful camp: the demand by the Americans for seven and one-half parcels had effected in the end the loss to each of them of an extra half parcel! Thus, as Stan and I grimly agreed, even an enemy authority can mediate the divine justice in human affairs. The camp then settled down to enjoy their packages, and much of the bitterness was forgotten in the wonder of so many badly needed and wanted things.

The whole rather sordid story ended on a note of humor. In the later stages of the controversy, when the great mountain of goods had been gone over, it was discovered that among the piles of clothing and shoes that came along with the parcels were two hundred pairs of boots from the South African Red Cross. This was a needed reminder to many Americans that there were benevolent souls in Red Cross chapters outside the boundaries of the United States. To the delight of almost everyone, the two South Africans in our midst posted the following notice:

DUE TO THE PRECEDENT THAT HAS BEEN SET, THE SOUTH AFRICAN COM-MUNITY IS LAYING CLAIM TO ALL 200 OF THE BOOTS DONATED BY THEIR RED CROSS. WE SHALL WEAR EACH PAIR FOR THREE DAYS TO SIGNAL OUR RIGHT TO WHAT IS OUR OWN PROPERTY, AND THEN SHALL BE GLAD TO LEND SOME OUT WHEN NOT IN USE TO ANY NON-SOUTH AFRICANS WHO REQUEST OUR GENEROUS HELP.

These conflicts—first over space and then over food—made me think a great deal more deeply about men and their life in community, and about the kinds of beings they really were.

Surely I had learned that men are neither so rational nor so moral as they like to think. Their minds and their ideals alike had too often shown themselves to me to be the instruments of their total self. And that self had manifested itself as consistently concerned about its own welfare, and thus hardly free to respect or be just to its neighbor, although it was "free" enough to find rational and moral reasons for what it did!

What then, I asked myself, is the cause of this unhappy situation? Why are we not what we want to be, or pretend even to ourselves to be? Could it be our lower instincts that cause the trouble? Is this, as we often popularly say, "the ape man in us"? Or, to put the same thought in more sophisticated language, is it an inheritance of animal instincts not yet brought under rational control? I was aware that the modern intellectual is apt to conceive of our problems in this way, and to believe that when we learn through scientific inquiry how to deal with these lower instincts, we shall have solved our most important dilemmas.

Our experience had shown me, however, that this departmentalizing of ourselves into a set of instincts, on the one hand, and an impartial inquiring and controlling mind, on the other, was far too simple a dualism to explain the actual complexity of human behavior. The selfishness that had shown itself so widely among the internees was by no means merely "instinctual." Its roots lay in fears concerning the self's security which only a self-conscious and intelligent being could experience. It would thus be more illuminating to classify the demand for seven and one-half parcels as a "human" rather than an "animal" reaction.

Only the human mind could look far into the future and see that four or five large parcels would run out over several months' time; then, noting that distant peril, decide that at least seven would be needed for its security. A merely instinctive or animal reaction would have required only a momentary satisfaction. It is above all our frightened human spirits which, when we become fully aware of present and future perils, move quickly to protect themselves against all the contingencies of life.

Man's mind thus adds dimensions to his instinctive "will to live" that quite change its character. Here the will to live, because now conscious and intelligent, becomes the much more dynamic will to power and will to possess an infinity of goods. Men and animals both want to survive, and in both this might be called "instinctual." But because he is made up of spirit as well as instinct, mind as well as organic drives, man is much more dangerous to his fellows in his efforts, and much more rapacious in his demands for goods. To call this behavior "instinct" is to minimize the relative innocence of our animal cousins, and to exonerate the spiritual, mental, and conscious elements in our nature which are even more deeply involved.

As I now saw it, therefore, man's problem is not just a matter of enlightened minds and devoted wills controlling a rebellious instinctive nature. Rather man is to be seen as a totality, a unified being made of body and of instincts, of consciousness and subconscious, of intelligence and will, all in baffling and complex interaction. And it is that total psychophysical organism, that total existing self in its unity, which determines whether the "higher" powers of mind and of will are going to be used creatively or destructively.

Thus a man's moral health or unhealth depends primarily on the fundamental character, direction, and loyalty of his self as a whole; of the "bent," so to speak, of this deepest level of his being where his spiritual unity is achieved. But sadly enough, it seemed just as plain that this fundamental bent of the total self in all of us was inward, toward our own welfare. And so immersed were we in it that we hardly seemed able to see this in ourselves, much less extricate ourselves from this dilemma.

Having found these truths about human existence enacted before my eyes, I began to recall some of the theological ideas I had almost forgotten in the bustle and activity of camp life. Among the most relevant, it now seemed, was the old idea of original sin.

When its relevancy was so striking in this new context, it seemed ironic that of all the ideas linked with Christian belief, this one should probably strike the average man as the most dubious. Of course, much of its traditional form now seems to us outdated. In all probability there was no such single pair of progenitors as the man Adam and his wife Eve; in any event, this is a matter for the biological and anthropological sciences to determine. Few of us wish to or can believe that their one act of disobedience brought about a fall for the whole race continued in us by inheritance. Blaming our troubles on an inheritance from Adam is as futile and evasive as blaming them on our evolutionary animal predecessors!

Yet, when one looks at the actual social behavior of people, this theological notion of a common, pervasive warping of our wills away from the good we wish to achieve is more descriptive of our actual experience of ourselves than is any other assessment of our situation. What the doctrine of sin has said about man's present state seemed to fit the facts as I found them.

Certainly in camp everyone alike was involved in the problem; none was entirely righteous. "Good" people and "bad" people found it incredibly difficult, not to say impossible, to will the good; that is, to be objective in a situation of tension, and to be generous and fair to their neighbors. In all of us, moreover, some power within seemed to drive us to promote our own interests against those of our neighbors. We were not our "true selves," the selves we wanted to be or liked to think we were. We were caught willingly and yet unwillingly in a self-love from which we could not seem to achieve our own release, for what was wrong was our will itself. Whenever we willed something, it was our own distorted will that did the willing, so that we could not will the good. Though quite free to will whatever we wanted to do in a given situation, we were not free to will to love others, because the will did not really want to. We were literally bound in our own sin.

This was, I knew, the way Christian thought had long viewed man's predicament. It was also precisely what the facts of my experience seemed to substantiate.

When I saw this congruence between the Christian description and our actual experience of ourselves, I realized that it was just this situation which the idea of original sin had always sought to make partially clear. The reality to which the symbols of the "Fall" and of "Original Sin" point is not really the particular and dubious act of Adam. Rather it is this fundamental self-concern of the total self which, so to speak, lies below our particular thoughts and acts, molds them, directs them, and then betrays us into the actual misdeeds we all witness in our common life. The particular past act of Adam and Eve in the garden, and the Augustinian notion of an inherited corruption, were explanations or theories used by Christian thinkers to explain how this undeniable reality in human existence came about, how we got into the difficulty we are so clearly in.

And, as I ruefully concluded, the problem pointed to and described by these symbols is still very much evident in our ordinary experience, whatever modern knowledge may have done to the saga of Adam and his mistake.

VII ✍ Sugar—and Politics

Politics is seldom dull; in Weihsien camp it was never so. From the day we arrived to the end of our stay, the issues of power, law, and government were the most fascinating and baffling that we faced. Day in and day out we were confronted with many problems that most students of society discuss in the abstract. We, however, had to solve them in practice. How do you form a government? How are leaders best picked? Why is democratic rule preferable—if it is? How does a government generate enough power to rule and yet not be allowed too much power lest it become despotic? How is the moral dimension of life interrelated with the role of law and force in human community?

These were the questions that we had to wrestle with daily. It cannot be said that we ever solved any of these problems. For unlike questions of mathematical theory or engineering, political problems, since they are concerned with people and their relationships and not with things, admit of no final solutions. We did, however, learn a lot at first hand about the kinds of issues with which man's political capacities must always deal.

Not every camp faced these peculiarly political problems. Many civilian camps were not allowed such freedom by the Japanese in governing themselves. Although this internal freedom was a great boon to us, it did present us with the problem of generating enough authority among ourselves to govern our little society efficiently.

Ours, as a civilian internment camp, was on this question quite unlike a prisoner-of-war camp. The governmental hierarchy of an army camp is assigned to it at the outset in its clearly delineated military ranks; thus its leaders are determined by the presence of the officer corps. All that is needed to make things run well is the officer's good horse sense and instinct for applying wisely and humanely to a new situation the various set rules of army life. To him belongs the problem of ruling and possibly— when it comes to dealing with the enemy—of diplomacy. But the *political* problem is not his and never will be while he wears his stripes. As history shows repeatedly, the difference between rule in army life and politics in civilian life is frequently not under-

117

stood, and even the most successful generals have not always been able to master the art of politics.

The prime concern of politics is not *use* of power but *generation* of power, with the achievement and maintenance of authority. The great "political" geniuses also may be able to rule well—as may, indeed, a king or a general. But what makes them so-called "political animals" or "born politicians" is not this capacity to rule, but the ability to draw power to themselves, to assume and keep—by one means or another—the role of leader. This achievement of rule, of legitimate and controlled power, establishes the political problem, both for a man and for a society. This problem must be resolved by every society, if not politically, then by the "man on horseback." Thus democracy and politics, so often set in opposition to one another as ideal vs. sordid reality, work together—or fall together.

Democracy is that structure of social rule in which authority and power are established by none but political means. Here the ordinary citizen—as opposed to the hereditary ruler—draws to himself through persuasion and/or political pressure (not through the use of force) the consent of others that legitimatizes his rule. As every American president knows, the acquisition and retention of power depend on his political acumen, on his capacity to draw to himself without force the power to get done what he has to get done. If he is not equal to this political task, he cannot long rule in a democracy.

Our camp community faced the political problem in its most elemental form. When we arrived, we did not have even the beginnings of a government. Aside from our common Western origins, we could scarcely have been a more heterogeneous crowd. Usually in such inchoate communities, a rough, preliminary rule is established and maintained by those who hold the force of arms. Later, when a common ethos appears, this authority founded on force can be replaced by one based on consent. With us, however, such an early basis for order was impossible. In an internment camp, enemy soldiers hold all the instruments of force. It is they, therefore, not the fledgling government, who preserve order. We soon discovered that such a government as ours, one with responsibility but no visible means of enforcing its authority—much like the problem of the present United Nations —faces a trying and baffling task.

Through this experience I learned several things. First, that any stable government or system of law must seek to guide itself as best it can by the principles of justice and equality. Secondly, that in the last analysis government can rest only on the united *moral* strength of the community which it governs. But, thirdly, that the capacity to rule is also dependent upon the possession of force. Force must be available in extreme cases to compel compliance to the will of the government and it must be present to punish serious offenders against the community's laws. In the creation of legitimate governmental authority, the interplay between these moral and compulsive elements creates the most fascinating of problems. Morality can never replace force, but it must provide the deep basis for the creative use of force.

The first time I saw clearly the fundamental need for the element of force in any governmental rule was in my experience on the Housing Committee. In order to do our job of making housing more bearable—i.e., in order to achieve more justice—we had to move people around continually. As I have indicated, I at first believed that people would simply move when such an action had been proved "just" to them. After I was disabused of that fantasy, I thought that probably (here possibly memories of school discipline were responsible) people would comply willingly when those in legitimate authority told them to do so. We *were* the appointed authority. Yet we were invariably told to go mind our own business.

Thus arose for us the problem of power. If the committee is to do what it thinks just, it must be able to get people to comply with its plans. But if people won't be persuaded, and if they can't be compelled, how is the justice to be enacted? For the first time it appeared to me that, contrary to most pacifist and anarchistic theory (to which I had been sympathetic), legitimate force is one of the necessary bases upon which justice can be established in human affairs.

One day after we had been in camp about four months, Mr. Izu casually told us that in ten days' time forty Belgians were coming to the camp and that we were to clear ten rooms for these families at once. We gasped. Having seen how difficult—not to say dangerous—it had been to get more space for our own overcrowded people, how did he expect us to get all those rooms for strangers on such short notice?

"No, matter," shrugged the impassive Izu, "the rooms must be found." With irrefutable logic, he added, "Is it not more just to move other people now than to let the new arrivals sleep out in the cold and wet when they get here?"

He was right: rooms had to be found. This was clearly more

important than the delicacy of the *way* in which they were to be found.

When we scanned our map of the compound, we found only two possibilities. We could move about thirty bachelors out of small rooms into dorms; or we could move about the same number of single women. Since it was clear that families could not be moved into dorms, and since by the same token the Belgian families could not be housed there, this wholesale move of either male or female single people was the only available alternative. But which group should we move?

This was a tormenting question for one intent on doing the "right thing." It was obvious to anyone with a sense of fairness that it would be more just to move the men than the women. The latter were on the whole older, less robust, and they suffered a great deal more from the rigors of camp life. Every humane consideration led us to decide to leave the women alone and to tackle the thirty bachelors. If governments were run solely on moral grounds, this is what we would have done at once. But, as we discovered, they are not; power is also part of the political equation. The question "Can it be done?" is as relevant as the question "Is it right?"

We talked to the men. I was by now not at all surprised that they refused categorically to move out of their single rooms in spite of the fact that they were crowded three to a small space. Rational argument and moral pressure were useless. The men merely found new reasons why it was most just that others be required to move.

"Didn't we send our wives home as the government ordered before the war?" protested one. "Haven't those damn women stayed on in China in spite of the clear command of the Consulate to get out? We *had* to stay—they didn't. We're not moving for them!"

"But many of these women were secretaries and teachers who were as badly needed here as you executives," I argued.

"That may be, Mac—but we're not moving. And there are thirty of us who will knock the stuffing out of any committee that tries to get us out."

What were we to do? This was no case of individual families too disunited to oppose us. These thirty men were well aware of their strength *en masse,* and they would fight. How could we get them out? We thought briefly of calling out the guards. But just as quickly we gave that one up. It was too dangerous. A free-for-all with the guards might end anywhere, with someone wounded or even killed. Not unmindful of our own image as well, we knew it would be fatal for any internee to be responsible for bringing the guards into a physical tussle with his mates. Only if we were sure there would be no physical resistance could we consider calling on Japanese power for help.

Frustrated, we went to the Internee Discipline Committee to see what they might be able to do for us. Could they conscript enough men from the camp to go and move those recalcitrant bachelors out?

"Not on your life," said Ian Campbell, the realistic head of discipline. "We would have to get at least fifty to move that crowd. Any group of husky men would sympathize with those bachelors. In fact they would probably help them against you. I have no idea of letting such a fight as that get started here—much less encouraging it. No, brother, the best thing for you to do is to move the gals quietly and forget it."

"But that isn't *right!*" I exploded. "I'll be damned if I'm going to force those women to move. It's unjust! I know perfectly well it's only because we *can't* move the men. What will I say to them? How can I convince them it's right, when I know damn well it isn't?"

"Well, then, what's the answer? Are you going to let the Belgians sleep in the cold because you can't get rooms fairly?" asked Campbell with a smile, knowing he had me. "Is *that* just, letting them suffer—and much more than the single women will—to ease *your* conscience? No, my advice is go ahead and move them."

I didn't like it a bit, but I had to admit that Campbell was right. In the end I recommended to Shields that we move the women. As always, they were more docile than the men. But we on the committee could hardly rejoice in our action, or even sound convincing to our own ears, when we sought to persuade the skeptical women that moving them was the "right thing to do."

I thought about this case a great deal because it seemed to me both utterly outrageous and vastly significant. Political action did involve compromise. To my surprise, I saw that our action—uncomfortable as it was for everyone—was in fact more moral than if we had taken the less practical idealistic route. For no program in the life of a community is really just if that program cannot be enacted. Ideal solutions can always be conceived by liberal onlookers, and they may appeal to our minds when we contemplate them. But they are politically useless and of little moral value if they can in nowise be put into effect. Such solutions cannot claim the word "just," for they are never either relevant or real. To refuse to move the women on idealistic grounds would not have been just; it would merely have resulted in the irresponsible—and much more unjust—political act of leaving the Belgians homeless. In this case, compromise of one's moral principles appeared to me to be morally necessary.

The reason behind this surprising irrelevance of "pure" justice was, I decided, this strange factor of power. Politics is essentially the art of the possible—not of the ideal. Fundamentally it involves *enacting* solutions to community problems in actual life, rather than *thinking out* solutions to intellectual problems in the realm of thought—although the enacting should be well thought out too! For this reason, political action is limited by the amount of power available to put the solution into effect. Here our ability to be just is directly proportional to our ability to perform. Thus, I came to believe, are power and social justice not opposed, as pacifists often contend, but are interrelated.

That neither the course of events nor even we ourselves could easily be molded according to our best ideals and standards was a new thought for me. Every political decision, I was learning, must take place within the given context of its situation, within the balance of social forces operating at the moment. Each decision can only choose the best among the possibilities that that particular situation makes available. We do not act in political life *because* our act is just. We act because the pressures of the moment force us to resolve in one way or another some vital problem in the community. Then we hope, and strive, that the resolution which we can effect is in the measure possible to that occasion, the most just solution available. But the main thing is that the act resolve the given problem creatively, and that life go on—in this case, I concluded ruefully, that the Belgians can at least get in out of the wet.

Those of us who were on committees at the beginning had been appointed to our posts rather than elected. Although I was a convinced believer in democracy, the fact that I was appointed had hardly bothered me. Nor did it at first occur to me that a more democratic way of choosing our camp government might be preferable. I liked my job; I was delighted to be a "big shot." The thought of a possible election probably signaled more of a threat than a promise to the average committeeman.

I soon noticed, however, that my own attitude was changing, as was that of the other men in similar work. The remarks people made to us when we sought to deal with them did the most to effect this change. When we tried to move anyone, or change anybody's status for the worse, we were met by suspicious questions about ourselves:

"Where do you get the authority to come in here and tell me to move?" someone would say. "Why aren't you moving, too, if it's so all-fired important that we move? And why aren't your friends being moved? Incidentally, I notice those other committeemen aren't moving either!"

Such a fog of suspicion could never be dispelled so long as we held office by appointment. Then the question "How did you get your authority?" was not answerable. Our authority derived merely from the other committeemen and not from the persons with whom we had to deal; in the most concrete sense, it was an illegitimate authority.

One reason that democracy is essential as a form of government suddenly dawned on me: under it, authority is derived from the very people who suffer from its exercise, and a rational answer can be given to the question of its *legitimacy*. If I had been elected, I could have said, "How did I get this authority? From you! And if you do not feel we are doing an honest job, pick someone else at the next election."

Amusingly, therefore, the very men who at first basked in the security of having been appointed found they preferred the risk of elected status. This was not because of "faith in democracy," though most of us had that, but because of the need to compel the carping public to share in part with us some of the onus for the unpopular actions we must take. As the supplies man remarked: "Then the people who always complain will have helped to put me here in this post. I can more easily overlook their carping at what they call my inefficiency and dishonesty!— because *they* have elected me, and so it's their fault as much as mine!"

For these reasons, after six months in camp, it became a regular practice, twice a year, to elect the nine chairmen of the committees. Gradually, the same process of "democratization" took place in all those positions of responsibility where conflicts could occur, where complaints were common and suspicions likely.

Being the manager of a kitchen was, for example, a post of real responsibility. All the kitchen's supplies and the appointment of its laboring force were in the manager's hands. Naturally, with the supplies meager at best, diners wondered—sometimes silently and sometimes aloud—whether all the supplies were reaching the diners' menus. The political result of these suspicions was, as in the other cases, the establishment of a full-blown democracy in our kitchen.

The unintended founder of our kitchen's democracy and the "heroine" of the tale I am about to relate, was the weightier half of a most extraordinary couple, the Witherspoons. Mrs. Witherspoon's husband, a lawyer, was a small, seedy man with a tiny mustache; and he was, apparently, a born pilferer. It was well known in North China society that he had been ejected from the club for stealing soap. No Old China Hand would play cards or golf with him because, so the report ran, he invariably cheated. But the good lawyer who, fortunately, had given up serious practice years before, was a frail reed indeed compared to his massive lady.

She was a heavily girdled, wallowing, mastodon of a woman, with white hair, a hard, strong face, and an even stronger will. Neighbors reported that her poor spouse was buffeted about like a canoe in a hurricane when she went after him. He would shoot out the door of their small room followed by a torrent of verbiage. Then, puttering about in the still waters of the tiny garden at the end of their small plot, he would ease his harried soul by talking back to her under his breath while she bellowed at him from within. Rumor had it that she drove him to go on his petty pilfering raids, and would threaten in stentorian tones not to let him in the door if he came back empty-handed. In any case, it was true that he had been tried and convicted of several attempts to snatch from the kitchen more than the couple's rightful portion of food and to lift supplies off the carts as they came by.

This strange pair had arrived late in camp, and had come well stocked with supplies, especially sugar. By April, 1944, however, these stores apparently had run out. Suddenly Mrs. Witherspoon began to take an active interest in the sugar issued to the kitchens.

Rumors began to circulate among the diners that they were

not getting all the sugar issued to the kitchen because the cooks were taking some home each time a sweet was made. All such rumors could be traced back to Mrs. Witherspoon. Finally, in May, after smoldering all winter, she declared open war. In a concerted house-to-house campaign, she fomented accusations that the kitchen management had been stealing sugar and then falsifying the careful books that were kept in the locked store-rooms.

We who worked in the kitchen were well aware that small amounts of sugar—along with larger quantities of meat and vegetables—disappeared regularly. But the charge that the management was organizing and abetting this state of affairs rather than seeking to prevent it, we *knew* to be false. Since the diners were hardly satisfied with the sweetness of our paltry desserts, however, these tales found a ready hearing. The result was that just when the food in the kitchen was at its best, suspicion began to poison the atmosphere.

"Is it all there, bud?" "Just see, Mac, that they don't steal the salt, too—eh?" We didn't know with whom we were more angry—the unscrupulous Mrs. Witherspoon or the gullible diners who believed her rumors.

The staff called a general meeting of the diners and demanded that the kitchen as a whole take action on this matter. First, we suggested that a committee representing the diners be elected to investigate the kitchen and propose ways of its improvement. Next, we stipulated that the Discipline Committee be requested to investigate our practices so that Mrs. Witherspoon's accusations would be confirmed or forever silenced.

Then began a fantastic, dreamlike investigation. It was one not unlike those of the McCarthy era, where the accusations to be proved or disproved were so mammoth and incredible that no one could believe them except those who wanted to. At the same time, disproof was exceedingly difficult to establish conclusively. Now that she had the attention of the Discipline Committee, and was the center of every camp discussion, Mrs. Witherspoon was delighted to be quite specific in her accusations, which only made them more incredible. She did not hesitate to specify just what sweets over the last three months had received less sugar than recorded by the cooks, and how much had been purloined by the staff in that period. The amount she named was gigantic: three hundred pounds—almost equal to the total received by the kitchen during that time!

I remember my feelings of incredulity when I read her statement.

"Damn," I said to Stan, who was on the cooking shift with me. "Six of those desserts she mentions *we* made! Remember on that cake last week, you and Laura were weighing that sugar into the bowls while I was marking down the figures? The old gal's nuts, no doubt of it. But how do you *prove* it? How can you prove you *didn't* steal something, if you were there and were handling it?"

"Yeah, that's a tough job," Stan said with a sigh. "But look at it this way. To get away with that sugar while we are making a cake, think of the others we'd have to have in on the deal—twenty women volunteers, and the eight men on the shift, not to mention the two cooks, the manager, and the two storekeepers! You might make such an involved plot work once. But can you imagine that whole motley gang of about thirty-five people—most of whom can't stand the sight of each other—working secretly in cahoots for three or four months, with no one the wiser but Mrs. Witherspoon? No one will believe that, don't worry!"

Stan was right—few people *did* believe the woman when she was required to bring her vague suspicions into the form of a concrete theory of what had happened. During the investigation, her case disintegrated further. She was asked by one member of the Discipline Committee why she was so sure that twenty-five pounds of sugar could not have been put into a certain cake.

"Because it's impossible, that's why," she said somewhat irritably. "Look, the cooks say one hundred pounds of flour were put into the cake. Well, with twenty-five pounds of sugar that's one part sugar to four parts flour. Now see here, the most expensive cakes at home," and she brandished *Fannie Farmer's Boston Cooking-School Cook Book,* "have only two parts flour to one part sugar. And you can't tell me that that cake last week wasn't a lot less than half as sweet as the kind of cake I'm talking about. Why, you could hardly taste the sugar. I'll bet there were at least eight or nine parts flour to one part sugar. In other words, only about twelve pounds of sugar were used!"

To prove it, she opened her cookbook and pointed to a recipe which called for one cup of sugar and two cups of flour. I must say I was slightly shaken by this—never having seen a cake recipe before. I agreed that our cakes were by no means half as sweet as a good cake at home; so if the recipes there really called for two parts flour to one part sugar, our one hundred pounds to twenty-five pounds *did* look suspicious.

Then as I watched the face of my cooking partner, Laura, I saw her bewildered look give way to an amused smile. She said to Mrs. Witherspoon with some asperity:

"You poor lady. If you had ever looked inside a cookbook before, you would know that a cup of sugar weighs twice as much as the same bulk of flour. Fannie's recipe is set in terms of bulk and reads one *part* sugar to two of flour. Translated into weight, which is the measure we use, the same recipe would read entirely differently: one unit flour to *one* unit sugar. For a cake for eight hundred persons that would have meant using one hundred pounds of sugar to one hundred pounds of flour. It would have been a *much* sweeter cake than we could produce with our paltry twenty-five pounds of sugar. No wonder it didn't taste like Fannie's cakes to you! It had less than one-fourth the sugar in it that she called for!"

It was evident that Mrs. Witherspoon had been an expert on telling the No. 1 boy to order the cook to make a cake for tea. And that was the limit of her culinary experience.

Finally, Mrs. Witherspoon was asked, why, beyond her cookbook calculations, had she been so certain that this stealing was taking place? Had she seen someone taking sugar, or heard credible reports of its use by the staff in their rooms? Her only answer was, no, that like any diner she had eaten the sweets and her taste told her the sugar was missing. Now we knew there was little to be gained by arguing with her about taste. But we did concoct a way of measuring to the satisfaction of the committee the reliability of her taste buds.

The next morning, without any prior notice and in the presence of the Discipline Committee, we sweetened the cereal ration with a large portion of sugar. That afternoon Mrs. Witherspoon was asked whether she had eaten the cereal that morning. When she replied that she had, she was asked: "And did it taste sweet to you?" "Not at all," she retorted huffily, and she promptly gave her oath that she had tasted no sugar in it.

To her astonishment, both she and the case were summarily dismissed. As Campbell said with a twinkle, "The one ground for theft you proffered, my good lady, was the accuracy of your taste buds. These have now been shown to be unreliable at best. Since you have adduced no evidence, there is no basis for further investigation. Unfortunately, there are neither libel nor perjury laws in this camp, else you might be in serious difficulty. Let me merely say that this committee will not be interested in any further accusations or complaints from either you or your husband."

The most tangible result of this hullabaloo about sugar was the radical revision of the political structure of the kitchen. The Diners Committee that had investigated the matter with the Discipline Committee recommended that henceforth the post of manager be elective. As they said in their report, by this means not only would the electorate be guaranteed the opportunity regularly to change kitchen administrations—the diners also would be reminded of their own responsibility for the government of the kitchen and, therefore, would contribute by assent to the legitimate authority of the manager in kitchen affairs.

And so it went. Gradually, every position in camp which might become a focal point of conflict, suspicion, and turmoil, became an elective office. When the first election of the kitchen manager was held, I thought to myself, "It may have been, as I recall Reinhold Niebuhr once saying somewhere, the goodness and rationality of men which made the rise of democracy in human affairs possible. But certainly in our camp, it has been the grousing, the orneriness and the outright resentments of men that have made it necessary. Democracy forces the strong to give up power, and the carping public to take it on—and with it a sense of responsibility. Perhaps part of the superiority of democracy to the other forms of government lies just here: it reduces the chances not only of a greedy tyranny inflicted from above, but also of a resentful revolt from the bottom."

While politically we became a democracy, economically our society remained completely socialistic throughout its course. All the means of production were managed by representatives of the community as a whole and not by private individuals who owned these means. Also, it was up to the camp government to see that all services were available to each internee, regardless of his capacity to work. We were in effect an economy in which "from each according to his ability and to each according to his need" (as the Marxist doctrine stipulates) was the unquestioned principle by which both our labor and the distribution of our goods were organized.

Any other social and economic structure was so inconceivable that even the most rabid capitalists—and there were plenty of them among us from the ranks of businessmen of North China—

never questioned its rightness for us. The particular capitalistic way of looking at the ownership of the means of production was completely irrelevant. To have considered, for example, the kitchens or the bakery as the private property of those skilled enough to rebuild them and strong enough to run them, and consequently, to have allowed these "owners" to sell their products to others, would have been quite unthinkable. To refuse food, heat, or water to those too young, too old, or too feeble to earn their keep by work, would have seemed abysmally cruel to the hardest-hearted among us.

I had heard often enough from the lips of conservative leaders in America that there is only one "natural" economic order, namely that of competitive free enterprise. It was the one way *any* society can be organized, they maintained, and still remain healthy and creative. But our experience indicated that the system that may work in one context may not be constructive in the next. In America the geographical and economic situation have made possible the development of a most creative system of private ownership. It may well be, however, that in other countries with different situations, other economic solutions are more creative than the one we ourselves prefer—as, one hopes, both America and the Communists are learning. In a lifeboat, capitalists as well as socialists will, if they are to remain men and not beasts, share their water as a common possession rather than regard it as the private property of those who brought it aboard.

Although no pattern other than the one described was remotely possible, this one, we found, was by no means ideal. In fact, it revealed some fascinating problems—problems perhaps more frequent in noncapitalist societies, but perhaps also common to almost any sort of economic structure.

The paramount one was that of the efficiency of labor. How do you get lazy men to work and to work hard, if you don't hire them, if you don't pay them wages and are thus unable to fire them? An answer to this question was not easy to find. No one in the camp ever discovered a way to stop a lazy man from being lazy.

The most commonly suggested solution was to put a slacker on one of the toughest jobs:

"Make the bum sweat just like the rest of us. Don't you see, what he *wants* is to have the sort of easy job you've given him!"

This recipe sounds great—in theory. But putting one of these fellows on a hard-working shift in the bakery or the kitchen was like putting an uncoordinated and flabby man into the line of a top-flight professional football team. In a high-powered job, a lazy fellow who didn't carry his weight always caused endless confusion and trouble. In the end, the whole shift would threaten to quit unless he were removed.

The most famous case of this sort was that of a Hungarian named Kovaks. He enjoyed a riper reputation for a shady past than anyone in camp, and was the proud possessor of passports from four different nations. A wide, squat man, he had curly reddish hair, a flat face, and hard, cold, unblinking, indeed, almost reptilian eyes. He was a nervous, bustly sort of fellow, affable, but completely inattentive when one talked to him, as if he had on his mind a deal that had to be consummated that very night. He was altogether useless on any job.

One time when I was manager of the kitchen, I agreed to try him as a pan washer (the man who kept all the important cooking utensils clean for their continual use in the kitchen). I shall never forget his first day. I got to the kitchen about eight, right after roll call, to see how things were coming along for breakfast and lunch. I found the head cook in a fury. Taking me over to the sink, where a pile of unwashed pans was already mounting, he said:

"Who's the goddamn pan washer and where the hell is he? He was supposed to have gotten here two hours ago to clean up for breakfast! My helpers are going to have to do this work, which they won't like at all— and neither do I!"

Making a mental note to tell Kovaks when he finally appeared that he simply must get there on time, I went out to attend to something else. About two hours later, I came back to find the pantry still empty, except for the stack of dirty pans, which was now immense.

"Hasn't that lazy bum showed up yet?" I asked.

"Oh Lord yes," groaned the now resigned head cook. "He turned up about nine. He came in here and asked me what he was supposed to do. I led him to the stack of pans in the pantry, and told him to get to work. He took one look at that pile, put his hand to his head, cried out, 'Mein Gott im Himmel!' and fled on his fat legs. We haven't seen the bastard since, and I don't expect to. That's the last time, Gilkey, I'll take on a chap like Kovaks as a part of my outfit!"

When I got over laughing at the picture of Kovaks' thunderstruck awareness of what *work* meant, I realized what the cook was saying: no lazy man can be used on an important job. The only thing to do was to assign him such a completely insignificant task that when he failed to appear, it didn't matter.

An ironic twist to this story was that on the day Kovaks arrived—he was sent into camp late—his first question was about the black market. From that day to the end, he was busy fifteen hours a day, rushing around buying and selling all manner of things illegally. But when it came to assigned work, for which he received neither the satisfaction of excitement nor the reward of hard cash, he refused to stir himself.

Then there was Jacobson—what could one do with a person like him? He was a wealthy American businessman from Tientsin who must have worked hard for his small fortune, but who found that the mere prospect of manual labor in the camp made him slightly queasy. A man in his middle forties, Jacobson had evidently in Tientsin been running slightly to fat. But he was now so well thinned-out by camp life that his formerly rotund face hung down in soft folds with the infinite sadness of a sorrowful basset.

Jacobson had been given almost every job in camp—except the hard ones. He finally ended up in the kitchen as a "vegetable helper," one of a pair of older men who helped the women vegetable teams by carrying and washing the baskets of vegetables. When I came on as manager, I was a little puzzled that a man in his forties should have this sort of light job, usually reserved for men in their sixties. I asked the doctors if there was anything wrong with him. No, they said, he had been repeatedly checked by them and there was absolutely nothing wrong with him organically. I approached Jacobson on the issue one day, and this is what he told me:

"Yes, it's true. Neither doctor in camp has been able to find out what is wrong. It's quite mysterious really, Gilkey. You see, after working a bit, I begin to feel weak and nauseous." Gingerly he would touch his stomach as if it were all starting up again. "I begin to feel dizzy, as if a fainting spell were coming on. I sit down for a while and have a smoke. Then the funny feeling goes away, and I can begin to work—slowly and easily, you know, because anything else brings it back that much quicker. I try not to talk about my troubles with anyone, Gilkey. I guess that's why so many people say I'm lazy and just don't like work. But you understand, I'm sure."

And with this he got up slowly, with a hand on his tender

stomach, and walked deliberately back to the old bathtub in which he and his elderly partner were scrubbing potatoes. Looking up at me with a brave smile after he had bent stiffly over the tub to begin his scrubbing, he said with infinite sadness, "This was a damnably large issue of potatoes today!"

Such cases as Kovaks and Jacobson were immune to the pressure of public opinion. Almost always the worst malingerers were well known throughout the camp. They were called slackers —and worse—by everyone, and often to their faces; but this never made them work harder. They continued cheerily to nurse their ailments, to avoid every kind of unpleasant labor simply by refusing to do it. The reason, of course, that they could thus withstand the hostile attitude of other workers was that they had their own set of friends who completely shared their revulsion concerning work. Therefore they did not care what the others thought. They felt, reasonably enough, that a soft job was more important than the respect of those in whom they had no interest.

We never really solved the problem of the lazy worker. To take a job away from him was no punishment. It was what men like Kovaks and Jacobson really wanted, since they knew they would be fed whether they worked or not. In the end, watching Jacobson slowly picking up a basket of leeks, I concluded that only the devolopment of some kind of real incentive, whether in the form of material reward or of inner morale, could ever change lazy people into hard workers—as the prospect of a cash return would surely galvanize Jacobson into action once he was free!

Ultimately, the question of efficient labor leads to the deeper questions of motivation and the meaningfulness of work. About this problem, classical socialist theory has, in my view, been far too cavalier and idealistic. Socialist writers have thought, in optimistic fashion, that once men are enabled to work for their own community rather than for masters, they will labor for the sheer joy of it. Our work was communal enough for anyone; no owners reaped the reward of others' labor. But there was precious little evidence of this sheer love of work. At any rate, it became clear to me that the question of incentive remained one of the most serious problems for societies that offered total security regardless of work accomplished. Correspondingly, the question of humane treatment of both its victims and its misfits haunts those economies which offer rewards only for work well done.

A somewhat related but equally stubborn labor problem was

that of the inefficient worker—the man who was willing enough, but who simply wasn't much good. How does a manager deal with him?

As I found out soon after I took over, a manager received plenty of free advice on all his problems. One day I became conscious that the line of people waiting for hot water was unusually long. Stepping up to the boiler to see what was the cause of the delay, I found out quickly enough: there was a new stoker on, and he couldn't get his fire hot enough at the crucial hour of four o'clock when the whole British empire was waiting, wanting its tea. I felt sorry for him; he was my old boss cook Edwin Parker, the art dealer. Edwin was a hard and able worker in other lines, but he couldn't get the hang of stoking. While I stood there, I heard a familiar voice down the line sounding off. It came from a Yorkshireman named Thomas, a nice fellow but one with a tendency to gripe when things weren't going the way he thought they should. Now, he was saying in a loud, disgruntled tone, "An efficient management would have gotten rid of that sort of stoker and put on a chap who knows his business!"

Remarks like that tend to stick in one's mind. Two days later, Edwin told me he was fed up and wanted to quit. I went around to the Labor Committee to see whom I might get to replace him. This process consisted first of finding out who was for the moment off a job, or who wanted a change, and then asking to have him assigned to the kitchen. Since we couldn't compel anyone to take a job, and had no rewards to offer, it was not always easy to persuade someone to take a job like stoking. But when my friend Matthew Read, the second man on the Labor Committee, told me that Thomas was leaving his present job, Thomas' own advice came back to me and I laughed. Telling the Labor Committee—a two-man affair—the story, I said, "For goodness' sake, give the job to Thomas. He thinks all you need to do here to run a kitchen is to hire efficient labor."

"Yes," said Matt, "we have plenty of problems with managers all right, but not of this sort. Our labor troubles stem from the fact that we have to use inefficient people because there just aren't enough of any other kind. We'll give the job to Thomas—maybe then he'll look more tolerantly on the way things are run here. And mind you, this is one case where you won't have to talk a chap into being a stoker—Thomas won't dare refuse!"

Poor old Thomas! He went on the job as green as the art dealer had been. For the first week his fires wouldn't boil the water at the right time. I used to drop around the hot water room to see how things were going about the time the line was getting really angry. It was a terrible temptation to say, "Well, it's certainly a relief finally to have a man on the job who really knows his work." But Thomas tried hard. Knowing as well as I why he had been put on that job, he would look at me so sheepishly that I never had the heart to rub it in.

As this and many similar experiences made me realize, there were just so many working men in the camp, no more, and all the labor had to be performed by that one small group. Some of these men were good workers, some were not; no amount of "efficiency experting" on the part of management could increase the number of the former or decrease the number of the latter. At bottom the labor problem, like all the others that I encountered, boiled down to the question of the kind of people who make up the society—their capacity, their training, their skills, and their willingness to work.

Another problem generated by our particular form of society was that of distribution. Since we were not a price economy where the ability to pay determines how goods are to be spread around, we had to distribute our supplies according to some other principle. In such a situation, we all assumed quite without thought that the sole fair and workable principle was that of equality. But to my astonishment, as case after case showed, equality is often less than "fair," and, when that is true, the problems of distribution are baffling indeed.

Distribution in the kitchen was our worst headache. It seemed that in this department we could never avoid cataclysmic crises. Eventually, we had to appoint a special "dining room manager." He was Bertram Carter, the charming and diplomatic representative of Thomas Cook and Sons in Peking.

Our problems were gigantic. When there is plenty to eat, as in the armed services, the size of a portion is irrelevant, since one can always get more. But when there is less than enough, all servings must be exactly equal, 1/800th of the total amount made. In the case of most dishes it is impossible to gauge with any accuracy what that 1/800th of the total is.

If we guessed wrong either way, there was always trouble. When we served too little and ended up with a surplus, the remainder was served in "seconds." But then the families who collected their food and ate it at home, on hearing of this later, would rightly complain that they got less than their full ration. And if we served too much, a worse tragedy resulted: the end of the line would get nothing, and furious was a mild word for their feelings! The only way to handle this situation, we decided, was to have intelligent elderly men (trained accountants and bankers were best) to stand by the serving table and count the people as they came along, keeping careful check on how much had been given out, and increasing the serving or decreasing it proportionately as we went along. But even this made people angry: for late diners might find their portions less than what early ones received or vice versa—and again we would be accused of being unfair.

One time after a whole group of people had berated us because their portions were unequal, I said to Bertram, "My God, Bertram, the root of the demand for equal treatment as we saw it tonight is not the outraged sense of justice for the other fellow, as I had always thought. It is the frustrated desire to get for yourself all that is coming to you. It is of more moment to us that our neighbor doesn't get a bigger share than we have, than it is that he gets as much as we do. Self-interest, of course, is *also* the root of our desire to get *more* than our neighbor—and that is one reason, isn't it, that life is so damned complicated! For then there really isn't as much difference as we like to think between the ordinary guy demanding justice for himself and the heel who wants to take more than the next guy. One's a kind of polite, respectable, legal sort of self-interest, the other's a rude, antisocial and illegal one—but both are motivated by the same thing."

"That's right," said Bertram, "and remember the potatoes."

He was speaking of our most glaring case of the interrelation of self-interest, equality, and the stupidities in life. Until the last year of camp, the kitchens received about once every two weeks an issue large enough to give every diner one whole potato apiece. This meant that we could either bake the potatoes in the ovens and so give the diners a delicious change, or else boil them in their skins and serve them that way. In either case, they were far tastier than peeled and chopped up in stew, and more healthful into the bargain because the skins were not thrown away. Everyone agreed that this was marvelous—but every time we tried it, we were assailed by complaints.

What we were up against, was the hard fact that the good Lord makes potatoes in different shapes and sizes. Those who received the smaller potatoes were outraged—at us, at the Japanese, at the world—and invariably they lodged the strongest sort of protest at this unfairness. Again and again we tried to explain that if potatoes were to be served baked or boiled whole, and everyone wanted that, then some people had to get the smaller potatoes. But this point was far too logical when rights are abused and tempers aroused. Finally, quite against our own better judgment, that of the doctors, and the real desires of the diners, we had to peel, slice, and serve in equal portions all issues of potatoes.

Though it seemed silly to worry about the size of the potato serving, I also realized that in an affluent society we may be relaxed about our dinner servings because there is more if we wish. But with the *basic* essentials of life, such as our salary, a promotion, or an honor in our profession, we are just as furious if some colleague gets favored treatment over ourselves.

Pondering further on this point, I thought of the strange fact that in history, justice seems to ride on the back of self-interest rather than on that of virtue. The drive on the part of under-privileged groups to receive a greater share of this world's goods and privileges is surely a movement toward greater justice in human affairs, and for that reason, it has always seemed to me, should be supported by every morally serious person. Nevertheless, however virtuous the "cause," it is well to recall that those who justly clamor for more equality are as much motivated by self-concern as are those more fortunate ones who stubbornly seek to preserve their unequal privileges. Thus, contrary to our usual opinion, the justice of a group's cause, which requires our support of it, does not indicate any greater amount of virtue or any less amount of self-interest on the part of that unfortunate group. And somewhat grimly I thought to myself, "It's a safe bet that when they in turn become top dogs, they probably will defend their new privileges as desperately and unjustly as their former masters defended theirs—and then the just man may well find himself on the other side."

The strangest thing I was discovering about the principle of equality, however, was how often it was actually unfair. Whenever, in fact, the needs of people really differed from those of their neighbors, it was manifestly unjust to give them equal portions. From the beginning it was agreed that infants, pregnant women, the sick, and the aged needed special kinds of food, especially food containing more of those elements most desired by all, such as proteins, fats, and sugar. To satisfy these special needs, the diet kitchen was established in the hospital, and everyone accepted the principle embodied there that a "just" distribution should in these cases be unequal, that is, determined solely by special needs. Noting the vast difference between the principles governing that kitchen from those operative in our own, I thought, "Here is a case where seemingly love would appear to have triumphed over law. Even better put, where love has become embodied in organized practice. Here a generous concern for the unique needs of individual cases has replaced our practice in the kitchen of governing all cases by the one general rule of equality."

I soon realized that as usual I had been too optimistic. Life cannot be run in a way that so easily dispenses with strict principles, with general laws by which individual cases are determined. Thus the diet kitchen in itself was a welter of ironclad rules. People claimed over and over, on no valid grounds, that *they* were special cases, and demanded "their fair extra portions." The ironic consequence was that strict rules had to be established to determine who really deserved the status of an exception to the law of equality. No one without a doctor's prescription could qualify for the diet kitchen or for extra rations in the main kitchens.

The same was true of all exceptions. Special events such as birthday parties and anniversaries always called for small extra rations from the kitchens: an extra potato, a bit of extra flour, and so on. Experience quickly showed that no such exceptions could safely be made unless some general laws were established to govern them: *only* birthdays and wedding anniversaries, and only a cup of flour, etc. Otherwise, every one of the 799 other diners would have been clamoring for these extras, and our supplies would by no means have gone around. A kind of special mercy is necessary in the equitable running of any large organization, but benevolence to special cases cannot be "freewheeling."

As Matt and I decided when we used to mull over all this in the evening, even exceptions to the law have to be determined legalistically. It seems impossible ever completely to leave the realm of law and enter the paradise of love where each is merely given what he needs and asks for, because in his self-concern, what a man asks for will always be more than he needs and also more than he sees his neighbor getting.

The reason the Marxists can never reach their idyllic level of "communism" beyond what Marx called "the selfish calculation of bourgeois rights" is not because of problems in production. Rather it is because the dominance of self-interest in mankind will always make the law necessary to protect men against their rapacious neighbors.

What baffled us the most in this area was the problem of exceptions for the heavy workers. With some justice, they always felt they deserved a larger ration of food than those who did not work so hard or actually needed or wanted less. There seemed no way that such a just but unequal distribution could be handled officially. A separate line for the heavy workers was often suggested, but the difficulty of defining fairly that favored class made the solution impossible, and we felt it would raise so much jealousy among the rest that it was never even tried.

The eventual solution was "unofficial." That is, workers simply carried home extra rations of the supplies connected with their particular work. Stokers carted off coke from their fires, helpers in the kitchen took seconds, bakers got a private loaf, fitters availed themselves of extra wood or stove pipes, and so on. These were called "perks," from the word "perquisite," and in moderation they were generally accepted morally and legally as a justified reward for hard labor done.

As might be expected, this practice gradually got out of hand. Men on their day off would demand these extras; men who never had done heavy work were found helping themselves; and more than "leftovers"—that is actual raw supplies—began to appear among the usual "perks." At this point the others' gorge rose; accusations of corruption and embezzlement were hurled at bakery, kitchen or fitter's shop; and a widespread reaction against the practice as a whole set in. A concerted effort was made to ban the entire practice of "perks" by declaring them illegal.

The new law banning all "perks" quickly defeated its own purpose. That purpose had been to prevent the normal "perks" from mushrooming into outright stealing. But the law itself, by calling "perks" a crime, blurred fatally just that distinction between stealing and the mild "perks" it sought to preserve. By blurring that distinction, it made impossible the prosecution of the serious matter of stealing.

One of the stokers in the kitchen was a former official in a Far Eastern shipping line, a rather high-class type with a good education. Shortly after the law went into effect, he was caught taking home buckets of lump coal (rather than the coke made by his fires) from the kitchen yard.

At his trial he defended himself by maintaining that his act was not stealing, but the common "perk" for his stoking job. Thus, said he, what he did was merely something that every stoker did by common practice and so his case was no different in kind from tens of others. Consequently, he continued, while he recognized that "perks" were now against the law, he demanded that every stoker in camp stand with him in the dock, or else he would claim that he was being tried unfairly.

His sharp defense—one could see the advantage of a trained mind—put the court in a tough spot, as it was calculated to do. The Discipline Committee had no intention of prosecuting all the other stokers whom they knew were continuing to take home "mild perks" as usual. What the committee wished to prosecute was stealing, and the members were certain that what this man had been doing was just that. They had, however, to acquit him, for they could not define legally the subtle but important difference between a normal "perk" and stealing so long as the law regarded both as crimes. What was needed was a legal definition of a legitimate "perk" so that anything beyond that could be effectively prosecuted. The mistake had been to seek to abolish an accepted pattern of the community's life rather than to control it within reasonable bounds.

Shortly after the conclusion of this case, another man was caught taking raw supplies home from the kitchen. When he, too, claimed that this was his rightful "perk" and that he was then "no different from any other kitchen worker and so could not be prosecuted unless they all are," this mistake in the law became plain to everyone.

As we all knew, "perks" had not ceased because of the law against them. On the contrary, all that had occurred by the promulgation of an idealistic law was the removal of the law from its relevance to the social scene—and *that* was a serious matter. For then, practices which the community would not accept were legally identifiable with continuing practices that it did accept, and so the law became incapable of coping with precisely those actions it was designed to prevent.

By common consent, therefore, the law against "perks" was abolished. A more sensible and effective effort was made to control them instead. Having been officially recognized, they could then be carefully defined. During the last year, the administration of each utility made out a careful list of the "perks" recognized on each of its jobs. If, by common practice, any job had had no "perk"—for example, it was difficult to find one for the latrine cleaners—we managers had to dream one up, for a "perk" had now become everyone's right! This was hardly ideal legislation, justifying as it did an unequal distribution. But because "perks" were legally defined, stealing could now be dealt with by the law.

We discussed at length how the distinction between "perks"— a relatively unjust and so socially acceptable practice—and stealing—a radically unjust and so socially unacceptable practice— might be drawn. This was not easy to do. Amount was not involved, nor could we rest content merely with the arbitrary principle of the authorization of management—such and such is a "perk," such and such is not. Finally, it was generally agreed among us that the dividing line came between raw supplies and goods about to be served, on the one hand, and prepared goods that remained after communal use, on the other. No worker in the kitchen was allowed to take home raw meat, vegetables, and so on, or to go off with his extra before serving time. His "perks" came from a division of whatever was left over *after* serving, and if we ran out or only had barely enough, he got no "perks." If, however, there was some left over from the initial serving, then the kitchen staff got first crack at second portions. Correspondingly, stokers could not take home any raw coal, but only the coke produced by their fires.

This principle at first glance looked ironclad. But human nature can work its will even within such rules. When we made cakes in the kitchen, we always made extras so there would be some left over! And stokers dealt with their fires in just that loving fashion which produces fine coke! Still this was a fairly sensible way of handling the problem and it infinitely clarified the legal situation with respect to the utilities.

Matthew Read and I used to talk by the hour about the strange relation of law to society which this whole problem highlighted. Somewhat to our surprise, we found we agreed that the law was made necessary because of self-interest, and that therefore its primary function was not, as I had always thought, that of stating what is abstractly just and right, but rather that of controlling self-interest, and molding it into socially creative rather than socially destructive patterns.

An idealistic law may state beautifully the abstract principles which should be operative for a perfect society. But as our experience was continually demonstrating, then it would fail to fulfill its necessary function as law, namely, that of controlling the self-interested and potentially dangerous predatory activities of man against his neighbor.

Law, it seemed to us, must be just in the sense that in controlling behavior it should mold behavior in more and more creative and equal directions—else needless suffering result and society be engulfed in conflict. But first of all, law must be an agent of control. Thus it must be practical. It must be in touch with actual patterns of behavior if it is to be the controller of them. Consequently effective law is almost always a good deal less than the ideal.

Man as a personal and social being—and also, as I believe, as a child of God—is responsible to his neighbor. For this reason, creative law must move *toward* the ideal. But man, as I was learning, is also a sinner seeking more than his neighbor at his neighbor's expense. Therefore, effective law must be "earthy" enough to exert that control over his behavior which is essential if there is to be any human society at all.

VIII ✍ Threat of Anarchy

Weihsien camp's greatest difficulties with law and order had to do not so much with the justice as with the strength of its laws. The main problem was the political one of generating governmental power, rather than of ruling with wisdom and justice—though that was by no means easy. It seemed strange that in an enemy internment camp, the peril of anarchy was much more immediate than the threat of tyranny. And yet, as we gradually and anxiously came to realize, our small civilization was endangered because it seemed unable to develop strong laws that could be enforced.

Stealing was what made our need for stronger government so

acute. As rations became shorter, the tendency to steal grew. By the last year or so of the war, it was becoming a threatening social problem. It was, indeed, not only the most understandable but the easiest thing in the world to bring off.

Stealing was easy because camp supplies passed through a multitude of hands. They were distributed to the kitchens, the bakery, and other utilities by gangs of men, and worked on there by innumerable shifts of butchers, cooks, bakers, stokers, and general helpers. At any one of these points, it was ridiculously simple for one man or a group of men to slip off the job for a moment with a bucket of coal, a sack of flour, a piece of meat, a basket of potatoes—or whatever the supplies might be.

The only time as manager of the kitchen I ever managed to catch anyone red-handed was when a practiced pilferer made the mistake of jumping the seasons in her apparel. One hot August day, I saw one of the vegetable women, a big, rather tough middle-aged Russian, the widow of a British army sergeant, working in a large overcoat while she was chopping carrots. I do not fancy myself as a brilliant investigator, but the overcoat made even me come awake with suspicion. So I asked her to open it. At first she refused, counterattacking with a torrential display of temperament. But being by now fairly sure of my ground, I insisted and began firmly to remove the coat from her broad back. At this she relented completely, and with many knowing winks and gestures, showed me her handiwork with real pride. On the inside of that coat I found fifteen large pockets sewn into its heavy lining. In every pocket nestled either a fat potato or a carrot!

Butchers had an even easier time of it with more valuable articles. Two of them worked alone in an isolated room for an entire day handling our most prized possession—raw meat. It was absurdly simple for one—when the other was momentarily absent —to run home with four or five good cuts from the three-day supply for the whole kitchen.

Often, when I saw these men running back to their rooms, bundled up in their heavy coats, I would wonder what other flesh might be accompanying their own. But unless one was sure of one's ground, a manager could hardly demand that the man empty his pockets. Ill-grounded accusations of theft are not calculated to build up a team spirit! The mechanics of prevention were difficult, as difficult as the mechanics of stealing were easy.

The people of the camp were strongly tempted indeed to take advantage of these many opportunities. They were almost always hungry and cold; while no one starved or froze, everyone wanted desperately to have more to eat and to feel the comfort of being really warm. When food and coal were there for the taking, even consciences that normally were strong would weaken. The power of these temptations was especially acute for men and women with families. Haunted by the thought of their children's discomfort, they could scarcely be expected to refuse to take with them some morsels to cheer up the house. It was a hardy and rare spirit that could, in such circumstances, ignore the immediate and pressing claims of his family. Noting the awesome strength of such temptations, as well as their devastating consequences to our social order, I was struck by the strange way in which the natural—and in most respects—noble loyalty of a man to his family can, unless tempered by some wider loyalty, become the springboard for dangerous social chaos.

Although stealing was understandable, its peril to the community was nonetheless critical. The supplies each utility received were pitifully inadequate and increasingly so. Edible meat, lump coal, sound potatoes, flour, oil, sugar, and the other staples were available in such small amounts that any cut in the supplies was serious.

If 150 pounds of meat—only a fraction of which was first grade, the rest being skin, fat, innards, and so on—was all that eight hundred people got for three days, then the removal through the butchers of that essential fraction, say twenty pounds, meant a staggering reduction in the rations of each of the diners. If our coal issue was mostly fine dust, to take home the few lumps scattered in the pile left the other stokers with an almost impossible task. Those of us who worked in the utilities saw at once the disintegrating effects stealing had on our whole corporate life. We feared its consequences from the very first case that appeared.

Initially, it was a puzzle to me why a community where stealing was so natural and posed so dangerous a threat to its life, should have had such great difficulty in establishing its own law. Why were people so apt to be against legal measures to prevent crime when such measures were so clearly in their own interest as members of the community? But as Matt and I thrashed out this problem, we came to see that in fact the law had always had an ambiguous, dubious role to play in our lives, and that this situation probably tended to weaken immeasurably its legitimacy and force among us.

In the first place, all public supplies and property had a strange dual ownership. They belonged both to the Japanese enemy and to our community, complicating endlessly for each internee the moral question, "Is it right to steal?"

To most of us, stealing from the Japanese seemed morally justified—if not, indeed, incumbent on us as enemy nationals. The Japanese had taken by force from the mission compound all the equipment we used; the metal and coal issued to us had been forced out of the Chinese. Even the food we received had been purchased with a false currency, supported only by the enemy's arms. Why not, then, gladly steal these things and in this way get back at them for the immeasurably greater theft of the wealth of the rest of the Far East? To cap all this, most of the internees had not forgotten the way in which their personal property and their businesses had been arbitrarily and ruthlessly confiscated by the Japanese authorities. The prevailing attitude of the camp was, therefore, that since the Japanese had no moral right to what they had commandeered in China, an internee was thoroughly justified in taking back from them all he could.

To this feeling of moral justification was added the less tenable but still widely held view that by stealing from their captors, each internee was by that much sabotaging the Japanese war effort and aiding the Allies. In the case of the pound or two of meat, this line of thought was optimistic to say the least. If stealing from the Japanese, however, had forced them to replace what had been taken, there might have been some point to the argument. But we never found an instance in which the Japanese replaced or restocked any supplies depleted by theft.

In every case the Japanese would say—and with some justification—that since they had already provided coal, bread, or food for our subsistence, they were not responsible for the subsequent theft of these items by our own people. Besides, they liked to add with sarcasm, in spite of the theft, these stolen supplies had still been consumed "by the camp." They agreed that in this case the distribution, being by and for the thieves, was unfair. But after all—and here they would smile courteously—it had been long agreed between us that the distribution of supplies would remain solely the responsibility of the internees themselves.

It looked, therefore, as if this argument were to a high degree an attempt to rationalize on patriotic grounds the desire to steal for oneself. This rationalization contained within it enough of a seed of truth so that with assiduous cultivation, it could produce a fine flower of legal disputation. To hear a perpetrator describe it, one would have thought that a theft at night of lump coal from the kitchen pile was, in fact, a dashing commando raid into enemy territory. One would think that in dodging the manager and the Discipline Committee, this patriot was in fact slipping through the fingers of the Japanese Consular Guard!

For all its benefits, the black market unquestionably contributed further to the general disrespect for the law. Almost everyone had in one way or another participated in this trade or enjoyed its fruits. Even though everyone knew it was illegal, and thus against his own sworn promise "to obey camp rules," it was regarded as both good and right. By means of a rigid distinction between "enemy law," to which we owed no moral obligation whatsoever, and our own "camp law," which still bound our consciences, most internees were enabled to cling to their respect for legality and morality in general, while at the same time snatching what they could from their captors.

This rather fine distinction, so obvious to the more respectable, middle-class leaders of the camp, was by no means so apparent to everyone else, as was illustrated by the sad case of Goodpasture. "Goody," as he was called affectionately by his friends, was a leading British importer, a man in his early fifties. While he was, I am sure, intelligent enough in affairs of trade, he was hardly a strong or dominating sort of man. A small, genial man with a smaller mustache, he had a much younger wife who did not appear overjoyed with her bargain. Consequently, Goody lavished most of his love on his twelve-year-old son, a young man with a promise of far more spirit, and certainly far larger biceps, than his mild, diminutive father.

In the early days, almost everyone was involved in the black market; Goodpasture, not wanting to pass up any good thing, began to participate, too. As Goody ruefully admitted later, however, he was not the most suave or adept of black marketers. He found it arduous at his age to clamber up to the top of the wall to negotiate with the Chinese farmers on the other side. Once up there, he always found that his Chinese was not as good as he had at one time thought it was. Designed in fact to give orders to rickshaw boys, it was hardly sufficient for these delicate discussions about times, places, quantities, and prices. He didn't really know what the Chinese were saying, and several times he discovered he had made agreements about prices and quantities he had no intention of honoring. His nerve wasn't as steady as it used to be either, and he had to rest a while after each sortie on the wall in order to get his heart quiet again.

He was about ready to give all this up when to his surprise and delight, he discovered that his young son could do everything he'd been trying to do, and do it with remarkable skill. Soon their roles were reversed, and Goody, Sr., was standing guard on the ground while Goody, Jr., risked his neck on the wall at night. As Goody used to boast quietly to his envious friends, "I'll tell you, chaps, the boy is becoming a pukka second-story man. You should see the way he clambers all over that wall, tells the Chinese what to deliver, and then bargains with them on prices. Some day he'll be paying his dad's chits at the club, hmmm?"

To the proud father, his son's activities seemed innocent enough. He had spent his life under the benevolent aegis of the majestic British law. Within its supporting structure, his own self-identity and self-esteem as a reputable businessman, as well as his profits as an importer, had grown as he prospered. To doubt this law or to question its hold over his own conscience could never have crossed Goodpasture's mind. Thus for him these nightly excursions were merely a temporary expedient, a kind of *entr'acte* brought on by the strange and totally abnormal conditions of an enemy prison camp. It never occurred to him that his son would view them in a different light.

To Goodpasture, Jr., however, camp existence was no *entr'acte*. This was *life*, the whole of life. The only law he knew was the Japanese law his father and he were engaged in flouting. The memories of British existence in Tientsin, related of an evening by his parents and their homesick friends, seemed to him both old-fashioned and unreal. What he had learned from *his* experience was that life was pretty chancy; its good things came only if a smart fellow took what he could when he could. Above all, he must keep clear of the clutches of the authorities.

Then the inevitable happened. There occurred a number of serious cases of theft from the rooms. The disappearance of clothes, watches, money and so on, became more and more noticeable. Finally, when a set of valuable tools was stolen from the carpenter's shop, it became plain that some rather practiced thief, or possibly a group of thieves, was at work. A concerted search was made. As a result, the carpenter's tools were found

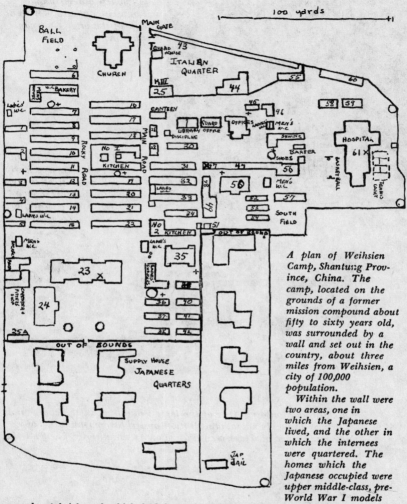

A plan of Weihsien Camp, Shantung Province, China. The camp, located on the grounds of a former mission compound about fifty to sixty years old, was surrounded by a wall and set out in the country, about three miles from Weihsien, a city of 100,000 population.

Within the wall were two areas, one in which the Japanese lived, and the other in which the internees were quartered. The homes which the Japanese occupied were upper middle-class, pre-World War I models made of brick and which had been the missionaries' residences. The rest of the compound, the working mission, contained living space allocated to the 2,000 internees, as well as schools, a church built some time in the early twenties, a small ballfield, an excellent and somewhat new hospital building, a bakery, and three kitchens. Families in the camp lived in rows of 9 by 12-foot rooms; the single people lived in dormitory rooms in the larger classroom buildings. The scale of the plan is accurate: the compound is only 200 yards at its widest point, and 150 yards long.

A small Chinese summer house in an area between two of the large classroom buildings.

The hospital. To the right, one can see clearly the wall with its electrified barbed wire, the guard-house, and the countryside beyond.

A classroom building. One of the largest buildings in the compound, this was probably the administration and classroom building of the middle-school. Here men and women's dormitories filled all the rooms.

A typical row of 9 by 12-foot rooms where the families lived. This sketch shows a patio in front, a stove and table where the woman is working, a small garden where vegetables might be grown, a line for laundry, and so on.

The yard of Kitchen I, the largest kitchen of the compound, where the author was cook and later manager. Two men are shown working, preparing lunch on the table.

Inside Kitchen I, which fea
800 people. This shows
large cauldrons in which
all the cooking was done
(the man is stirring one
here), the various pots used
for serving the food, the
stoke hole below the
cauldrons where the stoker
kept his fires, the pot for
water on the right-hand
side, and a lot of dirt and
mess all around.

The camp bakery (on the
right) and one of the men's
latrines and showers
beyond it. The bakery
held large ovens and a room
for making bread. The
water tower on the left is
for the men's showers;
a man is pumping water
into the tower.

The ballfield and a good view of the wall showing the electrified barbed wire, the guardhouse with the machine guns in it, and the defense stations of the Japanese guard. They never had to use these stations. The very small softball diamond was so close to the wall that there was some problem of losing balls over it.

THE BALL FIELD

Looking down the main road of the camp past the rows of houses toward the gate. The internees went outside the gate only to dump the garbage.

View of Blocks 21-22, showing two rows of 9 by 12-foot rooms and a women's latrine with the water tower behind it.

BLOCKS 21-22 - LADIES

Since not much has happened here in
this calm, enclosed life, there hasn't seemed
to be much point in keeping a day to
day record. Nevertheless there are some
aspects of a life like this that are interesting
and so are worth putting down. But first
the general circumstances of our interned
existence should be recorded.

The main factor that stands out is
that relative to what we all expected
should war with Japan break out, we have
been extremely fortunate. In the first
place the majority of us, those who were
already living in the south compound, have
been able to stay in our own houses
and so to keep up the usual basic
comforts of life as well as retain all our
belongings. Since we had all rather
expected to be carted off somewhere, presumably to some sort of 'concentration
camp' with only the things that we could
carry in our hands, this fact has been
a pleasant surprise.

Of course, those foreigners who had been
living in other parts of the main campus
had to move into this compound into the
houses already occupied with the
inevitable result that there has been a
bit of crowding. Fortunately however, each
of the separate groups has found itself

These two pages are from the journal kept by the author while
held in house arrest at Yenching University in Peking, before going
to Weihsien.

...with do the poor Chinese manage? And how
to the freighters in Peking - Tientsin who have
to earn & pay for their being manage?

Just a note on prices as of May 1945: eggs
$13.50; cigarettes $326.00, peanuts $55.00 lb. formerly $2.00),
soap $16, brooms 20.00 (50¢), peng mato 230.00 (4.00 before), mail
600.00 a lb, sugar 200.00, Am cigarette 100.00 a pack, equivalent
of one roll of toilet paper 29.00. And then a fine stock of brooms
came in at 600.00 a long broom! And so it goes! In June
peanuts $120.00 lb, I spent in other words $960.00
on 8 lbs of peanuts. At 160.00 lb, Am cigarette $1.00 gold.
$250.00 a pack or at the present exchange
We are now dealing in $1,000. bills as if they were
fifty Dollars.

Where does all this money come from? This
brings up the whole question of extra legal dealing
which is one of the most interesting chapters of camp
history.

BLACK MARKET

During the first few months of camp most of us were
astounded to find that food was coming into camp
"over the wall." It took quite a while for this information
to seep into the consciousness of all: at first only a few
"friends of friends" knew about it. But gradually it
became known all over. It started up in social
places - wherever there was a sheltered corner of the
wall with no guard in sight: Chinese contacts were
made, orders were placed, and the stuff was thrown
over one way, as the money was thrown over the other
way. The volume of business done in this manner
was truly staggering that first summer & winter.
Thousands of eggs came in regularly, jams, peanut
butter, sugar etc. For a period of about six months you
could buy these things almost at will if you went
to the right people.

Along with hosts of private individuals, who could
be seen walking near the wall daily waiting for
some sign from outside, there were 4 below three major

Scrubbing
vegetables

Cutting
Vegetables

A drawing by Miss Marie Regier, a missionary at Weihsien, showing women (who could be missionaries, bankers' wives, gay ladies, and so on) scrubbing and cutting the vegetables and washing them in the old bathtub.

stashed away in an old tunnel where teen-agers were known to gather.

Certain clues indicated beyond question that it was Goodpasture, Jr., who had put them there. A few days later some more objects were found in his mattress. His father was, as might be expected, both horrified and incredulous.

"Imagine my son stealing! And from our own people, too!" he moaned in genuine dismay. And his despair only grew when it became clear that the boy, now fourteen, had steadfastly lied to everyone—to the committee, to older friends, and to his father. To him there was no distinction between laws and between authorities; and he was willing to challenge the camp establishment as readily as he had been to defy the larger order upheld by the Japanese army.

Community morale is a vague, irrational matter of atmosphere and moral tone—not a matter of logic. It would seem that once a basic moral standard is flouted in one area it is difficult for standards to be upheld in some other area. I was made aware of this tone of unlawfulness when, as manager, I heard a stoker on the boiler side say to a friend as he was putting his coke "perk" into his bucket to go home for the night, "These committeemen and that damn manager say we shouldn't take home lump coal, do they? Well, every one of those bloody committeemen have stolen stovepipes in their rooms—stolen from the same bloody Nips. Why is the coal I take home so different, except that I'm not a pukka big shot! Probably old man Campbell is well supplied with coal anyway—the stoker on No. 2 boiler lives right next door to him—the very one who got Campbell his extra stovepipes!"

Once a general moral justification had been given to stealing from the Japanese and defying their law, then almost anything in camp which anyone wanted to steal could be argued around to being the property of the Japanese.

The conditions of camp life certainly encouraged stealing. But it was also true that the maintenance of our civilization depended directly on its prevention. The real threat that widespread stealing posed for us was not merely the amount involved. The greater danger lay in what it did to the utilities themselves as organizations of cooperative labor.

A moral disease such as stealing could have the same disintegrating effect on our utilities that a case of bubonic plague has on the human anatomy. During that last year, this effect was revealing itself. Our community never did, in fact, disintegrate. But the mechanism of its self-destruction was visible to us as the amount of stealing took a sharp rise in the last year of camp. The mechanism operates roughly like this:

As thefts increase, and the stolen goods are seen, heard about, or even smelled in the rest of the camp, inevitably rumors start to circulate. One hears that meat is disappearing "regularly" from the butchery, potatoes from the vegetable tables, and coal from the piles. Other workers, hearing these reports of goods enjoyed at home, begin to lose interest in resisting their own forms of the same sort of temptation. As a helper in the kitchen said once to Stan, "If all these other guys are taking stuff home to their kids, why the hell should mine go hungry? I'm going to get in on this before it's all gone!"

The virus spreads. Twenty-five pounds of meat stolen grow to fifty, and then to a hundred, and pretty soon the diners are getting noticeably less than their fair share of the issued supplies.

At this point the disintegration reaches a new stage. The character of the kitchen changes, and with that change its ability to maintain itself as an organization with integrity begins to weaken. Matt saw this in the Labor Committee office. Men who had worked for a considerable period as cooks in the kitchen and seemed happy on the job would ask to be transferred. When Matt wanted to know why, their answer would go something like this:

"The kitchen isn't what it used to be. Everybody is suspicious of everybody else. Most of all, the people suspect me, the cook. I'm supposed to be responsible for my shift—that means for the honesty of my crew. I don't know if they're taking stuff behind my back or not—probably a little, but I have no idea how much. If they're taking a lot, then we're a bunch of phonies, pretending to feed the diners but actually feeding ourselves.

"I'll tell you, Read, I'm no bloody missionary saint—oh, excuse me, I always forget you *are* one of those—but I will not be held responsible for something I don't approve of but can't prevent. That is why I want out—and there are plenty of others who feel the same way!"

When Matt told me of this conversation, my heart sank.

"Well, the disease is spreading, all right! In fact, it's going so fast that it's driving the remnants of remaining healthy, honest

cooks like Brockman, right out. My God, it even makes *me* want
to quit. If I can't control the stealing, I don't want to be
responsible either."

"Yes, and that's not all," said Matt. "A couple of shady
characters came to see us in the labor office yesterday—Old Tom
and a friend of his. They had heard that Brockman wanted to
get out. They were offering to set up a new cooking shift which
they would head. I told them no dice, naturally. Any shift run by
those two would syphon stuff out so fast it would be a lucky diner
that ever saw a chunk of meat. You can see what is happening. As
the honest chaps get uneasy and want to move out, the
scroungers move up—up from the ranks of helper and right into
the heart of the organization itself, to cook if Brockman quits
and, brother, if you quit and no one else will do it, they'll move
right into manager, too. Then the disease will have killed the
patient, and the kitchen as a means of feeding the diners will
have died. Immorality, my friend, is not merely the private
demon of the 'missionary saints,' Brockman flung at me. It's more
like a public demon, and it can bring a society to its knees as
surely as any physical plague!"

"But Matt, what would happen then?" I asked. "I agree that if
the utilities ever became a means of getting supplies to a few
instead of to everybody, they would have to be disbanded. It
would be better to divide the supplies individually as soon as
they are issued. But you realize, don't you, that such an indi-
vidualized economy wouldn't work. Each individual would get so
little—especially in oil and flour—that he couldn't possibly bake
bread or make stew for himself. Large families might make it,
but smaller ones or single people never could. Such a 'state of
nature' before society, à la Locke, where everyone does everything for himself, would mean malnutrition and ultimately
starvation. No, we have to live corporately, as a social community, or we're extinct!"

"But if we are to remain a communal organization, there must
be enough law enforcement to keep that stealing from spreading
further," said Matt. "You managers better begin to work with
discipline a little more closely, I think. Unless there's law around
here, there won't be much of a camp left!"

As I went home that night from Matthew and Edith's, I felt
more worried than at any time since we had first arrived. How
could the stealing be stopped? How could we watch each corner

of the kitchen every day? And if we couldn't, how could we develop enough strength in our laws to control this disease that was threatening slowly to choke us?

How were we to enforce our laws? During the early stages of camp, the forms of punishment boiled down to varieties of "moral pressure," or more accurately, the "pressure of public disapproval." If men were caught and convicted of any sort of crime, their names would be posted along with the crime on the bulletin boards of the camp. Recalling how such unfavorable publicity would have affected careers or social ambitions in Peking or Tientsin society, most of us thought this threat would be sufficient to control behavior. Since I had never been really hungry or cold before, and since I had felt in my family, at school, or on a faculty the deadly results of social disapproval, I assumed that I'd rather face anything I could think of—hunger or cold—than the humiliation of such posting.

I began to wonder about this when I noticed in the kitchen how informal forms of moral pressure, in this case the obvious disapproval of his mates, failed to get Jacobson and his like to work. It was plain that such men would rather have easy jobs than the approval or even the admiration of everyone else. Feeling that this independence from the crowd's approval was in some respects strong and possibly creative, I began to wonder even how ethical was the pressure of public opinion as an instrument of shaping social behavior.

It was, however, the ineffectiveness of moral pressure in our situation that most impressed us. Mere public opinion seemingly almost never changed anyone's antisocial behavior. A second incident involving Mrs. Witherspoon illustrates this ineffectiveness.

As was mentioned earlier, after the two men escaped from the camp in April, 1944, every internee had twice each day to gather with his group at a set spot, and to stand in designated rows for about an hour while the camp was counted. Since the Japanese were now very strict about this whole matter, if any individual in a group was late, the whole group had to remain an extra three-quarters of an hour.

Most people came to their place in roll call as soon as the great bell began to ring, and waited for the guards to arrive. Not so Mrs. Witherspoon. Unfortunately for her section, her back window overlooked the ballfield where they were gathered. Thus she would stay in her room, "combing her hair" as she explained, until she saw the guard run up. Then she would leave her room, and stride as quickly as she could down her row and onto the ballfield. Like some great rhino seeking to be unnoticed, she would attempt to squeeze her wide bulk invisibly into her place in the line at the last minute. Naturally, since she was hardly designed by age or bulk to be a sprinter, she was late time and time again. The guard would get to her place before she did, or he would see her wallowing in that direction, and each time he was infuriated and made the entire four hundred people remain overtime. Her neighbors were thus daily enraged with her, and did not attempt to hide the fact. The internee warden repeatedly pleaded with her, begged her, tried to order her to appear with the rest when the bell sounded. She always refused.

In desperation, the warden and the Discipline Committee called on the chief of police. They told him that the community had sought in vain to get this woman to cooperate. Since the community was unable to control her, it should not be held responsible for her, said they. Therefore the section should not be punished for her stubbornness. Having watched her antics once from a distance, the chief agreed. In broken English, he put the point quite well, "Group have not responsibility for her; she have none for them."

If moral pressure could affect the antisocial, this thick-skinned lady would have wilted quickly enough.

Another instance in the winter of 1944–1945 showed even more clearly the futility of looking to community pressure as the sole basis for law. This was a case of stealing that involved as ill-assorted a pair as could be imagined.

One of them was John Chamberlain, the well-to-do representative of a large British machinery corporation. Chamberlain was the perfect picture of the British colonial. Even after two years, his scuffed shoes were always shined, his threadbare trousers creased; his worn shirts immaculately pressed. An ascot tie was always at his throat, a silk kerchief in his pocket, and his mustache was neatly trimmed to the last stiff hair. He had always been gay as well as immaculate. But now the gleam in his eye had, so to speak, enlarged. The bouyancy and charm were still very much present, but unsteadier, more wayward, and so more forced.

The other member of the pair could hardly have been a greater contrast. He was Willie Bryan, a swarthy Eurasian from

Shanghai. There were many Eurasians in the camp. Often they were incredibly handsome people with striking black hair, beautifully molded features, and a golden skin. Willie's brother George, who worked on my shift in the kitchen, a friendly, nervous guy, was like that.

But Willie himself was one of the ugliest and most sinister-looking men I had ever seen. He slouched, where Chamberlain stood straight; he was dirty, unshaven and unwashed, where Chamberlain was groomed and clean. Willie had probably dressed in silks in Shanghai; but here he was too lazy to care. Though not particularly large, Willie was strong; above all, he moved with a catlike grace which showed he could handle himself, and was probably adept with the large knife he always kept by him. His eyes were small, insolent, humorous, and most of the time languid. But they could gleam red with hostility when Willie got angry. A large scar ran across his face. Everyone knew Willie could be intensely dangerous if he wanted to. He came to camp with an awesome reputation—for gambling, gunrunning, narcotics, and all the rest. People spoke *of* him with affectionate fear—and *to* him with hopeful respect, as if intimacy with him might afford some sort of protection, even while they were also trying to make it clear to him that, as a Eurasian, he was far below their social level. His actual character was not easy to assess. Most of the time he was a cheerful, friendly person in a sardonic sort of way, and good company. But one felt an inner coldness and cruelty that may have been the cause of this universal reaction of fear.

Once I saw the whole supplies gang, of which Willie was the leading spirit, drop off four bags of lump coal at the door of a Greek boy on the gang as the carts wheeled by. Willie and the boy leaped off, stuffed the bags in the door, and were back on the cart almost before I could catch my breath. I reported this incident to discipline and showed them the bags. After that, when we passed on the street, Willie would only spit. We never exchanged a word again. I was glad this had not happened in Shanghai.

One night a middle-aged woman, an Anglican missionary, saw John and Willie taking lump coal from the supply pile. She reported this at once to the Discipline Committee. The lawyers in the camp had devised for us an intricate judicial system. Now began its first real testing.

According to this system, any serious accusation against an internee must first be brought before the Discipline Committee, where the accuser would have to state his case and be examined by the accused. If in the mind of the committee there was sufficient evidence, the case would be brought before the camp court. This court consisted of five judges to be chosen by lot from a panel of some forty "honorable men." Since this panel of forty had long since been selected by the nine-man committee, the court was ready to function when a case came up once the five judges for that particular case had been drawn by lot.

The day after reporting the case, the woman duly accused Chamberlain and Bryan before the Discipline Committee. At that meeting the two of them offered as a defense the justifications we all knew so well: (1) Coal was the recognized "perk" of the supplies gang. If they were to be convicted, the entire laboring force should be similarly treated, although it was pointed out by a committee member that lump coal taken at night hardly counted as a "perk." (2) They were actually helping the Allied war effort since the Japanese would have to replace the coal from their own supplies. They felt, as Willie sardonically remarked, that they should be feted, not punished, by the camp for having risked their skins to relieve the Japanese of some of their coal! In spite of these arguments, the committee agreed that a case had been made against them, and that the trial would start the next day.

The camp buzzed with excitement. These were two of the most colorful characters around; this was our first serious criminal case; and everyone was intensely curious about the way the untried judicial system would work. The committee room where the trial was to be held was jammed. A crowd, including everyone not at work, gathered outside. People stood looking in the windows, talking out the possible legal tangles. All were generally delighted that these two heroes had unwittingly caused that item longed for by every internee: an Event!

The five judges arrived and nervously took their seats. Then the Discipline Committee appeared. Ian Campbell, as chairman, was prosecuting attorney. Everyone fell silent, waiting for the trial to begin. At that moment someone noticed that the chairs that were to hold the two defendants were empty!

For a time the court waited, embarrassed and not quite sure what to do. Then Campbell, obviously upset, dispatched the constable, an enormous, jovial British police chief from Tientsin, to round them up. The constable came back abashed and genuinely puzzled.

"Chamberlain and Bryan won't come," he announced. Then,

in a tone of bewilderment, he added, "They told me I couldn't *make* them come until they were convicted."

Obviously, the officer had been rendered completely speechless by this argument.

"So I said," he continued, " 'Don't you want to come—to defend yourselves in the court? How can you get a fair trial if you don't defend yourselves?' "

" 'Oh, the hell with that'—pardon Your Honor—said Bryan. 'That ruddy court can't do anything to us anyway, so why should we give a damn what sort of a sentence we get?' " The constable repeated this bit of realism as if he completely failed to comprehend it with his mind, but his awed tone showed that somewhere, viscerally, he understood what was being said. The assembled judges, muttering "Oh" or "Shame" at this, were obviously in a state of deep shock. If you are a magistrate, it is one thing to be defied, feared, maligned, and even hated. But to be ignored as too piddling to warrant an hour of anyone's attention is a mortal blow to the self-esteem of any guardian of law and order. Against this humiliation, as Bryan well understood, there is no defense.

The ensuing trial could hardly be called dramatic. The onlookers were torn between amusement and disappointment; the participants were embarrassed as they went through the motions of the trial procedures. Chamberlain and Bryan were seen now and then, lounging lazily outside the windows. Needless to say, a verdict of guilty was handed down to the empty defendants' box; the expected penalty was imposed. The names of the two men were to be posted as convicted of stealing.

After the court adjourned, I was among a sizable crowd watching an irate Campbell post this notice on one of the camp's bulletin boards. A huge, handsome man, with innate courtesy and a good deal of common sense, and a not too well-concealed awareness of his own prestige, Campbell was the epitome of the massive, respectable power of the colonial ruling class. He now despised Chamberlain, who had so clearly let down his class. Willie was too strong ever to despise; but Campbell was too much on the side of law and order to like Willie, and far too much the "gentleman" to respect him. But we were all a little tainted, and Campbell was no exception. Although he tried to look down his nose at Willie, Willie wasn't having any. The confrontation of these two men was thus a classic: the one representing the mighty of the world who wield law and order, often for their own benefit, and the other, from the ranks of the "wicked," who sense the flaws in the mighty and hate above all their smug respectability.

Behind me I heard someone snort. Turning my head, I saw that it was Willie. He was reading the notice over Campbell's shoulder. When Campbell turned to stare at him coldly, Willie laughed sardonically, full in Campbell's face. You could feel in that laugh all the age-old Eurasian resentment against the entrenched power and respectability of these representatives of the British empire.

"So those five bastards under the guidance of the head bastard here convicted me of stealing, have they? The ruddy hypocrites! Why, I helped two of them scrounge the bricks and pipes for their stoves from the supply house—and they have the nerve to say 'naughty, naughty Willie' to me!" And as the crowd stared in amazed silence—even Campbell was made speechless—Willie walked away laughing as undismayed at this posting as he was deeply wrothful at the hypocrisy of life. Basically, I am sure, he was content to savor his total triumph over an impotent and barely respectable law and order.

That evening, Matt and I talked over the problems of "moral pressure" as a basis for law.

"We make a great to-do about the force of public opinion," said Matt, "but when the chips are down, it's a skittish and unreliable thing at best. It may light on some unfortunate with a surprising and unjust weight, and at the same time remain indifferent to a real menace. Society seems to disapprove with equal relish the genius and the criminal, the saint and the malingerer! And it will always express sympathy for the outlaw if the government happens to be unpopular. In other words, more often than not, society approves and disapproves of precisely the wrong people. A thousand factors may divide and confuse public judgment. Through this maze of loopholes, the offender like Willie escapes, unscathed by a pressure too diffuse to touch him."

"Even more, Matt," I put in, "the Willies of the world can always find plenty of friends—those who are accustomed to the illegal, those who hate the government, and those who just plain like him. You know, I think the only place this moral pressure or moral force really works is where the government is immensely respected, where an absolutely unified public opinion can be created, and where each member is so intimately related to the others, and so dependent on them, that disapproval really hurts him.

"This works only in small and select groups such as families and schools, corporations and totalitarian states. Most of them, schools and corporations at least, are fooling themselves when they think no force but moral pressure is used, because the school can always use the coercion of expulsion if the moral pressure doesn't work. In a camp like this, where you can't expel anyone and where there is no unified public opinion that can hurt anyone, to count on moral pressure alone is hopeless.

"The real difficulty with the concept of a social order based on moral pressure is that it assumes that everyone is already moral. Look at the way Willie laughed at those poor chaps who were the judges. If their *moral* condemnation of Willie is to stick, they have to be clean themselves—and who *hasn't* been involved in some shadiness in this place?

"Anyway, what does moral condemnation mean to a man who doesn't care about being moral, or even being thought moral? Will he change his tune because of it? Never! He couldn't care less! Without the threat of some sort of harm to the offender, without some form of force, no system of law is possible in a world where universal morality cannot be assumed. And if it could, then after all, no system of law would really be necessary!"

Like most people, we thought that a legal and political problem such as ours called for an administrative solution.

"Too much stealing? Then get a larger police force, patrol the kitchens and the supply dumps—and keep the bums from taking the stuff out!"

That was the solution offered by almost all who after this trial found themselves pondering the problem of stealing. It seemed obvious to all of us that enough dependable men circulating around the camp at all hours would be able to do the job.

With real hope, the camp committee and the managers of the utilities sat down one night to make out a list of men for the proposed police force. The meeting lasted only about a half hour. We began, of course, with a discussion of the men who would be put on the force, that is, who would be "good chaps, dependable and honest," as the secretary of the camp committee said, comfortably wetting his pencil, preparing to write. But the moment names were suggested, we found ourselves in trouble.

"Jones, oh good heavens no! It's no good letting *him* patrol the camp alone at night—you'd have to put someone else on to watch him."

"Smith? Yes, of course. Good man, absolutely reliable. The heart of the supply gang. Won't allow any stealing when he's around. No sir!"

"But look here. If you move him off that gang to watch some other chaps at their work, the members of the supply gang will really start moving stuff out. Why put him somewhere as a nonworking policeman when he's already keeping the lid on things where he works?"

So it went. Every time we came to the name of a man whose integrity was in question, all agreed it would be worse to make him a policeman than to keep him on as a worker—for who would watch the watcher? Every time a man of integrity was mentioned, the head of his utility would complain that his organization would collapse without this man and men like him. The meeting broke up because no list could be made; there were no names anyone wanted to put on the list.

"You know," said Matt as we walked home that night, "no group can legislate itself above its own moral level. You don't get honesty by shifting a man from a worker's uniform to a policeman's. Solutions to the problem of law and order won't come because men take on other jobs. They will come only if the community has a sense of responsibility to its own welfare. No increase in the police force will add to that! . . . Old Irenaeus once said, 'Only the immortal can grant immortality to the mortal.' We might paraphrase that in our situation, 'You can't handle the problem of corruption except by incorruption.' And among us wayward humans, this makes it tough to build a lasting social order."

What *were* we to do? Evidently if stealing were to be prevented, it would be only because people feared the punishment following on their act. It was not at all easy to conceive an effective mode of punishment in an internment camp.

Our first efforts to find a real penalty were futile. To the mild slap of moral disapproval through posting was added the denial of the convicted man's few extra privileges in the camp: the right to shop in the canteen, to use the barber shop, library, shoe shop and sewing room, and to attend entertainments. But how silly all this turned out to be! His friends could buy him cigarettes, soap and toilet paper at the canteen, and surely, as we agreed, the risk of losing his chance for a haircut would hardly deter a man bent on stealing ten pounds of first-grade meat!

Next the Discipline Committee began considering setting up

their own jail. It would not be difficult: all that was needed was to clear a room, put in some furniture, and get a good lock on the door and some bars on the windows. But as they thought it over, it became plainer and plainer that a jail inside a camp wears a different face than one outside. Most of the men I heard talking about it agreed that to get out of work, to get away from the worried "little woman" and have some time to read and chat with friends, would be a distinct pleasure. Besides, as everyone realized at once, being locked up in *our* situation had a certain glamour; it was sure to make a hero out of any otherwise uninspiring individual. For everyone rallied round the man clapped into the Japanese jail, and the difference between the two was too subtle for public opinion. Probably friends would bake him small cakes, and generally turn the whole thing into a lark. Worst of all, the committee realized they would have to explain to the Japanese why he was in jail, leaving the possibility open that they might wish to punish him on their own. As a result, the committee reluctantly decided to give up this notion. Every obvious means of punishing lawbreakers disintegrated in their hands.

The camp committee called another meeting to discuss further penalties. The most frequently mentioned of these was that of reducing a convicted man's food ration. But it was thought wiser to move into such stricter measures gradually, and that a trial balloon might be launched to gauge the camp's sentiment. Also, this might give the committee time to make the camp aware of the seriousness of the situation. After debating several alternatives, the men agreed that cutting off a man's comfort money seemed to be the best first step. Some of the lawyers in the camp—who also attended the meeting—were told to redraft the camp constitution accordingly.

This was not a simple matter legally, since comfort money came to each internee from his own government through the Swiss. It was not clear by what sort of right the camp committee could interfere. But, as we managers of the kitchens pointed out, since the same problem would arise if we sought eventually to cut a man's food rations, given him by the Japanese, we might as well tackle the central issue at once: Did the camp want to grant its government this sort of authority in order to prevent stealing?

The legal basis for the new law devised by the lawyers that night centered on the duties of the Finance Committee. That committee's main function was to organize and distribute the comfort money brought to camp by the Swiss. It seemed legally sound to deny a convicted man the service of that committee along with other camp services, and thus make it impossible for him to receive his comfort allowance. On this basis, the lawyers reworked the constitution formed early in the camp, and so by the end of the evening, we had a new and stronger document. We went home feeling much relieved.

With this new constitution then, the camp committee and those others of us who were interested "went to the country," as they say in England. A series of general meetings were held at which the new constitution was explained to the public, and the reasons for its more stringent parts elaborated in great detail. Campbell and John McCracken, then head of the General Affairs Committee, hammered constantly at the theme that this was a moment of decision for the community. It faced breakdown and anarchy, the slow decay of its necessary institutions, unless the stealing were stopped, and firm law was the only way to stop it. Others of us argued the same case in small groups. We seized every chance to bend someone's ear on the matter, pleading that now our community had the opportunity to vote for its own survival. We were confident of a stunning victory at the referendum ten days later, especially because there seemed to be no concerted movement opposed to our proposal.

We could hardly believe our eyes when the results had been tabulated. The new constitution was defeated by a large majority. Quite evidently, the camp simply did not wish to have the strong government which might have saved it.

Over and over Matt and I discussed these results: Why had they voted this way? Surely they wanted to eat—and surely they had understood that rampant stealing was certain to lead to anarchy? To answer this question, we talked to many about how they voted; gradually we began to see what was going on.

Of course, there were people who gave the familiar legal argument that no internee government had the right to take away an internee's money: "This money is sent to me by my own government, and no ruddy committee or court is going to lift it off me!"

It was plain that one reason for the vote was the refusal to recognize the authority of an internee government over their own lives and acts—a refusal that indicated strikingly the very conditions the new constitution was designed to correct. Apparently, as long as men did not feel a sense of identification with and moral responsibility for the community of the camp, they would continue both to steal from it and to vote against punishments for stealing.

Even more apparent from our conversations was the fact that a great number of internees saw themselves as suffering, rather than gaining, from this new law against stealing. While no man wishes his goods to be taken from him, equally, no man wishes to be punished for stealing if he is contemplating it as a real possibility. Obviously a great number were contemplating just that. The trial balloon had certainly been a success, but it had not brought us the message we wanted.

It seemed clear that the community did not want a more effective law, for the same reason, ironically, it so desperately needed it, namely, that it was morally too weak to keep from stealing from itself. We were faced with the uncomfortable and frustrating truth that a democratic society can possess no stronger law than the moral character of the people within it will affirm and support.

This fascinating, if discouraging, legal development demonstrated clearly to me that any civilization rests only on some ethical basis. Talking to Matt one evening after the vote, I said, "It occurs to me that the old idea, taught us in so many political science classes, that constitutions and laws create community, is false. You know the social contract theory: Men come together, form a political community by contract, and on this constitutional and legal base the community and its cooperative life are established.

"It should be turned around. A good constitution is the expression of a deep underlying moral will of a community, not its cause. Only where a certain ethical self-control exists do the people want an effective law; and so only then is a social constitution possible.

"One of the mistakes of our liberal culture was not so much its emphasis on moral power as that it gave that power the wrong role in society. Moral pressure can never replace police, courts, and other ways of enforcing obedience—these will always be necessary. Rather moral power is their foundation, or at least the foundation of a firm, just system of laws that will curb the more selfish tendencies of men. If it is true, as we've seen, that no society can survive on moral pressure alone, it is equally true that it cannot live without some deep moral consensus lying back of and supporting its necessary governmental structures."

When this constitutional change failed, we realized that the survival of our small civilization now depended solely on the integrity of its individual members. In a most direct way, the work of our utilities rested upon the honest men in our midst.

They alone could prevent wholesale stealing, not only by refusing to steal themselves, but also by making clear that they would report anyone who did. This was no easy task in a small camp where feelings were strong and where a man was thrown constantly together with the person he might have reported. If the numbers of such men did not decrease, the tide of stealing might be contained. If for any reason their numbers declined, then nothing could prevent the collapse of our utilities.

This point was increasingly apparent to me during the last year whenever we would look for a new stoker, cook, or kitchen helper. The question uppermost in the minds of the Labor Committee and the managers was no longer, "Has he the skill to do his job?" but rather, "Has he the honesty to be trusted with these supplies?" For the skill, while important, could be learned, but the integrity could not. Yet it was indispensable to our common life. However highly developed our technology might have been, a technique was of no real service in the hands of a dishonest man.

The ultimate roots of social law and order extend down to the same moral and religious depths of the self where lies the basis of cooperation and sharing. If a man is committed only to his own survival and advancement, or to that of his family and group, then under pressure, neither will he share with his neighbor nor be obedient to the law. Had our community been made up solely of such men, all cooperative action devoted to the production and distribution of food, and all courts and laws devoted to the maintenance of order would have become inoperative.

My early indifference to the moral element in society faded, as our splendid institutions were threatened with collapse from within. I had thought that the only vocation that the camp could not use was the religious calling. But now it was clear that all the many secular vocations and skills the camp needed were of use to us only if the men who performed them had some inner strength.

Hardheaded men of affairs are inclined to smile at the moralist and religionist for concentrating his energies on the problems of morality and conscience far removed from what he considers to be the real business of life: that is to say, producing food, building houses, making clothes, curing bodies, and defining laws. But as this experience so cogently showed, while these things are essential for life, ultimately they are ineffective unless they stem from some cooperative spirit within the community. Far from being at the periphery of life, spiritual and moral matters are the foundation for all the daily work of the world. This same hardheaded man of affairs will probably continue to smile—but the effectiveness of his day-to-day work will still be based on that ethical core.

My thoughts seemed to have run into a strange dilemma I concluded ruefully a few days later. Two things that apparently contradicted each other had become transparently clear in this experience. First, I had learned that men need to be moral, that is, responsibly concerned with their neighbors' welfare as well as their own, if human community was to be at all possible; equally evident, however, men did not or even could not so overcome their own self-concern to be thus responsible to their neighbor.

How was such a dilemma possible, and above all, how could it be resolved? The presence of this contradiction did not represent an error in thought, I was sure: experience pointed too clearly to the truth of both sides of the paradox. Perhaps then human life is itself a dilemma, in some strange but actual contradiction to itself, and unable in its own terms to overcome the contradiction. In that case, attempting to smooth out the contradiction in thought will only result in falsifying the reality we are describing.

A resolution of such a contradiction in existence could only take place in life, not merely in thought about it. A better philosophy, a clearer and more coherent way of thinking about things will not be enough. Only a change in the mode and character of man's existence will resolve this sort of problem. If the self were to find a new center from which both its own health and security as well as its creative relation with the neighbor might flow, such a possibility alone could provide the answer to this dilemma. And I began to wonder if there was such a possibility of a new center for human existence—or was man left with a crippling self-contradiction which he could not himself resolve?

IX ✍ Saints, Priests, and Preachers

A community needs ethical people, but does the secular world need religious people? Are the saints really good, is religious piety a requisite for communal virtue, do we need God in order to love our fellow man? These questions occurred to me with increasing frequency as the deep significance of the moral dimension of life came clear to me. I looked around to find enlightenment.

I had to admit to myself that no easy answer to these questions could be found merely by noting the way in which different types of people, religious and irreligious, behaved. It was not possible to study us and say, "There, that proves you must be religious, for only the pious are good." People continually leap out of all the categories we try to put them in, and behave in totally unexpected ways.

The most important lesson I learned is that there are no cut-and-dried categories in human life, no easily recognizable brand names by which we can estimate our fellows. Over and over "respectable people," one of the commonest labels applied in social intercourse, turned out to be uncooperative, irritable, and worse, dishonest. Conversely, many who were neither respectable nor pious were in fact, valiant. At the same time, many obvious bums were just plain bums. It was the mystery, the richness, and the surprise of human beings that struck me the most when I looked round at my fellows.

Perhaps the most surprising of all was Clair Richards. She was a handsome, strong, self-sufficient, and possibly to some tastes hard-looking British woman in her thirties. As she swirled around the camp in her tight skirts and low-cut blouses, you knew the moment you saw her that she enjoyed going to bed with men. But I must say, the frank and competent stare that met you when you spoke to her, plus her booming voice and rollicking laugh, tended to make a man, at least a young man, wonder more about his own capacities than about her obvious attractions. Inevitably, stories of a lurid past in Peking and

163

Tientsin, of her having been the intimate of leading industrialists and diplomats, followed in her wake. How true or untrue these were, I shall never know.

Clair, moreover, thoroughly enjoyed her role among the more proper, bespectacled women of this predominantly Anglo-Saxon camp; despite their evident disapproval, she never made any effort to hide her many gifts. It is safe to say that when she swung into view, the words "character" and "moral" were not the first to pop into the minds of the envious, horrified, or interested observer.

Early in 1944, Kitchen II found itself in serious difficulties. The food was sloppily prepared and unimaginative—just when Kitchen I was developing all of its new ideas. The staff of Kitchen II was poorly organized and sullen; new rumors of stealing were heard every day. A meeting, called to name a new manager, appointed Prentiss Row, a tall, elegant English gentleman in his early sixties, wealthy, white-mustached, suave, humorous. I thought him too much the detached aristocrat to weld together this chaotic kitchen, but he did so with amazing shrewdness, toughness and, above all, imagination.

I was even more surprised when I found that it was Clair to whom he had given charge of women's labor in the kitchen. This was a hard, thankless task. It took courage enough to enforce the working rules which had grown lax through the slackest of habits. It took a sense of humor to do this without causing too many conflicts; and it took a rugged and undeviating honesty to stem the mounting tide of stealing. Despite her well-advertised labels, Clair had these virtues and to spare. Clair, with Row, completely changed both the morale and efficiency of that kitchen force. Looked upon by most of the pious as so wicked they were embarrassed to be seen talking with her, she had in fact a higher moral character than they did.

Another equally surprising woman flew an entirely different sort of flag. She was Jane Bright, an intense, scholarly, devout Quaker in her late forties, who had been professor of history at Yenching University. Jane was a kind of slim Margaret Rutherford, with a firm jaw and a long stride, addicted to brown tweed suits. I had often seen her in former days at Yenching, striding through the little village near the university, or bicycling the six miles to the city. She was usually alone except when accompanied by her Chinese friends among the students or in the village.

They would gather at her house for lessons in reading and writing as well as in history or the Bible.

Shortly after Weihsien camp started, a group of us decided to offer a series of lectures on contemporary philosophical and Christian thought. Jane, with no formal theological training, was well-enough informed on the vastly technical subject of modern biblical studies, to deliver two excellent lectures without any books available for review. An ascetic, intellectual missionary, Jane was the last person one would have thought capable of coping with the rough, secular world.

Nevertheless, on two occasions Jane proved herself the most remarkable woman I have ever had the good fortune to know. Probably the hardest single job for a woman was that of director of women's labor for the entire camp. Heaven knows that women are no more selfish or any lazier than men. Among women, however, nervous tensions seem always closer to the surface. In the women's labor office more explosions, if not more real difficulties, occurred than in the men's labor office. To be done well, this job needed the kind of objectivity, balance, and kindness that rarely go with a tough hide and a strong will. Halfway through the internment, this missionary took over the women's labor office and handled crises which, for any ordinary mortal, would have resulted in total disaster.

One victorious accomplishment of hers especially impressed me. Over a period of time, White Russian women had somehow claimed as their prerogative most of the jobs connected with serving food to the long lines in Kitchen I. I had never quite believed that Dostoevski's characters were real until I met their counterparts in camp.

"Temperamental" is the wrong word; it connotes the Anglo-Saxon ideal of self-control, for it implies that the dominance of life by intense emotion is somehow abnormal. With these women, one realized that life *was* emotion. Strong, probably sensual, often warm and as often hostile, these women were living embodiments of powerful feelings. Reason was in them no instrument for the *control* of feelings. Reason gave feelings wings, carrying their emotions, whether those of affection or those of anger, to heights unimaginable to the British or New England women around them. Thus they were the epitome of friendliness and charm to those whom they liked, vindictive and ruthless to those who had crossed them. A person on good terms with them ate like a king. But by the same token it was fatal if one were not: a mild spat could mean a half cut in servings, and a real fight spelled almost total hunger. Gradually the complaints from the diners about favoritism began to mount, and we had to change our serving teams.

This sort of wholesale shift of labor, involving some twenty serving women, was the kind of nightmare calculated to make an administrator blanch. Other jobs had to be found for these women that they would accept, and replacements for them must be discovered that would satisfy the griping diners. Above all, these people had to be somehow persuaded to leave a job generally regarded as abounding in "perks," as easy, and as prestigious for one that would certainly be less so.

One could look forward to weeks of tantrums, scenes, and even the eventuality of dragging these women from their posts physically. They knew what the complaints were among these thin-lipped Anglo-Saxons, and they were not about to admit that the griping was justified by giving in. I shrank from facing Jane with this horrendous prospect, but I had to do it for I certainly didn't want to tackle the problem myself!

When I explained the situation to her, she merely set her British jaw and said, "But it wants doing, doesn't it?"

A week later, to my utter astonishment, she informed me that the whole move had been arranged. And when I heard what the solution was, I had to admit that it smacked of genius. In our kitchen were some fifteen daughters of fundamentalist missionaries. They were innocent, pretty, well-mannered, and under no stretch of the imagination could they be considered competitive with these potent Russian women; nor could they ever be accused of coveting this position in order to make a good thing of it.

Even the Russians had to admit to Jane that these girls would make ideal servers, and no diner in his right mind could accuse one of these innocent virgins of favoritism. Although they remained unhappy about it, the Russians found themselves stripped of all counterarguments. Jane effected a shift, almost without a murmur, that would have wrecked any lesser soul. In much the same way, she kept the reluctant female labor force functioning and tranquil for the duration.

But this was not all. The greatest achievement of Jane's rare combination of tact, toughness, and compassion, showed itself in connection with a housing problem. In one dorm were some twenty-five women who just could not get along with one another. Not only were there the usual factions of missionary vs. businesswoman—this group also contained three middle-aged women who were literally impossible to live with. The conflicts made life almost unbearable for all concerned, and no solution seemed possible.

When we on the Housing Committee were about to despair, a deputation from the dorm made up of representatives of each faction came to the quarters office. To our surprise, they asked that Jane Bright be prevailed upon to move in with them. As one of them said, "She has the respect and affection of all the contestants; she may be able to calm things down a bit."

Without a murmur this doughty Daniel moved into the female lion's den—and there she remained. Jane had both firmness and love; that was her secret. No serious trouble ever arose in that dorm again.

What human eye, deceived by the superficial labels that we like to apply to people in society, could have seen the real worth and ability of these two women? To the pious, Clair was too immoral to be good. To those who were not pious, Jane was too devout to be realistic or effective. Both judgments were wide of the mark.

What is "character"? Its qualities seemed strangely elusive—like the Holy Spirit, they apparently blow where they will. Society usually associates character with breeding, good family, education, religious belief, and the like. These judgments may have some validity in the long run. But in the case of individuals, general categories are seldom dependable.

In the last desperate months of camp, the survival of our kitchens depended almost entirely upon the loyalty and honesty of a handful of people. They were by no means solely the well bred, the well schooled, or the pious. Among this small group there were aristocratic, educated, and religious individuals, to be sure. But just as conspicuous were persons of an altogether different stripe.

The two women who ran the storeroom in our kitchen, for example, could not have been more diverse. One was Mrs. W. T. Roxby-Jones, wife of a courtly gentleman, important in the Kailon Mining Company. She was a handsome, gracious, middle-aged lady, charming, intelligent and well bred. Mrs. Roxby-Jones worked day in and day out, keeping account of our oil, our sugar, and other specially prized stocks, and advising the cooks. She was beloved by all.

Her partner in this central work at the vitals of the kitchen was Mrs. Neal, the wife of a salty British tar. They had been the keepers of a lighthouse off the China coast. They came to camp late because he could not be replaced immediately. Both were unschooled, rough, and earthy; what she said and the way she said it were as different from the cultivated manner of Mrs. Roxby-Jones as could be imagined. But the same undeviating honesty, sense of cooperation, and responsibility were there—as well as the same capacity to laugh heartily with a group of men. It was impossible to say who contributed the more to our common life.

The most remarkable male in the kitchen was a former British army man, Dick Rogers. Dick was a rough-looking fellow, with a heavy chest and bulging muscles. He was slow of speech and unsubtle of thought. But in the life of the kitchen, he was a giant among men. He was so honest he was asked regularly to sleep among the stores—the hunks of meat, piles of coal and sacks of sugar—so that they would not be stolen at night. He was so hard-working that, besides his own steady work, there was no job in the kitchen he did not perform whenever anyone fell sick or quit.

It never occurred to Dick to take time off as everyone else did. When he finished one job, he merely looked around for another that had to be done. Yet this tower of strength in our community, whose integrity strengthened and inspired that of many weaker persons, was, in the context of life outside the camp, a man always wrestling with the problem of drink. The irony was that many a pious diner, whose regular ration of good food depended on Dick's strength of character, still thought of him as immoral because he drank. One diner observed sadly, "Pity, a man like that; looks so strong, but too weak to resist temptation!"

If justice is to be done in human affairs, it is truly fortunate that we are in the end judged by the Lord and not by one another!

Considering the difficulty of cataloging people in neat pigeon-holes, it was not strange that there were also innumerable surprises in the behavior of the religious ones among us. These formed a large and easily identifiable segment of the camp; there were about four hundred Roman Catholic priests and nuns, at least during the first six months—and about the same number of British and American Protestant missionaries and their families. In this large group of "professional" Christian workers were all sorts of people.

Among the priests, for example, was every type, from tough ex-barflies, cowpunchers, and professional ballplayers to sensitive scholars, artists, and saints. The Protestants embraced every variety, from simple, poorly educated Pentecostal and Holiness missionaries to the liberal products of private colleges and suburban churches.

Understandably, in this large group of humans were a few whose morals and whose honesty could be validly questioned; there were others who were unable to cooperate with camp policy, where that step involved some personal sacrifice. Missionaries seldom stole goods; but on occasion they could be as lazy as the next fellow, and they were often as unwilling as anyone else to give up space for those who had less.

To be fair, however, such cases were the exception. It seems to me that on the whole the missionaries were more honest and cooperative than any parallel secular group. But the missionary community did have its own characteristic weaknesses as well as its own unique strengths. We continually pondered and talked about these characteristics in Weihsien.

The Catholic was the most intriguing group, by far. A heterogeneous collection of Belgian, Dutch, American, and Canadian priests, monks, and nuns, from about every order and vocation, they had been herded into our camp from monasteries, convents, mission stations, and schools all over Mongolia and North China. Reared as I had been in a non-Catholic culture, it was an experience to live next to these bearded men with their long robes and frequent prayers, their gruff masculine heartiness and ready humor. They seemed a strange mixture of worldliness and saintliness; perhaps that was what made them so fascinating. What was more relevant, they were, especially in the early days, invaluable.

Unlike us laymen, the fathers had long been disciplined to cooperative, manual work. They had baked, cooked, gardened, and stoked in their monasteries and in their chapter houses. There they had become accustomed to the rigors of an austere life. Camp existence with its discomforts, its hard labor, its demand for cheerfulness and a cooperative spirit was merely a continuation of the life to which they were already committed, but one with more variety and excitement. With their rules relaxed, new faces to see, and above all with the added zest of the continual presence of women, their life in camp was perhaps not less but more happy than that one they had left behind. Consequently, the natural good cheer of these men increased rather than waned. The younger ones frankly loved their life there—"in the world" as they often quaintly put it. Many told us they did not look forward to a return to the relative quiet and seclusion of their monastic existence.

This zest for life and for work had a tonic effect on the disheartened layman, unaccustomed to manual labor, and cut off now both from his usual comforts and from the possibility of achieving through his daily work at the office his normal goals of new wealth and success. The high spirits, the songs and jokes of the younger fathers, like those of boys released from boarding school, helped immensely to get things going.

Life was much more than daily chores, fun, and games for these men, however. They had a strange power as a group when they wanted to exert it. In the early days, when the black market was flourishing mightily, the guards caught two Chinese farmers and shot them. Using them as an example, they tried to frighten us out of trading over the wall. The day after the incident—the whole camp had heard those fatal shots, and was pretty fearful of what might happen next—the Japanese lined us up outside our rooms for a special roll call. For an hour we were kept waiting, wondering what the next move would be. I looked up and down the row of about a hundred men standing there with me. I thought to myself that it would be hard to find a tougher-looking bunch anywhere. Many of them were ex-British army men and ex-American marines; they looked as ready as any to have it out with the guards if need be.

At last a Japanese officer appeared. He walked up and down in front of us screaming, stamping his foot, waving his sword—and then coming right up within six inches of one immobile internee's face and screaming all the louder. Quite frightened, the internee translator, a likable half-Japanese, half-British boy from Tientsin, said that the officer was telling us that if anyone was caught on the wall, he would be shot like the farmer. During this harangue, not one of these tough men moved a muscle or uttered a sound. We were impressed that the officer meant what he said.

No one fancied himself looking down the barrel of that officer's revolver by reacting in any unseemly way to his outburst.

After five minutes of this torrent of howls, yells, and shrieks, we were all dismissed. The officer and his two guards moved off to the hospital to give the same lecture to the Catholic fathers assembled there.

For about fifteen minutes we sat on our beds talking quietly and soberly about this new turn. Suddenly we heard a deep roar from over near the hospital. It had a sound like laughter—laughter from hundreds of male throats. As we ran out the door, the cascade of sound mounted steadily in volume. Then, to our complete puzzlement, we saw the officer and his guards fleeing past us in obvious panic.

Consumed with curiosity, we ran over to learn what had transpired. We found the fathers stretched out on the ground, literally holding their sides, gasping and weak from laughter. Soon one of the American fathers got enough breath to tell us about it.

"That squirt was yelling and carrying on," he said, "when suddenly we noticed that the Belgian Dominicans over to the right were slowly moving toward him. So, as though it was a signal, we all started slowly to surround him. Before the little guy realized it, he was enveloped by a crowd of big, bearded monks. We were all staring down at him with popping eyes and laughing. We kept moving closer and closer in massed ranks, laughing louder than ever. We must have frightened the daylights out of him—you know the way they are about 'holy men.' Anyway, just about the time he was engulfed to the point where he could hardly see the sky any more, he lost his nerve. I saw him push his way out frantically, and flee in your direction. It was beautiful!"

After this event, even the most anticlerical looked on the fathers with new respect. What difference a deep sense of unity, a sort of subconscious common consent, can make! Had any one of our line of "single men" started to move toward the officer or to laugh, we others would merely have looked at him admiringly. With a pang of sympathy, we would no doubt have asked ourselves, "What will the Japs do to *him?*" When the same thought crossed a father's mind and he began to act on it, every one of the others acted with him in concert—and the enemy was routed!

It was difficult to say just what it was about the fathers that so completely won our hearts. In part, it was their cheerfulness and their personal selflessness, a kind of noncompetitive character that was at the same time strong and masculine. In part, it was their accomplishments in the black market, which delighted as well as fed most of us. Their unbeatable baseball team may also have contributed. But probably primarily it was the remarkable way they manifested strength of character without some of the weaknesses that often accompany piety.

The Catholic fathers possessed a religious and moral serious-ness free of spiritual pride, they communicated to others not how holy they were but their inexhaustible acceptance and warmth toward the more worldly and wayward laymen. Nothing and no one seemed to offend them, or shock them; no person outraged their moral sense. A person could count on their accepting him, as he could count on their integrity—and such acceptance of others is sadly rare on the part of "moral" people. Consequently, no one felt uncomfortable with them, or sensed that sharpest of all hostilities of one human being to another—that nonaccept-ance which springs from moral disapproval and so from a feeling of moral superiority.

The fathers mixed amiably with anybody and everybody: with men accustomed to drinking, gambling, swearing, wenching, even taking dope, men replete with all the major and minor vices. Yet they remained unchanged in their own character by this intimate, personal contact with "the world." Somehow they seemed able to accept and even to love the world as it was, and in this acceptance the presence of their own strength gave new strength to our wayward world.

How much less creative, I thought—and how far from the Gospels—is the frequent Protestant reaction of moral disap-proval, and of spiritual if not physical withdrawal.

Although they did try to be friendly, the Protestants neverthe-less typically huddled together in a compact "Christian rem-nant." Not unlike the Pharisees in the New Testament, they kept to their own flock of saved souls, evidently because they feared to be contaminated in some way by this sinful world which they inwardly abhorred. In contrast, the Catholic fathers *mixed*. They made friends with anyone in camp, helped out, played cards, smoked, and joked with them. They were a means of grace to the whole community.

Looking at them, I knew then that one man could help another man inwardly not so much by his holiness as by his love. Only if his own moral integrity is more than balanced by his acceptance of a wayward brother can he be of any service at all to him. Honest Protestants, I thought, could well admire and seek to emulate this ability of much of the Catholic clergy to relate creatively to the world. How ironic it is that Protestantism, which was established to free the gospel of God's unconditional love for sinners from the rigors of the law, should in its latter-day life have to look so often to its Catholic brothers to see manifested God's love for sinful men.

All in all, therefore, the Catholic fathers played a most creative role in our camp life, and the internees responded with genuine affection. It is true that many of the peculiar and difficult problems of traditional Catholicism and its relations to non-Catholics were not evident in our situation. Wisely at the start, the "bishop" in charge determined not to try to control in any way the political or the moral life of the camp as a whole. As a minority group, they carefully refrained from any action against the freedom of expression of other faiths.

The one Achilles' heel which I saw in their relations with the rest of the camp concerned the problem of intellectual honesty, one which every authoritarian form of religion must finally face. Among the Protestant missionaries, diversity of opinion was so prevalent that at first it seemed embarrassing when compared to the clear unity enjoyed by our Catholic friends. The fundamentalists and the liberals among us could work together, to be sure, when it came to services in the church and other common activities. But still their frequent bitter disagreements were painfully obvious and damaging. This was especially clear one night when a liberal British missionary gave a learned lecture on Christianity and evolution. The next night a leader among the fundamentalists responded with a blistering attack on "this atheistic doctrine" because it did not agree with the account of creation in Genesis.

A day later I happened to be sitting in the dining room next to a scholarly Belgian Jesuit. We had often talked together about theology and its relation to science. The Jesuit thoroughly agreed that the lecture by the fundamentalist had been stuff and nonsense. He said that the quicker the church realized that she does not have in her revelation a mass of scientific information and so allows science to go on about its business without interference, the better for both the church and the world.

Two nights later, however, the leader and temporary "bishop" of the Catholic group gave *his* lecture on the same topic. He was a big, jovial, American priest, large of heart but not over-burdened with education, either in science or in theology. As he declared, he was only "going to give the doctrine I learned in seminary." Apparently the series so far had sown confusion (as well it might) in the minds of his flock, and so he had "to tell them what the truth is." I gathered that to him truth was equivalent to what he had "learned in seminary." Knowing him, we were not surprised that his lecture, although based on dog-matic ecclesiastical statements of various sorts rather than on particular verses of Genesis, repeated idea for idea the funda-mentalist's position of a few nights before.

From that time on my Jesuit friend sedulously avoided the subject of science and religion. Nor would he criticize in his temporary "bishop" the very concepts he had ridiculed in the Protestant. Both critical faculties and independence of thought seemed to wither, once a matter had been officially stated, even on such a low level of ecclesiastical authority as we had.

Over a year later, this same priest to my great surprise revealed again the difficulty an authoritarian religion has with intellec-tual honesty. There was in camp a good-hearted but not intellec-tually very sophisticated British woman—divorced and with two small children—who was increasingly unhappy with her Protes-tant faith. As she explained to me once, her Anglican religion was so vacillating and ambiguous that she found no comfort in it. It seemed to say Yes and then No to almost every question she asked. Such vagueness on matters of great concern to her failed, apparently, to provide needed inner security for a lone woman in that crumbling colonial world. So she was searching for some-thing "more solid," she said, to hang on to.

I was not surprised when she told me this same Jesuit priest had begun to interest her in Roman Catholicism, nor even when a month or so later she said she had been confirmed. But I was surprised when she showed me with great pride the booklets the priest had given her to explain certain doctrines. Among them was one she especially liked. It described in great detail—and with pictures of Adam, Eve, and all the animals—the six days of creation and all the stirring events of the historical Fall. Here were statements clear and definite enough for anyone looking for absolute certainty. But whether she would have found that certainty had she heard the priest talk to me of science and theology, I was not so sure.

One thing I learned from this incident was that a mind needing security will make a good many compromises with what it once knew to be false. When these same views—now expounded by the priest—had been expressed by the fundamentalist, she had felt them to be absurd. Clearly, the fundamentalist's faith did not offer her the certainty she yearned for. With the Jesuit, she was willing to pay the price of her own independence of thought, which she had formerly prized, in return for the greater gain of religious assurance. The same price, of course, was paid by the priest. For the sake of the authority and growth of his church, he paid heavily in the good coin of his own independence and honesty of mind. Perhaps she, as a lonely woman in need, gained from her bargain. But I concluded—although no Catholic would agree with this—that he, as a highly educated and intelligent man, was quite possibly a loser with his.

Certainly the most troublesome, if also exciting, aspect of our life for the younger Catholic fathers was their continual proximity to women—women of all ages, sizes, and shapes. With their rules relaxed so that they could work, they found themselves mixing with women to an extent which they had not known for years.

In the Peking kitchen at the start of camp this created a touching but also touchy situation. Among our group were some ten to fifteen very conservative missionary families, all of whom had teen-aged daughters. There were also a number of boys their own age in the camp—sons of families in the Tientsin business world. But these girls were too unsophisticated and far too "moral" to enjoy their company. To these girls, therefore, the American and Canadian priests in their early and middle twenties were an absolute Godsend. Neither party wanted anything serious to develop in their relationship, both had strictly honorable intentions, and heaven knew none of them courted trouble. Thus, trusting completely the other's nonserious intentions, and realizing subconsciously their immense need for one another, young Roman priests could be seen taking the air of a fine evening with Protestant daughters, both enjoying this companionship to the utmost. Soon they had paired off into "steady" couples. Only after several months did any of them realize to what extent their real affections had become involved.

Almost everyone in camp rejoiced over this situation as by far the best answer to the inevitable needs of each group. The only exceptions to this general approval were, needless to say, the rather strongly anti-Papal fundamentalist parents of the girls, on the one hand, and the Catholic authorities, on the other, both of whom regarded the whole development as one of the major calamities of church history!

Perhaps the most astounding ecumenical gathering ever to take place was the meeting in the kitchen one night of the outraged fathers of the girls and the stony, embarrassed, and inwardly furious Catholic prelate and his staff. Knowing they had problems in common, they got along well enough and spent the evening trying to find means to break off these "courtships." Actually, there was little that either side could do while the summer air remained heavy with romance. But apparently there was agreement on one thing: the quicker the division of Christendom between Catholic and Protestant was enlarged, the happier all would be!

The transfer of the priests, monks, and nuns back to Peking in September, 1943, six months after camp began, ended this idyll as well as all the other benefits that this interesting group brought to our lives. To their dismay, all but ten or so of them were called back to their monastic and chapter establishments. Apparently the papal legate to Tokyo had convinced the Japanese government that these men were neutral "citizens" of the Vatican state, instead of the Americans, Canadians, Belgians, and Dutch that the Japanese had thought them to be. Therefore they were no longer considered to be "enemy nationals." We chuckled over this interpretation in our dorm, remembering the many times that the Catholic hierarchy at home has paraded its stanch "Americanism."

The day of their departure was for each of us one of the saddest days in camp. As the four hundred of them climbed reluctantly into their trucks, there was hardly a dry eye anywhere.

Men, women, and children lined the streets to wave forlornly and fondly to these good friends who had loved and helped them time and again. The missionary girls wept openly, without embarrassment, as they saw their trusted and trustworthy companions leaving them. Both priest and girl friend looked glumly into a future bereft of such friendship. As a British banker standing near me said when the trucks had driven away, "I wish to God the Protestants had gone off instead." So deep had been the imprint which these Catholic fathers made upon us.

X ✑ More Saints, Priests, and Preachers

It was hard to classify the Catholic priests in any simple way, but it was impossible to pigeonhole the Protestant missionaries. They were a far more varied lot in background, in education and, above all, in the way they approached both their Christian faith and the business of living. As I came to see when I discussed this subject with others, one's assessment of them tended to be greatly influenced by one's feelings for missionary work itself, for its value and its legitimacy.

If a person does not believe in whatever it is the missionary is devoted to spreading, he is not inclined to like either him or what he does. Then the role of the missionary seems arrogant, fanatical, imperialistic, and futile; and the missionary himself hypocritical and foolish. People then say, "What right do they have to jam *their* religion down others' throats, to import Western faiths to China?"

When, on the other hand, men are primarily dedicated to spreading ideas in whose worth one does believe—such as modern medicine, democracy, modern methods and views of education, technology, and the like—one tends to overlook their particular faults as humans and, above all, to approve the changes in another society that their work brings about.

The Christian religion has had a considerable impact on the cultures of the Far East. But probably its influence has not been nearly so destructive of the patterns of life in these ancient cultures as has the introduction of industrialism, the natural and social sciences, universal and modern education, democratic and socialist concepts, and medicine. The purveyors of these latter commodities are as truly "missionaries" of the West as were the evangelists. The fact that we neither scorn nor castigate them as arrogant imperialists (although many Orientals may well do so) only shows that we consider these ideas necessary to a rich, full life, in much the way that an earlier Christian culture considered Christianity a necessary foundation for human fulfillment.

My first impression of mission work on arriving in China had been most favorable. The university where I taught—Yenching University in Peking—had been founded by mission organizations and was still in part supported by them. During the period of the Japanese rule, it was the only free university in North China. The many mission stations that I visited also seemed to be the transmitters of much of what I thought valuable in civilized life. Mission schools provided an introduction to the physical and social sciences and to history. Mission hospitals provided the only modern medical care available in many regions, and their clear humanitarian, idealistic, and democratic ideology planted the seeds of social progress in that as yet unreconstructed Oriental culture.

The value of these contributions seemed to me obvious. It appeared to me arguable that most of the democratic humanitarianism on which Chinese reform movements were then based owed its rise largely to the influences of the Christian religion brought by the missionaries. Above all, it was evident that among all the Westerners of many nations who had left their massive imprint on China, the missionary was the only one who had had a sincere wish to help the Chinese rather than either to dominate or to milk them.

The Chinese had to buy their tobacco, their oil and coal, and many other items at prices set by Western interests; if they went to Tientsin or the other treaty ports, they had to obey the law enforced by British police and in British courts. But no one ever *had* to go to a mission school, hospital, or church. However confused and deplorable the West's relations with the Orient may have been, it has been fortunate for all concerned that when the Westerner first entered the Far Eastern scene, a missionary stood beside the gunboat captain and the commercial trader.

I found, moreover, that the missionaries who represented the major churches of Britain and America (I had little contact with Scandinavian or German missions) were on the whole a rather remarkable group of people. Endowed with both humor and talent, they had had to provide their own entertainments in the course of their normal life in the Far East. It was natural, then, that they were the ones who took the lead in our intellectual, dramatic, and musical enterprises.

When over one hundred American missionaries departed in the first evacuation, many laymen in our Peking kitchen maintained that our kitchen community had lost not only its brains but its zest as well.

As one Britisher admitted ruefully, "All we're left with now are the business folk and we British. My word, old chap, they can't either cook or laugh, what?" It had surprised many like him to find that these liberal missionaries were not only interesting and capable people very much aware of the modern world, but fun to be with.

There was no denying, however, that most of the Westerners in China detested the missionary and never were able to speak of him except in scorn or ridicule. It simply never occurred to any of the nonmissionary personnel (with the possible exception of a few Episcopalians) to attend church. The Sunday services were for professionals only, and when I went I saw very few amateurs there!

There had developed in the Far East a chasm of distrust and contempt between merchant and missionary that was incredible to anyone brought up in a society where the layman often attends church and where the clergy, while not necessarily admired, are at least tolerated and accepted. Certainly this chasm negates the present Communist Chinese picture of the merchant and the missionary as a cooperative team of imperialist aggressors. Curious as to the sources of this gulf, I talked with everyone I could about it. Gradually I began to see the picture each of these communities had of the other, and why their mutual antipathy was so great. Both pictures were exaggerations of an essential truth, and so by their very extremity revealed the causes of the trouble.

The picture which the missionary had of the Western lay businessman was not unlike that which the Communist regime in China has of him. Both groups see him as hard, immoral, addicted to drink, interested only in mulcting wealth from the poor Chinese while arrogantly excluding them from his cities, clubs, and vacation spots, and remaining indifferent to both the values and the needs of their indigenous culture. There were certain elements of truth here, although the picture was wildly exaggerated.

The businessman in the Far East was apt to be a less responsible member of his total community than he would have been at home. It seemed never to have crossed his mind that he might become part of the wider Chinese culture around him; he built his own world, which he never left. His life was circumscribed by the narrow confines of the business office, the club porch, and the social life among the treaty-port elite. Outside that small circle of foreign equals, there were for him only the Chinese subordinates in his office whom he did not understand and so tended to distrust, and beyond them the great sea of Chinese "natives" in whom he had little interest except as a market. In his environment—"a little bit of Surrey in North China, old boy"—there was no wider community within which he might, as he would at home, adopt a responsible role commensurate with his wealth and advantages.

The merchants' picture of the missionary is more familiar to us all. To them the missionary was a loveless, sexless, viceless, disapproving, and hypocritical fanatic. He was repressed and repressive, trying to force others into the narrow straightjacket of his own list of rigid "do's and don'ts," and thus squeezing out of his own life and out of theirs all its natural and redeeming joys. At first, in Peking, I found this picture incredible; it seemed so clearly not to fit the liberal group I knew. But acquaintance in camp with a much wider circle of missionaries showed that it did contain some truth. It revealed, therefore, in exaggerated but striking terms what I came to consider the greatest single spiritual problem confronting the Protestant faith.

In any case, with these two pictures vividly in mind, I could understand as never before the genesis of the gulf between the two communities. As I sometimes humorously imagined, it probably started when the first fundamentalist missionary confronted the first tobacco merchant over the prostrate form of a Chinese—each of them seeking to purvey to this hapless Oriental precisely what the other most abhorred!

The first missionary who fitted in some form this stereotyped picture was a "faith" missionary in our dorm. His name was Baker, and he was a cheerful, hard-working, friendly man from the American midwest. He was rather handsome in a rough, homespun way, with curly brown hair and an open face. On the whole, his simple, unaffected cheerfulness and good will made him well liked by his fellows, both at work and in the dorm. As one of them remarked to him one night, to his infinite shock and horror, "The only thing wrong with you, Baker, is all that stuff you believe!"

Baker's religion was rigidly fundamentalist and conservative, and his moral standards equally strict. Any deviation from his own doctrinal beliefs or any hint of a personal vice spelled for him certain damnation. From his bed in the corner, as we "bulled" together around the stove, he would cheerfully assure us that anyone who smoked, cussed, or told off-color jokes was certain to go to hell.

Near him in the row of beds were two American ex-marines named Coolidge—and so called "Cal"—and Knowles, and a Scottish atheist named Bruce who, despite his name, assured us he was not of Celtic origin: "Goddamn it, I'm a Jew, I'm a Jew," he said to Baker one day when the latter tried to convert him. None of these three—neither the large humorous Coolidge with his white goatee, nor the short Knowles with his tough Brooklyn accent, nor the rotund bright-eyed Bruce—by the wildest stretch of the imagination fitted Baker's concept of the "moral man." They all smoked, drank (though opportunities in camp were very rare), swore, and laughed heartily in the nonstop ribaldry of male dormitory life. The rest of us were delighted that they were there. To Baker, however, they were a continual affront and frustration. They actually seemed not only to enjoy their vices but to rejoice in them, despite the missionary's clear warnings of the fate in store for them.

Blinded as Baker was by his own code of trivia, it never dawned on him that each of these three men in his own way was intensely moral. Each believed in fair play; each knew the importance of honesty; none of them would have stooped to anything that was shady or mean. They understood the significance of justice and of creative government in our community and, with much profanity, would always support both. Above all, when given the opportunity through the parcels to share their meager rations with others, they were quicker than Baker to do so—with a great deal of cynical comment and much embarrassment. To Baker they were simply damned souls—and that's all there was to it.

One night matters came to a head in a discussion six of us were having about how we should treat the Japanese when victory was won. This was a somewhat academic issue for us as their prisoners but still one fraught with intense feeling. Coolidge, Knowles, Bruce, and I found ourselves in general agreement: the Japanese were hardly lovable at that point. They appeared to us cruel and aggressive. We felt that the militaristic and imperial elements of their culture would certainly have to be dealt with severely if we won.

But, as Bruce said, "After all, they *are* human beings, and we are by no means perfect. Really the only thing to do is to try to forget this whole business and to bring them back again into the world of civilized and peaceable nations as quickly as possible."

I was impressed. But Baker violently disagreed with this view. "Why," he said, "they're all pagans there, and filled with all kinds of immorality. In fact, they're hardly human at all—look at the way they behave! No, I don't feel any responsibility to them as brothers. If our world is to be ruled by righteousness, we must rid it of these unrighteous groups as best we can. There's no question but what we should crush them completely in order to weaken them permanently as a nation. If necessary, I'd even say we ought seriously to consider depopulating the island."

The rest of us stared wide-eyed, frankly horrified at this outburst. Bruce remarked sarcastically: "Well, brother Baker, if *that* is what your God has said to you, I'm glad for the sake of my ruddy soul that He has never spoken to me!"

This bizarre view of Baker's was by no means typical of even conservative missionaries. What *was* typical of much conservative religion, however, was the radical separation in Baker's mind of what *he* thought of as moral concerns and what were, in fact, the real moral issues of our camp life. For him holiness had so thoroughly displaced love as the goal of Christian living that he could voice such a prejudiced and inhuman policy with no realization that he was in any way compromising the character of his Christian faith or his own moral qualities. As Cal put it with a laugh, "Thank the Lord he's only a harmless missionary."

"Providence" was a word often on Baker's lips, and I must admit he had about as strange a view of it as I had ever heard. Baker believed that since every good thing came directly to the saints from the hand of God, it showed little Christian faith for churches to finance missionary work by the usual means of raising money, investing it, and paying salaries. If God wills that the work continue, Providence will directly provide the means thereto, said Baker.

He also argued that it would be disobedient to God's will to agree to go home if the government so ordered; Providence might intend him to stay. For this reason he consistently refused to make this promise. Providence was to him a direct divine guidance bureau for his own life, thrusting him through the enemy territory of an alien world on the heavenly mission of evangelism, and paying his expenses on the trip.

Because of his refusal to go home when so ordered, Baker was given no comfort money by the United States government. In consequence he was unable to buy any of the essentials available only at the camp canteen, such as toilet paper and soap. These items were, to be sure, not very exciting; but it was hard to do without them, and no one wanted to encourage any near bunkmate to try! Some few internees, such as the Greeks and the Palestinians, whose governments were not able to send funds, failed to receive comfort money through no fault of their own. Each month, therefore, the camp collected a small percentage or "tax" of the comfort money given to the rest of us in order to provide some money for these less fortunate internees. Without much argument, Baker was allowed to collect an allowance along with them. His reiterated opinion that it showed an absence of faith for other missionaries to accept *their* comfort money naturally caused some comment in the dorm.

The crowning touch occurred one day when he came in with his rations purchased from the canteen. Having dumped them with a satisfied sigh on his bed, he looked around earnestly and remarked to all and sundry, "As I have said so many times to all of you, God's Providence will always provide for those who have faith in Him."

Considering that it was *our* comfort money that had bought these goods for him, we took it somewhat amiss that these same contributions were used by him as the final proof that as good Christians we should never have accepted comfort money in the first place—for the Lord will provide. As Bruce, the Jewish atheist, remarked in his Scottish brogue, "At any rate, this is the first time that my wee wallet has been the direct instrument of Almighty Providence!"

Like every great idea, providence has had its perverted forms. The special providence that provides toilet paper and soap to the saints through the kindnesses of the damned, but leaves all other men than the favored few alone, is a pathetic parody on the magnificent concept of God's sovereignty in the whole of history.

Legalism was, however, the most prevalent failing of the conservative missionary, and its distressing effects were felt by most of the community. By legalism, I mean the practice, exemplified by Baker, of judging one's own actions and those of everyone else, by a rigid set of prescribed and usually trivial "do's and don't's." The saddest example had to do with our monthly cigarette ration.

Each internee was permitted to buy at the canteen a certain rationed number of cigarettes, enough for the light smoker but woefully inadequate for the pack-a-day man. Consequently, many of the heavier smokers were always trying to get nonsmokers to let them purchase an extra lot of cigarettes with their ration cards. Since most of the missionaries did not use tobacco, they seemed fair game. Probably over half of them offered their cards goodhumoredly and made no issue of it. But a significant number of the conservative ones refused, saying, "I would never allow cigarettes to be registered on *my* canteen card." Apparently they feared that this would act as a "demerit" to be held against them at some later balancing of the celestial books. Most laymen naturally felt that this was pretty narrow and, as they put it, ". . . no more than we might expect from the ruddy missionaries." But on the whole not much comment was made.

When, however, sixteen packs of American cigarettes arrived in each of the Red Cross parcels, a complex moral problem was presented to the pious. What were they to do with them? Certainly their rigid law against smoking demanded that they should destroy these cigarettes—especially when they had refused to lend out their ration cards because smoking was sinful.

On the other hand, it was very tempting not to destroy their cigarettes. Lucrative deals were now possible, since heavy smokers offered tins of milk, butter, and meat in exchange for a pack or two. Was a man not justified in trading them so that his children might have more to eat? Apparently the missionaries decided that he was. Almost all who had refused to lend out their ration cards before now exchanged their sixteen packs for the immense wealth of tins of milk or meat. To the cynical observer it almost seemed that to these pious associating themselves with smoking was not a sin if a profit was involved!

On our cooking shift was a most pleasant, open, kind fundamentalist named Smithfield. He was a red-haired fellow, hard working, cheerful, and an excellent ballplayer. One day a fellow on our shift pressed him about how he dealt with the seemingly clear contradiction involved in the selling of cigarettes.

"Look, Smithfield, if smoking is sinful, then how can you encourage it by trading cigarettes? And if fags aren't really so bad—which you seem certainly to believe by trading them—then why don't you guys admit it, and let others use your cards to get an extra ration? You can't have your milk and your virtue both, you know!

"You know what I think? I think you don't feel they're really wrong at all. Would you be a 'pusher' of opium for milk as you now are of cigarettes? Of course you wouldn't! No, you guys just talk a lot about cigarettes and those other vices because, by avoiding them, you've found a fairly painless way of being pious. You don't really take your moral talk seriously at all, Smithfield!"

Smithfield, though an intelligent man, never saw any contradiction at all in what he did.

"I don't want them on my card because to use tobacco is
sinful," he stated confidently, "and I'm not going to touch sin if I
can help it. And as for the trading—I sold them for milk because
my kids need milk. Isn't that reason enough?"

I couldn't help thinking that Smithfield's sharp questioner had
been on the right tack. It boiled down to how seriously the missionaries took their own moral code. Filled with all manner of
relatively petty "do's and don't's," that code seemed too trivial to
bear the weight of righteousness which they sought to pump into
it. What had happened, I decided, was that somehow in the
development of the Protestant ethic, the magnificent goal of
serving God within the world had been perverted or lost in the
shuffle.

Instead of bringing love and service into the world through his
calling and his family life, the Protestant began to try to keep
himself "holy" in spite of the world. As he began to accept more
and more of the world's fundamental values of property, security,
and prestige, inevitably the "holiness" he sought in the world
became more and more trivial. He ended by concentrating only
on avoiding the vices which might prevent him from being
respectable.

After all, to love your neighbor within the everyday world is a
risky and explosive thing to do. It might upset firm property
rights, the barriers of class and race, and cast doubt on the
sanctity and righteousness of war and violence! No class moving
upward in society can easily afford love as their goal! But in
"holiness" they can combine moral fervor with social expediency.
The "holy man," properly defined by prudent churchmen, could
be propertied and prestigious as well as being a pious pillar of
the church.

Through some such development, I thought, Protestantism has
produced a degenerate moralism, a kind of legalism of life's petty
vices that would be boring and pathetic did it not have such a
terrible hold on so many hundreds of otherwise good-hearted
people. For many of them being a good Christian appeared to
mean almost exclusively keeping one's life free from such vices as
smoking, gambling, drinking, swearing, card playing, dancing,
and movies.

So much are these legal requirements of purity the working
criteria by which they judge themselves and their neighbors ("He
can't be a Christian, he cusses") that multitudes of Christians feel

they can, amid all the ambiguities of life, exactly determine the status of a man's immortal soul by his attitude to these vices. In this way, those of the legalist mentality would sooner attend the White Citizens' Council than be seen in a bar; they would think it better to be involved in an aggressive war than in a game of cards; they would rather be caught underpaying their help than be heard to swear. To hear the clergy of this persuasion preach, one would gather that, in a segregated, militaristic and, in many respects, economically unjust American society, they have come close to bringing in Utopia when they have succeeded in barring the legal sale of liquor!

I learned from this experience that the fault in this Protestant ethic was not that these legalistic missionaries were too moral. Rather, it was that many of them were not free of their law to be moral enough. Their legalism prevented them from being as creative as the sincerity of their faith should have made them. Everyone in camp—missionary and layman, Catholic and Protestant—failed in some way or another to live up to his own ideals and did things he did not wish to do and felt he ought not to do. It was not of this common human predicament that I was thinking. What I felt especially weak in these Protestants was their false standard of religious and ethical judgment that frustrated their own desire to function morally within the community, for this standard judged the self and others by criteria which were both arbitrary and irrelevant. In the end, it left the self feeling righteous and smug when the real and deadly moral issues of camp life had not yet even been raised, much less resolved.

It had long been evident that our community was faced with moral problems deep enough to threaten its very existence. And yet a significantly large group of Christian leaders was concerned exclusively with moral issues and vices not connected with these deeper problems of our life. For this reason their very moral intensity tended to make both themselves and the serious morality which they represented seem to be a socially irrelevant segment of life rather than the creative force they might have been. The constructive moral forces in our life were only weakened and the cynical forces strengthened when missionaries judged honest, hard-working, and generally self-sacrificing men as "weak"—and even went so far as to warn their young people not to associate with them!—because they smoked or swore.

"If *that* is morality, then I want none of it," said a man on our shift disgusted with this narrowness. Serious religion in this way became separated from serious morality, with the result that both religion and morality—and the community in which both existed—were immeasurably debilitated.

The most pathetic outcome of this legalism, however, was the barrier it created between the self-consciously pious and the other human beings around them. Almost inevitably the conservative Protestant would find himself disapproving, rejecting, and so withdrawing from those who did not heed his own fairly rigid rules of personal behavior.

Once I watched with fascinated horror this process of rejection and withdrawal take place when a nice young British fundamentalist named Taylor joined our cooking shift. Taylor wanted with all his heart to get along with the men there, to be warm and friendly to them, as he knew a Christian should be. All went well for the first few hours or so; no one told a dirty joke or otherwise made life difficult for Taylor. But then when we were ladling out the stew for lunch, a few drops of the thick, hot liquid fell on Neal's hand. Tom Neal was an ex-sailor of great physical strength and brassbound integrity. Naturally this British tar made the air blue with his curses as he tried to get the burning stew off his hand. When the pain was over, as it was in a minute or so, he relaxed and returned to his usual bantering, cheerful ways.

But something was now different. Taylor hadn't *said* a word, nor had he moved a muscle. But he looked as if he had frozen inside, as if he had felt an uprush of uncontrollable disapproval. That feeling, like all deep feelings, projected itself outward, communicating itself silently to everyone around. An intangible gulf had appeared from nowhere, as real as the stew both were ladling out of the cauldron. Of course Neal felt it, and looked up closely and searchingly into Taylor's withdrawn and unhappy eyes. With surprising insight he said, "Hey, boy, them words of mine can't hurt you! Come and help me get this stew to the service line."

Taylor tried to smile; he hated himself for his reaction. But he felt immensely uncomfortable and spent the rest of his time with us on the shift spiritually isolated and alone. He was happy, so he told me one day, only when he was with the other "Christian folk."

Not a few missionaries seemed to exult in their code, using it, one was tempted to believe, as an instrument of pride against their neighbors, as a means of disapproving of the other person and so of elevating themselves spiritually in their own eyes—and, they were sure, in the eyes of God as well. But others were victims of their own law, in "bondage" to it, as St. Paul says. Though they wanted to accept their fellow men, their whole legal understanding of religion prevented this, forcing on them willy-nilly this sense of disapproval, this unwilled rejection, and this hated, inevitable barrier. Such men were not hypocrites—as others often felt who found themselves judged by these unknown laws. They didn't *want* to judge others—they couldn't help it.

It was ironic that these Protestants here described seemed to incarnate even more than their monastic brothers the very view of Christianity they repeatedly deplored, namely, a Christianity which removed itself from men to seek salvation away from the actual life of real people. In their frantic effort to escape the fleshly vices and so to be "holy," many fell unwittingly into the far more crippling sins of the spirit, such as pride, rejection, and lovelessness. This, I continue to feel, has been the greatest tragedy of Protestant life.

Among the missionaries were indeed many who seemed free of the proud and petty legalism characteristic of numerous others. When this was the case, they contributed a great deal to our life: not only rugged honesty and willingness to work, but also the rarer cooperative and helpful spirit of persons dedicated to a wider welfare than their own.

Those missionaries were most creative, it seemed to me, whose religion had been graced by liberalism in some form. By this I do not mean to include people with any particular brand of theology. Rather it seemed apparent that people with all sorts of theological opinions, liberal or orthodox, could be immensely impressive as people so long as they never identified their own beliefs either with the absolute truth or with the necessary conditions for salvation. These people were able to meet cooperatively and warmly with others, even with those who had no relation to Christianity at all. Whatever their code of personal morals might be, they knew that love and service of the neighbor, and self-forgetfulness even of one's own holiness, were what a true Christian life was supposed to be. Unlike the pious legalist, they attempted to apply no homemade plumb lines to their neighbors' lives, but sought only to help them whenever their help was really needed.

It was always an amazement to me that the Salvation Army group, of whom there were perhaps ten families in camp, with their own strong orthodoxy of belief and strict personal code, were perhaps the "charter" members of this creative group. Possibly it was the influence of their ministry to the down-and-out in every society; more probably it was because they were able to accept and even to admire persons whose beliefs and habits differed from their own. Whatever it was, they won the affection and esteem of the camp as did no other Protestant group. Whenever a layman would express his distaste for the missionaries, he would always carefully exclude the Salvation Army workers. When the camp elected a seven-man committee to distribute the Red Cross clothing—a job calling for the highest integrity—two of the four missionaries selected were from the Salvation Army.

Perhaps the unique contribution of what I have called this creative group of missionaries—which included persons from almost all denominations—was their willingness to help others when there was special need. Most internees would help their families and friends over a difficult spot. But it rearely occurred to them to take the time and energy to put themselves out for someone they did not know.

There were, of course, innumerable such cases, varying greatly with the need involved. In the dorms there were always older or otherwise enfeebled people who for a period could not fetch their food or stand in line for hot water. In some cases, such a person needed constant attention and help. In other cases, mothers got sick and had to go to the hospital or at least to stay in bed. Someone would have to care for the children, clean up the room, and do the family laundry.

The folk around these incapacitated people in the dorm or on the block would, to be sure, do these chores for a day or so. But almost always, after an initial burst of energetic good will, their enthusiasm would wear out. Soon some missionary, perhaps unacquainted with the weakened one, would be seen taking this responsibility, and after a while getting another one to relieve him.

The most dramatic case concerned a White Russian couple who separated with some bitterness, the man moving into a dorm across the compound from his wife and child. A powerful fellow with a marvelously developed physique, he was quiet, introverted, and moody. No one felt he knew him—who he really was or what he might do.

As time wore on, he regretted his move into the frustrations of the dorm and, understandably, wished to return to his family. But his wife was having none of this, for whatever reasons, and refused to allow him in. Furious and distraught, he even attempted suicide. Everyone who knew the situation agreed that someone *had* to move in with his wife to prevent his breaking down the door and either molesting his reluctant spouse or disposing of her. But who would enter that emotional maelstrom as "an act of kindness"?

A firm and capable British missionary woman agreed to sleep there, and for the rest of camp remained in this, at best, difficult post. In time she and the Russian wife became the best of friends; and all agreed that "no one but a missionary would have taken on *that* job!"

Aside from their readiness to clean up the latrines at the start of the camp, the most generally useful case of this willingness to tackle jobs no one else would undertake was the missionaries' work with the teen-agers.

We had in Weihsien a fairly tough bunch of "drugstore cowboys." Many factors encouraged their development. Camp life is, on the surface, intensely dreary and boring. There is nothing new, unusual, or really fun to do; the day is filled with unpleasant chores. Consequently, teen-agers found themselves continually bored, looking around for something, *anything*, exciting. Since all of them had at one time or another played around with the black market, none of them had much respect for law or conventional moral codes.

There was, moreover, little room for family life. A couple who arrived with a boy of twelve or thirteen were given one room for the family. The parents realized that there were neither taverns nor bawdyhouses, no drinking or drag racing to lead a boy into trouble. In the hopes of having their tiny room to themselves once in a while, they usually encouraged the kids to "go out into the compound and play with the other children." Because all lights were shut off at 10 P.M., and the curfew enforced, they did not pay much attention to the hour when the child came back.

After two years had passed, this crowd of kids, still wandering the compound after dark, were from fourteen to sixteen. They were much more experienced with each other and with the camp, and fully aware that nothing exciting could be found in that compound on a warm evening that they did not invent for themselves. Trouble was unavoidable.

About a year before the end of the war, it began to dawn on the parents that something explosive was going on among their teen-agers. As always, rumors filled the air, but then investigation by the Discipline Committee uncovered a lush situation. In the unused basement of one of the buildings, and in a small dugout air-raid shelter in another part of the compound, youngsters were gathering regularly for what we could only term sexual orgies. In the room of Mrs. Johnson, the poor Eurasian woman with three children, they were meeting early in the evening for intercourse on the small room's three beds while Mrs. Johnson kept watch at the door, her own children, aged eleven to fourteen, apparently taking leading roles in the affair. When the parents had said irritably, "Run along outside and find something to do," the kids had done exactly that.

The ages of those involved staggered that worldly camp the most. When the facts were brought to light, parents who had taken no interest in what their children were doing so long as they were out of the room, were horrified and furious. The parents held a mass meeting to deal with this crisis. Many an irate parent declared that "they" must be remiss in some way, and "they" should jolly well do something about it, and pronto! But it was interesting that not one parent came up with any concrete suggestions, and certainly no one volunteered to do anything constructive himself. The meeting ended on a note of unmitigated gloom. Short of an unworkable sundown curfew, what could anybody really do?

To no one's real surprise, the crisis was finally dealt with by the missionary teachers, none of whom had children of that age. They met together and devised a program of evening entertainment: dancing, square dancing, games, science study, language lessons, and so on *ad infinitum*.

To the anxious parents, none of this sounded nearly exciting enough to draw the minds of the kids away from their newfound diversions. As a result, there was initially a great deal of criticism of this missionary effort: "Typical, isn't it? Too little and too late!"

Fortunately, the teachers knew young people better, and so they kept persistently at it, organizing a game room and assigning evenings among themselves, Monday through Friday, for supervision. There were chess and checker tournaments, craft shows, dart contests, one-act plays and homemade puppet shows —everything that ingenuity could devise. Five or six good souls kept the operation going, spending two long evenings each week supervising these kids. The program worked, and from then on, despite regular and careful investigation, no more signs of our former troubles were discovered. As many parents, looking up in sad and worried anger from their bridge games, agreed, "It was about time they did something!"

The man who more than anyone brought about the solution of the teen-age problem was Eric Ridley. It is rare indeed when a person has the good fortune to meet a saint, but he came as close to it as anyone I have ever known. Often in an evening of that last year I (headed for some pleasant rendezvous with my girl friend) would pass the game room and peer in to see what the missionaries had cooking for the teen-agers. As often as not Eric Ridley would be bent over a chessboard or a model boat, or directing some sort of square dance—absorbed, warm, and interested, pouring all of himself into this effort to capture the minds and imaginations of those penned-up youths.

If anyone could have done it, he could. A track man, he had won the 440 in the Olympics for England in the twenties, and then had come to China as a missionary. In camp he was in his middle forties, lithe and springy of step and, above all, overflowing with good humor and love of life. He was aided by others, to be sure. But it was Eric's enthusiasm and charm that carried the day with the whole effort. Shortly before the camp ended, he was stricken suddenly with a brain tumor and died the same day. The entire camp, especially its youth, was stunned for days, so great was the vacuum that Eric's death had left.

There was a quality seemingly unique to the missionary group, namely, naturally and without pretense to respond to a need which everyone else recognized only to turn aside. Much of this went unnoticed, but our camp could scarcely have survived as well as it did without it. If there were any evidences of the grace of God observable on the surface of our camp existence, they were to be found here.

As I looked at those of us who represented the Christian world in Weihsien, with all our pride, our failings, and yet the graces that appeared now and again, I was continually reminded of Reinhold Niebuhr's remark that religion is not the place where the problem of man's egotism is automatically solved. Rather, it is there that the ultimate battle between human pride and God's grace takes place. Insofar as human pride may win that battle, religion can and does become one of the instruments of human sin. But insofar as there the self does meet God and so can surrender to something beyond its own self-interest, religion may provide the one possibility for a much needed and very rare release from our common self-concern.

XI ✍ Living for What?

Besides personal integrity, the deepest spiritual problem an internment camp encounters is that of "meaning." This word can signify many diverse things. There is the semantic and logical problem of the meaning of words, symbols, and propositions, with which recent philosophy has so much concerned itself. There is also the existential problem of the meaning of life. Though the two are not unconnected, it was primarily the latter problem of meaning that we faced in camp. Like all of man's deeper spiritual problems, it determined in large part the way we felt and behaved day by day.

The phrase "meaning in life" seems to be vague, though interesting, when we first encounter it, and it strikes us as difficult to begin to think about it. To begin, let us take it to refer simply to a sense of worthful purpose in what we do and the life we lead. A man possesses a sense of "meaning" when he feels there is a vital connection between the goals he values and the activities and relationships in which he is involved.

Then what he does each day becomes a coherent means to ends he really prizes, his life and work accomplish something of value to him and so "make sense." Consequently his energies and powers are called forth in creative effort; he is vigorous, hard-working, and, in the good sense of that word, ambitious. In this sense, meaning in life is the spiritual fuel that drives the human machine. Without it we are indifferent and bored; there is no ambition to work, we are inspired by no concern or sense of significance, and our powers are unstirred and so lie idle. Without "meaning" we are undirected and a vulnerable prey to all manner of despair and anxiety, unable to stand firm against any new winds of adversity.

I had not thought much about the problem of meaning in this sense before I came to camp. It appeared so evident to a middle-class college boy that life had one: you went to college, played tennis, got a job, married, became a success, and presto—*there* was meaning! How could anyone "lose" a sense of meaning, or think life didn't have any? Is it not obvious that people's careers and families are meaningful? The only real questions are: what career and which girl? Provided that we make sensible choices and work moderately hard, meaning in life seemed to me to flow as naturally as growing older, and ambition to be as normal as the desire to eat well.

After camp was well underway, I came to see how much more complicated this problem is. Fairly soon it became evident that the work we were doing was not meaningful to a great number of people. The surprising consequence was that the normal quota of ambition, the inner incentive in men to use their powers in work, simply wasn't there. I am not referring here to the problem of temperamental laziness as in the case of Jacobson, but to the apparent lack of ambition on the part of normally industrious men.

I noticed this first when I was starting work as a helper on a kitchen shift. As I mentioned earlier, our boss, McDaniel, announced he was quitting to "take up an easier job in the carpenter's shop." Naturally I was interested in seeing that the new boss be an able, energetic man; without that, our food would be worthless.

On our shift there was another helper named Rumsey, a British businessman in his forties with a real flair for cooking and an unusual ability for getting along with other men. Hard working and intelligent, he would be the first to undertake any difficult task when the cook called for volunteers. He seemed an obvious choice. So I summoned up my courage and told him he ought to apply for the job of head cook. His answer set me thinking.

"Oh no, not me," he said. "Why should I take on a responsible job rather than the one I have? If you're the boss, all you get for your pains are complaints, squawks, and headaches from the diners and the men you boss when anything goes wrong. No thanks! I don't mind hard work and I like it in the kitchen. But I prefer a manual job any day where you don't have any responsibility and no one bothers you!"

What surprised me about Rumsey's refusal was that he would have responded very differently to the same proposal in the outside world. Had he been presented with the opportunity to move from salesman to district manager, from office worker to vice president—with all the new responsibilities, headaches, and enemies such a move might entail—he would have jumped at the chance. Such a move would have had real meaning in terms of everything he valued—financial reward, greater authority and power, and enhanced prestige. Its added increment of woes would have seemed minor compared with these obvious advantages.

This pattern repeated itself over and over during the last year and one-half of camp.

There were few enough prestige jobs, but if any could qualify as such, they were the posts of the nine committee chairmen, our ruling body. They corresponded roughly to a combination of government official and captain of industry—and were prized and coveted as such by every leader from China's colonial world when we first arrived. Surprisingly soon, however, the same men who had struggled for these positions lost their enthusiasm, and during the last year and one-half almost no one was interested in becoming important.

We held elections for these nine key positions every six months. Repeatedly the men who held them announced their desire to step down. But there were practically no takers; the incumbent had to be persuaded to remain at his job. In each of the last three elections, with nine posts at stake each time, only one was contested. Ironically, what would have elicited all the energies and capacities of the able men among us in the outside world seemed to be only a burdensome responsibility here.

Matthew and I used to talk a good deal about this strange dampening of the fires of ambition. Certainly it showed, we agreed, that ambition is not what we usually think it is: a matter merely of temperament, as is one's energy and so one's capacity for hard work. Thus ambition is not to be understood as a kind of instinct which each of us possesses in varying degrees and which, like hunger or sex, will manifest itself with more or less constant force in whatever situation we find ourselves. Rather, even in energetic men, ambition varies with the meanings to which a man's life is devoted and with the relation of those meanings to the work he does. Ambition is called out only by strongly held values which a man feels are attainable through his efforts.

If, therefore, a difficult task seems to provide a man with no desired values, then his ambition for that task withers, however prestigious it may seem to be. Without a sense of the significance of what they do, men become too indifferent to use their full powers, and they do merely what they have to do to keep going.

But why, we asked, had the significance of work vanished for us so completely here? In seeking answers to this question, we came closer than at any other time to understanding the real tone, the deepest emotional fiber of internment camp life, and through it a glimmer of comprehension of the world outside.

Why do men work hard? What goals call forth their ambitions and so their energies? For most of us the answer involves two interrelated concerns: our progress in our careers and our status in the community in which we live. In these two areas, most of our hopes and fears, our real values and so our deeper anxieties are concentrated.

When we are honest with ourselves, the questions that motivate the hard work of most of us run something like this: "How can I advance in my business (or professional) career, and so gain more economic security and professional prestige?" Or, for a woman, "How can we as a family, and I as its representative, gain in social relationships and prominence in our community, and so achieve greater social status and security?" To be sure, we do the many things we do partly for enjoyment, and partly because we feel we should. But mainly we are "ambitious" and therefore active because we value these rewards which our activities promise to bring us: greater security and greater social status.

The rewards or the "meanings" which most of us seek through our work and our communal activities are in large measure tied up with the particular careers we have chosen and the immediate social context of family and community in which we live. The result of this intimate connection between significance and local context is that when we are completely separated from that context, when both our careers and our social environment have vanished, we find ourselves suddenly empty, our life and work devoid of meaning, and our energies without incentive.*

Matt and I pondered this for some time before its full significance for our life at Weihsien dawned on me.

"That is the significance of this camp and of this problem of work," I said. "Those walls seal us off from the immediate meanings of our lives as effectively as they shut out the woods and fields! What we do here as cook or baker has absolutely no relevance to our lives in the world.

"Does Robinson get more legal clients because he is a good stoker? Can Jones climb any more rungs on the ladder in the Kailon Mining Company because he wields a meat knife? Will Gardner sell any less tobacco if his bread fails to rise tomorrow? No! The careers we all follow and so the purposes that motivate most of us are as far from us as the moon, and nothing we do here seems to matter.

"The same is true of our little 'social meanings.' Oh, sure, the elite *do* gather together for supper and bridge on the front patio—we do have our rather cramped social seasons. But the social hierarchy here has been so overturned that the successes and failures of social existence really couldn't matter less, and bear no relation to one's status outside. What would it mean to be president of a garden club *here?* This life, Matt, is an interim, a treading of water until normal life begins again. This is what provides our basic emotional tone. It is merely a waiting—a present without meaningful content. No wonder no one is energetic or gives much of a damn!"

"Yes," Matt replied, "coming here is not unlike death: you can't bring your career or your social eminence with you. They were left at the gate, or rotting in the go-downs, the offices, and the clubs of Tientsin and Tsingtao."

And pondering this whole matter further, I went on. "At first I thought that the only groups who left their vocations outside

---

* Often the move from a small town to a large city produces the same enervating and dispiriting effect. Without the familiar context of social approval and disapproval, where neighbors "rate" our work and progress, and give it objective value in our eyes, the significance of what we do vanishes. We are alone among strangers who neither know nor care whether we rise or fall in the world; our own sense of the meaningfulness of our work dissipates into the familiar urban feelings of emptiness and despair, or the all too common dependence upon the external and often vulgar symbols of material success: a flashy car, a large boat, or a mink coat.

were the teachers and missionaries whose skills were apparently useless for our present life. I envied those men who could use their professional training so creatively while mine was of no practical value. I had to learn to cook! But you know, in a much deeper sense, though the technical skills of their trade carried over, the basic purposes that motivated many of them did not. And by golly, a trained man whose sole purpose in life was to succeed is more stranded, more useless to our community, than many of our simpler missionary friends who have had to learn a new trade. Those believers—figuring the Lord has something for them to do even here—may well be loaded with motivation that gets them to work and keeps them at it!"

On another evening Matthew suggested an interesting idea about the relation of meaning to morals or to self-control.

"You know, when people exist listlessly with no real goals of career or social prestige, it's a lot harder for them to be responsible. As we have found, it's tough to resist stealing when your family is hungry; it demands a stubborn integrity of quite a rare kind. And what does a man lose here if he's caught stealing? No one takes seriously what happens in camp or will remember it later.

"In ordinary life, on the contrary, a man really loses if he runs afoul of the law. There most of us are honest, not so much, perhaps, because of an inner integrity as because flagrant dishonesty or the breath of a scandal would hurt our careers—and that we really don't want! The determination to be socially respectable and possibly prominent is not one of mankind's most noble motivations. But as a social control, it may be the most effective. Here, where all work is a pointless series of chores to be done because they have to be done, what sort of driving personal purpose can overrule the yearning for food and comfort?"

"Yes," I said, thinking back to some ancient arguments on this theme between the Aristotelians and the Stoics, "for most average people, a sense of creative significance and strength of character both require a meaningful social context. The objective social or historical conditions of meaning and of virtue are as important as the subjective—a man's love of what he does. For only if he can find a creative role in some community—be it his local community, or the wider society of scientists, writers, or artists—can a man be a creative person inside. The fate that pushed us into Weihsien has wounded both our inner ambition and our virtue. It is not easy to be a complete man in a meaningless environment."

Similar conversations went on regularly. We were puzzled, among other things, by the problem of incentive. It was obvious that no great number of people would work for the sheer joy of it or merely for the sake of their brothers' welfare. Is the problem of meaning resolved then by the familiar capitalist solution: reward a man with money and the problem of the meaning of his work is resolved?

Some sort of economic reward appears essential for work, it seemed to us, since work was basically an economic activity designed to answer economic needs. But we also surmised that monetary reward alone would not begin to resolve the problem of the meaning of work as it had revealed itself to us there. That which motivates a man's work usually motivates his total life. As we say with more accuracy than we know, "A man throws *himself* into his work."

Work is not merely an economic reality, producing only material results and running only on material fuel. Its motivations lie in the most central meanings of a man's life, be they self-centered, trivial, or profound. If men work only for their own material profit and are motivated by no further goals, their only interest will be self-interest. Our experience had shown overwhelmingly that a society based on self-interest alone was, as St. Augustine pointed out long ago, a self-destructive society.

But a simple monetary reward posed a further problem; it was not reward enough. Not only does this reward tend to make a man selfish; even more, it tends to make him bored. The experience of an American culture which has achieved prosperity shows all too clearly that lives whose work has been motivated by the desire for money or success alone become progressively empty and meaningless.

Having achieved the comfortable home in the suburbs, two cars, an air conditioner, and a drawer full of Hathaway shirts, these wealthy members of society then embark on an unending quest for something more which will give their lives interest, passion, and exhilaration. Some may try to find this lost glow in the magic of the bottle, others in the excitement of the neighbor's bed; others in an endless round of social affairs and a seasonal shuttling to and from fashionable resorts; still others in the more advanced competition for success and power. Indeed, the really talented and well-to-do man or woman can combine all of these diversions in one life. These efforts reveal one common factor: the frantic attempt to escape from a pointless boredom when what one does has no important or significant meaning, when one's life is caught up in no great passion or concern. An increasingly affluent society, without concomitant spiritual growth, can only look forward to the wider spread of the same problem, not to its amelioration.

One evening a week or so later, our conversation took another turn. Matt said after a moment's thought, "Isn't this internment camp, though, quite atypical of the normal course of life where things *do* go on? Here ordinary goals—the struggle for money, for social development, prestige, and success—stopped dead at the gate."

I had been reading a good deal of history in my time off. Suddenly it struck me that in history's long view, our camp was not so atypical of life as we might think.

"No, I disagree. Situations like internment camps, though rare for most of us, are a part of life and far more prevalent than we in the West like to think. History, as we like to call it—though the ancients were more realistic and called it Fate or *Fortuna*—continually does strange things to those who live within it. Occasionally it shakes itself so violently that all the well-established structures and certainties of life, its securities, goals, and meanings, come tumbling down. Look at Germany in the Thirty Years' War, the South in the last century, and England and Europe now! A war, a revolution, a famine, a plague, a depression are the forms most commonly taken by these shattering historical events. Unhappily, they have been a regularly recurring aspect of man's existence, and there is no evidence that they are becoming less so. When these historical cataclysms come upon us, all the usual meanings of life plummet down.

"What is economic or social security when all is insecure? What is fame when the cheering crowds have taken to the hills? What is social prestige in a society which lives huddled in caves and subway stations?

"The people here could not bring their wealth, success, or prestige with them. We are not so atypical, for it often happens in the course of history that men cannot take their worldly values from one moment into the next moment. The great determining forces of history do destroy man's small edifices of security and meaning swiftly, as they once helped slowly to build them up.

"The devastation of the English colonial world, with all the values that supported most of those here in camp, illustrates this point. When such is their 'fate,' men are left with little reason for doing anything besides feeding their bodies—*if* their entire vitality and reason for being had derived from these things that fate snatched from them.

"How *can* a consistent and creative meaning run through the moments even of a chaotic time? Is a man really like Sisyphus of the legend, merely pushing the stone up the hill, only to have it roll back? Is he, as the ancients said, bound fast on the wheel that brings him up high, only to hurl him down again? Or is there a deeper meaning that makes use of even these fates for some hidden purpose? Golly, Matt, *I* don't know the answer, and I'm not sure there is one. But at least I now know what sort of problem the Jews and the Christians—yes, and the Stoics, too— are talking about when they speak of the Divine Providence which rules even the fates that push men around!"

Most internees found no particular significance in what they did there. They did their work because it had to be done; because there was no driving reason for *not* doing it. But there was one vivid meaning that kept every person spiritually alive: the hope for the end of the war.

Theologically speaking, we were an eschatological, and apocalyptic society. The todays of our life were gray and lifeless: only the tomorrows were crystal bright. We knew little of a present Providence or meaning. But we all understood the hope that this dreary time would come to an end.

Like most men who wait impatiently for the millennium, we were forever rearranging our schedule of expectation. Two days after the war started, eight of us at Yenching recorded some guesses as to when victory would come. Like most of those in the early church waiting for the Second Coming, the vast majority of the guesses were eager, optimistic, and quite wrong. Five of us were sure the war would be over in six months, one said in one and one-half years, and only one guessed it would take more than two years' time to win! I remember looking at these guesses in my diary in October, 1944, almost three years later, and writing a large "Phooey" under the lot of them.

Still, however distant the Great Day seemed to become as the years wore on, its luster never dimmed. We lived literally by our faith in it. Then everything that made our present life grim would be removed, and every good that we so sorely missed would be returned. Above all, we would be free to do what we wanted, to go where we wished. No biblical prophets strained toward the day of salvation more eagerly than we did, waiting for the end of the war when all joys would begin anew and all tears would be dried. We did not know the time or the hour, but inwardly we were more than ready.

XII ✍ Rescue from the Clouds

We were a people waiting for only one thing: news of the progress of the war and its approaching end. Just how much this obsession dominated all my own thoughts became vividly clear to me one day in the kitchen. Walking through the dining hall, I passed an elderly woman missionary scanning with great eagerness a letter in Chinese script which she had received from Peking. (A very few letters came into camp, almost all from the cities of North China.) As I walked by, she looked up at me with real excitement and said, "Oh, I've just learned the most wonderful news! Come and hear all about it!"

Thinking her Chinese friends had told her of some new Allied military victory we had not yet had wind of, I stopped abruptly and asked hungrily, "What is it, for goodness' sake!"

"Oh, it's wonderful! Thirty souls were saved last week in Peking at our church revival!"

I walked away, laughing at myself. "You *are* a pagan, Gilkey!" I thought. "There's only one kind of news you want to hear, and that has little enough to do with heaven or hell!"

Fortunately news of the events we hungered to hear of came to us in a variety of ways. For some unaccountable reason, the

Japanese continued to publish and send out to old subscribers the English-language newspaper in Peking. That event beloved of the Japanese news service, the dispatch of the entire American fleet to the bottom of the sea, was regularly depicted in lurid detail on its pages. These bizarre reports retained, however, one aspect of the truth which gave us our main clues to the war's progress. They always mentioned the spot at which the Allied defeat had occurred. When we read that fifty American ships had been sunk successively at Guadalcanal, Kwajalein, Guam, the Philippines, and finally Okinawa, we had a pretty clear picture of how things were going. And when we learned that thousands of United States bombers were being shot down regularly over Japanese cities, we knew the end was not far off.

Another source of news was even more reliable since it was the only way in which we could hear of events the official news service wished to suppress.

The Chinese guerrilla bands in the nearby hills tried to relay to us whatever news of importance they had picked up by radio from Chungking. Since no Chinese had any direct contact with us after the guards took over the black market, this was no easy task. Actually the way it was done had a charmingly "Cloak-and-dagger" air to it.

The only Chinese who came into camp were the coolies who emptied the septic tanks, carrying out the precious "night soil" in large buckets at either end of a long pole. These coolies had to be very careful since the guards watched them closely to see they made no contact with the internees. But they managed to find loopholes.

At the end of each block of rooms was a large wooden garbage box, equipped with long handles so that two men could carry it, and a wooden cover. Each day two male internees would carry their box out the front gate about fifty yards to a rubbish pile where it would be dumped. There, to our everlasting discomfiture, hungry Chinese outside the walls would pore over its sorry contents hoping to find some luxurious morsel among our garbage. It was by way of these boxes that the coolies managed to get news to the camp. One day I chanced to watch this fascinating process.

At a prearranged time the coolies marched along the street of the camp bearing their lush burden. At the same moment, two internees could be seen preparing to cart their garbage box out of the camp. Just for a moment, they left the cover off the box.

One guerrilla coolie who had made a great point of spitting on his march—and spitting is no rarity among the Chinese—spat into the open garbage box as he went by. The cover was snapped shut by the men who had been lighting their cigarettes. Then they, too, started their leisurely walk to the garbage dump. When they reached the pile, they sifted more carefully than usual through the mess in their box, and sure enough, there, somewhere inside, was a damp and crumpled note. The message was then rushed to the camp translator, usually a discreet missionary. If important, the contents would be divulged to the nine-man committee. In turn the committee would decide its value and probable reliability, and about the wisdom of disclosing the news to the camp in general. Such precautions regarding officially published news were deemed necessary because the Chinese air waves were full of wildly optimistic rumors and there seemed no point in building up hopes unnecessarily.

The news of the first negotiations about the armistice reached us through the coolies on Monday, the 12th of August, 1945. We knew that the end was near in the Pacific. But knowing nothing yet either of the atomic bomb or of the Russian entry into the Asian war, we had no idea it would come as quickly as it did.

I first heard the news through Albert Hoskins. The most respected missionary among the camp's general leaders, Hoskins had served on the Labor Committee a couple of times and was now the official liaison man with the guerrillas and the translator of all their messages—including the one that bore the great news.

On that Monday I happened to step out of the kitchen yard into the main street when Bert hustled by. He stopped and came to me, looking very nervous and excited. He asked in an unusually intimate whisper, "Can you keep a secret?"

I had no idea what it might be about. I was, in fact, a little bored with this drama, which seemed so unlike him, so I said, "Can I tell Matt or Stan?"

"No," replied Bert, "but you'd better hear it anyway. I promised the committee to tell no one except my wife, but it's no fun to tell things like this *only* to your wife, for you can't get at the politics involved. So come on, let me tell you!"

"Okay." I was now less bored and quite willing to listen.

"All right—hang on, 'cause it's big!" He paused for the effect to sink in. "The war is over! It just came through the coolies from Chungking. This time it looks like the real thing. We don't dare tell the camp until we get some check. Someone might take it into his head to pay an old score with a guard. Before we hold power, that could be fatal. We don't know what the Japs will do when they hear this. So don't tell a soul."

I can still feel the shock, the thrill, the tremendous excitement mingled with incredulous unbelief when I heard this. Could it be true? Was the world that good? Was the war really over, the worries gone, a new life possible? With these thoughts a wave of sheer joy surged through me.

How completely certain kinds of news—that a loved one has died, that a war has begun, or that a war is over—can stop one world and begin another! Nothing one is doing today will, because of it, be relevant or possible tomorrow; aware of it, one gasps at the sheer contingency of things, how they and all their works can so quickly pass away.

The minute I heard that news, the whole camp looked, felt, and even smelled different. Now it was over, and all that was left was the getting out, and much that had worried us for the future receded quickly into the past. Bert and I hurriedly discussed the political possibilities for our future: would they land in Tsingtao, would the guerrillas take over the camp, and so on. I went back into the kitchen as into an unreal world. I found men debating, as we had done endlessly for two years, how long it would be now that the attack on Kyushu seemed certain to come soon.

The news, of course, seeped around quickly enough. That night I went as usual to Matt and Edith's for supper, wondering how to deal with this "thing" about which I knew I must talk soon or go wild. Finally I said, "I have been told something I promised not to tell you."

"So have I, on the same conditions," laughed Matt. And so, legalists that we were, we spent the evening happily discussing "it" without ever breaking our not too solemn promises.

By the next day, everyone knew that negotiations were underway. On Wednesday, further word came to us of an offer of peace by the emperor. Rumors had, however, flashed across the war sky like lightning since December 8, nearly four years before; more confirmation was needed before anyone could rest easy.

On Wednesday evening, more or less by unspoken word, all the adults gathered outside the commandant's office hoping to hear some bulletin, if one came. If one did not, we intended to demand official word of some sort from the Japanese, for they had refused to utter one syllable on the subject since the first tidings had come in on Monday. While the whole camp was standing there, jovial but very tense and excited, Mr. Watanobi came out of his office. He was a well-hated but secondary official, small, arrogant, and mean. At one time or another about everyone had sworn to himself to beat him black and blue when the war was over. When Mr. Watanobi saw this immense crowd, he turned ashen. Then all in unison bellowed, "There he is, get him!"

Struck with terror, Watanobi turned in panic and fled toward the Japanese quarters, his small sneaker-clad feet twinkling white over the ground. The sight of this hated tormentor transformed before our eyes into a fleeing rabbit caused a howl of delight and laughter to rise. With that metamorphosis of our rulers, all threats on the lives or the limbs of the guards vanished. Nothing was said officially that evening, but Watanobi's terrified flight was generally regarded as the most promising clue to the real state of things that we could have had.

Although the coming of victory had been the glorious event for which all longed, it also had its serious implications to those few who dared to ponder them. Who knew how an enraged Japanese soldiery might behave on the eve of certain defeat? Allied forces were one thousand miles away by land; we were a hundred miles from the nearest seaport. Did the Allies know we were here? Did anyone in authority care that we were? Could troops get here in time if they did?

What was about as gruesome to contemplate—assuming the guards left us alive and simply departed—was the question as to whether we would continue to receive supplies, and above all, protection before rescue came. We were sure that if we were left alone we would starve quickly enough with no help, and that with no weapons we would be quite defenseless against marauding army bands. In view of at least the first of these problems, our leaders had made a valiant effort to save and to hide at least four days' stock of flour for such an emergency. Strangely, nothing at all resembling what actually happened ever seemed to have occurred to us when we stared anxiously into the future.

Thursday, the day after Watanobi's flight, was weird. Everyone expected the end of our world to come; yet, for the moment, we were still absorbed in the trivia of camp life. Then on Friday, the end came in as glorious a Parousia as the wildest biblical scenarist could have devised.

The day, August 16, 1945, was clear, blue, and warm, as such a day should have been. We all began our chores of cooking, stoking, and cleaning up slops as usual. About the middle of the morning, however, word flashed around camp that an Allied plane had been sighted.

Two or three times during the course of the war, we had seen one of "our" planes flying way up in the upper atmosphere, a fast-moving silver speck far out of identification range. We felt sure they were Allied because of their solitary height and their speed, a vivid contrast to the antiquated Japanese planes that chugged overhead, burning, as one wag put it, "coal balls." Those lonely high fliers sent an electric shock through the camp on those two or three occasions, for they were, from the beginning of the war to its end, our only contact with Allied military might. Yet at that distant height they seemed, like Aristotle's god, to be wholly indifferent to our presence in their world, indeed, if they knew about our existence at all.

The plane that had been sighted on that Friday was evidently quite different—or so the boy who spread the word made clear as he ran through the kitchen yard screaming in an almost insane excitement, "An American plane, and headed straight for us!"

We all flung our stirring paddles down beside the cauldrons, left the carrots unchopped on the tables, and tore after the boy to the ballfield.

This miracle was true: there it was, now as big as a gull and heading for us from the western mountains.

As it came steadily nearer, the elation of the assembled camp—1,500 strong—mounted. This meant that the Allies were probing into *our* area, not a slow thousand miles away! And people began to shout to themselves, to everyone around them, to the heavens above, their exhilaration:

"Why, it's a *big* plane, with four engines! It's coming straight for the camp—and look how low it is! Look, there's the *American flag* painted on the side! Why, it's almost touching the trees! . . . It's turning around again. . . . It's coming *back* over the camp! . . . Look, look, they're *waving at us!* They know who we are. *They have come to get us!*"

At this point, the excitement was too great for any of us to contain. It surged up within us, a flood of joyful feeling, sweeping aside all our restraints and making us its captives. Suddenly I realized that for some seconds I had been running around in circles, waving my hands in the air and shouting at the top of my lungs. On becoming aware of these antics, I looked around briefly to see how others were behaving.

It was pandemonium, the more so because everyone like myself was looking up and shouting at the plane, and was unconscious of what he or anyone else was doing. Staid folk were embracing others to whom they had barely spoken for two years; proper middle-aged Englishmen and women were cheering or swearing. Others were laughing hysterically, or crying like babies. All were moved to an ecstasy of feeling that carried them quite out of their normal selves as the great plane banked over and circled the camp three times.

This plane was *our* plane. It was sent here for *us*, to tell us the war was over. It was that personal touch, the assurance that we were again included in the wider world of men—that our personal histories would resume—which gave those moments their supreme meaning and their violent emotion.

Then suddenly, all this sound stopped dead. A sharp gasp went up as fifteen hundred people stared in stark wonder. I could *feel* the drop of my own jaw. After flying very low back and forth about a half mile from the camp, the plane's underside suddenly opened. Out of it, wonder of wonders, floated seven men in parachutes! This was the height of the incredible! Not only were they coming here some day, they were here *today,* in our midst! Rescue was here!

For an instant this realization sank in silently, as a bomb might sink into water. Then the explosion occurred. Every last one of us started as with one mind toward the gate. Without pausing even a second to consider the danger involved, we poured like some gushing human torrent down the short road. This avalanche hit the great front gate, burst it open, and streamed past the guards standing at bewildered and indecisive attention.

As I rushed by, I caught a glimpse of one guard bringing his automatic rifle sharply into shooting position. But his bewilderment won out; he slowly lowered his gun. It was the first of several lucky breaks that day, when split-second decisions had to be made in the face of absolutely new situations to which no page of the Japanese soldier's manual applied. By some quirk of Providence, as in this instance, the decision was the right one.

Oblivious to all this danger, yelling and shouting, jostling and pushing, we rushed through the narrow streets of the neighboring village and out into the fields. So intent were we on finding our parachuted rescuers that we scarcely had any time to savor the sweet feeling of freedom that colored so vividly those earliest moments.

Suddenly we had become part of the wider world; even the

Chinese village of eight clay huts huddled near the walls of the camp held mystery and fascination for us; its rude dirt street was beautiful. Every sight, every smell, every sound was etched on our consciousness. These sensations of freedom were like a tonic, building up our excitement to an ever higher pitch.

Human beings, however, react variously. I laughed when, rushing by a small Chinese hut, I saw dear old Joe Lieberman haggling with a farmer's wife over the price of a large melon. Joe was a moderately successful businessman from Tientsin. A good worker and an able cook, he was a man whose round face and body and spindly legs belied his energy and agility.

Always cheerful and accommodating, Joe still had about him just the slightest aura of shadiness. One could not help liking him. But also one could not help suspecting that some of the supplies that vanished from the kitchen fled with the help of Joe's shift.

Joe had a dollars-and-cents approach to life: every experience and most people were viewed through the distorting spectacles of money. When Joe heard the war was over, he got very excited. Surprised at this strong reaction to an event unrelated to financial matters, I asked him why. His answer was classic: "Boy, can I get some nifty bets in the kitchen on the day and hour of the end of the war!" Then he rushed off to cut himself in on the assured profits presented to him by the armistice.

And now this. Joe saw me watching him, and running to me with enthusiasm written all over his smiling round face, he said: "Boy oh boy! You should see the prices you can get on melons in this village!" So could the highest ecstasy in the life of humans be strained out into a shopper's bargain!

About a half mile farther on, we came to a field high with Chinese corn. My first sight of an American soldier in World War II was that of a handsome major of about twenty-seven years, standing on a grave mound in the center of that cornfield. Looking further, I saw internees dancing wildly about what appeared to be six more godlike figures: how immense, how strong, how striking, how alive these American paratroopers looked in comparison to our shrunken shanks and drawn faces! Above all, their faces were *new!* After two and one-half years, we had come to assume subconsciously that everyone in the world looked like the fifteen hundred of us—we *were* our world. I had forgotten that more variety than our camp features provided was possible.

Meanwhile, some of the more rational internees were trying to fold up the parachutes. Most of us, however, were far too "high" for the task. We just stood there adoring, or ran about shouting and dancing. Our seven heroes were concerned with other matters. They had descended into the fields with their automatic weapons at the ready, anticipating a Japanese attack at every moment. The last thing they expected to find was this onslaught of ecstatic internees whose dancing about was making it impossible for them to deploy safely in the *gao-liang* field as they had planned.

In any case, after gathering up their gear and talking to enough of us to get an idea of the situation, they asked to be guided to the camp—so they "could take charge there." This casual, matter-of-fact statement of intentions sent us into another transport of rapture. The Japanese would no longer rule us! With this word, our cup of ecstasy ran over. The internees picked up their discomfited rescuers on their shoulders, and in a wild cheering procession reminiscent of a victorious high school student body bringing home the winning coach and team, the internees wound their way back to the camp.

As we approached the camp, the effect with its contrapuntal motifs was a mad confusion. Below there were the joyous, abandoned internees singing and yelling like Maenads in a bacchanalia, conscious only that the Lords had come and wishing only to shout hosanna. Above, on their shoulders, were the grim, watchful American soldiers, their arms at the ready, alert for any hostile move on the part of the twenty gaping Japanese guards who stood by the gate as we approached.

This time the tension was even more marked. The guards had to decide whether to fire on the seven parachutists or not. At point-blank range, they eyed one another for a brief moment. Then, as the triumphal procession, unmindful of the military drama being enacted above their heads, proceeded to the gates, a Japanese guard saluted—and the gates were opened.

We first grasped the military aspect of the capture of the camp when the procession came to a halt just inside the gate. At that point, the young major in charge leaped to the ground and asked, "Where's the chief military officer of the camp?"

Somewhat awed, the internees nearest to him pointed to the neighboring yard where the Japanese administrative officers were. With a fine sense of drama, the major, who had a service pistol on each hip, drew them both, checked them out carefully, and then strode toward the head office. In his figure, every internee saw the embodiment of the righteous marshal striding fearlessly through the swinging doors into the barroom where a hated outlaw awaited him.

The scene that ensued was in the same great tradition—so we were told afterward by the major's interpreter. With both guns leveled, the major entered the room. There sat the Japanese officer, his hands spread out on his desk, awaiting his antagonist. Neither knew what the other intended to do, nor just what he himself would do in response—again it was touch and go. Through his interpreter, the major demanded that the Japanese officer hand over his gun and recognize that the American army was now in full charge.

This must have been a hard decision for the chief officer. Probably the Japanese had been taken so unaware by the parachuting a bare twenty minutes earlier that they had had no chance to communicate with their superiors in Tsingtao. Moreover, the chief himself probably had no accurate information as to whether Japan had really surrendered or not. If it was true, then to fight these seven men and possibly to kill them, would make it go all the harder for the chief and his men. But if Japan had not yet given up, then to surrender his well-armed force of fifty men to seven paratroopers would have been an act of cowardice and reason to commit hara-kiri.

For a full moment the commandant considered. Then slowly he reached into the drawer in front of him, as the major's trigger finger twitched. With a deliberate motion, the chief brought out his samurai sword and his gun, and solemnly handed them over to the major, who was astounded, relieved, and somewhat touched. At that remarkable gesture, the major handed back these symbols of authority, told the chief that they would work together, and stalked from the room. With that confrontation, the camp passed into American hands; henceforth, Japanese soldiers and G.I.'s alike took orders from the American officers.

When gods come to visit the children of men, it is only to be expected that the men will readily obey their slightest wishes and also that the women will be enraptured with them. Taken for granted in the pliable realm of mythology, such fantasies also turn out to be true in our mundane world when the moment is ripe. These seven men who ruled the camp for the next two weeks, were like gods among us. They were, in fact, as a group, large in physique, handsome, and capable.

I suspect that whatever they had done as our rulers, it would have been the same. Had they not come from the clouds to save us? Had they not braved incredible dangers to do so? Did they not represent massive and unbelievable power? Were they not the fighting men who had won the war for us, while we were cooking and stoking behind walls? Were they not tellers of wondrous tales, of marvels undreamed, of rockets and landing ships, of radar and of atom bombs, to us who knew nothing of the technology of the war? Did they not look so strong and healthy, so virile, so different from the shrunken humanity we knew? And finally, did they not promise us that we would all be flown to our homes in China, America, and England as soon as the planes were available—the "salvation" for which we had yearned? The only frame of reference in terms of which their status among us and their effect on the camp can be understood was that of deity.

One result was that the experienced British leaders of the camp, who in other circumstances would have had little use for such youths—and American youths in particular—treated these men like emperors. These usually impressive figures could be seen rushing about, doing silly little errands, compiling useless statistics, ever ready to accede to the slightest need or wish of the liberators. Middle-aged bankers, who were in frequent contact with the heavenly court, could be heard retailing the wonders of their wisdom to the little groups of awed fellow internees who were not fortunate enough to deal with the newcomers directly.

It was, however, the women of the camp who most instinctively recognized their divine status. Of all ages, whether from high society or low, married or single, proper or not so proper, all wanted nothing better from life than to adore. They followed the pleasantly surprised soldiers everywhere, staring at them in rapture, edging up to get a word from them, fighting for the chance to wait on them, and pushing their equally adoring children aside so as to be able slyly to touch or stroke them. As always, it was wonderful to have gods in your midst—unless, like the writer and a few others, you lost a girl friend in the process!

With the paratroopers' arrival, everything changed. A Chinese delegation from Weihsien city showed up the next day to offer all the vegetables and grain we could use and substantially more meat than we had ever received. And this, after the Japanese had told us over and over that such items were unobtainable. As carts of food began to roll into camp, all rationing ceased. From then on we were plagued by stomach upsets only because of the rich food. During that first week, we could not eat a full meal without vomiting—but valiantly we kept on trying.

The walls in effect came down as we found ourselves free to walk outside the camp and, within limits, to explore the villages and towns round about. Now, when the day's work was done, one could go on a picnic by the river some two miles from camp, or take the three-mile hike to Weihsien city for a Chinese dinner.

It was amazing to me, however, to find how quickly one slips back into the old indifference. I can remember on my second trip to Weihsien city telling myself to wake up and enjoy myself. This was stupendous, just what I had longed for! And yet, already I was taking it for granted and not *feeling* it at all.

So it was with most of these newly found good things. We should have gloried in them for months, considering how we had longed for them for years. But somehow the second or third time around they became as ordinary as if we'd had them all along. When we had been hungry, our one thought had been for three square meals a day. Lacking sweets, we had dreamed of chocolate and candy. Besieged with rumors, we had longed for news of the end of the war and of our release. Now we had all of these delights in abundance; yet we continually had to remind ourselves of this fact in order to appreciate them. We were not really any happier. Our wants and desires had only become a little harder to satisfy. Instead of freedom we now wanted "home"; instead of enough to eat, we now dreamed of cocktails and seafood. Now that we had the necessities of life, we tended to take them for granted and look for the luxuries—such are the insatiable desires of the human animal. Ironically, it is quite true that man does not live by bread alone; as soon as his craw is filled, his restless appetite will yearn for cake.

XIII ✐ Last Days at Weihsien

About a week after our rescue, word flashed around camp that eleven more planes had been sighted on the horizon. This time they were coming from the opposite direction, the east. As they flew closer, it became obvious that these planes were no ordinary B-24's but the famed B-29's whose origin must then have been Guam or Saipan in the Pacific. Magnificent and silvery as they circled far above us, they seemed almost to fill the sky. To our amazement, these monsters also opened their bellies, and great cases of goods, literally tons of it, hurtled down all over the countryside around us.

At once the men, greatly excited, ran out into the fields to bring these cases back into camp. This job had to be done quickly if it was to be done at all. When anything unusual happens in China, no matter how isolated or deserted the landscape might appear to be, in a few minutes' time hundreds of Chinese will appear from goodness knows where. It is hard to conceive of a more unusual event for the farmers of Shantung than that fleet of B-29's dropping cases of supplies in their fields. As poor as they were, such a scattering of good things was not an opportunity to be missed. Almost before we in camp had recovered from the shock of this bombardment, we found the fields already swarming with Chinese, understandably pocketing and lugging away as much as they could. Naturally we rushed out to salvage as much as we could.

It was only when we got out there that we realized what a job lay before us. Those drops must have been hastily organized. In most instances, two oil drums had been welded together to make a hollow metal container about the size of a large sofa. Since the giant drums had then been packed solid with tin cans, they must have weighed at least a ton. Then that great load was hitched to one parachute—which was clearly marked: MAXIMUM LOAD, 350 POUNDS. Of course the parachute cables snapped at once and the loaded drums plummeted to earth like bombs. We found them split asunder, their contents of crushed cans scattered everywhere. We spent a hectic afternoon gathering in all those broken tins and carting them the mile or so back to camp.

Our problems that day were not confined to the haul work. Soon after the first drop, the eleven planes circled around in a wide sweep. Then to our mingled joy and horror, the big devils headed back toward us with their bellies open again. The crucial difference was that the fields were now crowded with both Chinese and internees. Still the planes came on and emptied their lethal loads in approximately the same spots. Amid shrieks from the farmers and, I must admit, a great deal of trembling and frantic running on the part of the rest of us, the great drums crashed to earth all around us. None of them came near me, but some missed four of my fellows by no more than fifteen feet. I shall never forget the sinking feeling when I saw four double drums thunder to earth just behind a large crowd of Chinese. Why no one was hit, I never knew.

The B-29's were not the only Western artifact which the farmers had never seen before. Many of the goods in the cases were equally strange to them. One was eating happily the contents of a large tube when, spying an internee poring over the same broken drum, and wanting to show off his English, he pointed proudly to the word "cream" on the label. Unhappily, his vocabulary did not include the word "shaving" just above it. Still another "rescued" a box of medicines. Before a nearby internee could stop him, he had downed in one gulp an entire bottle of vitamin pills. When Knowles told this story in our dorm that night, Sas Sloan said from his double bed in the corner, "I wonder if that poor chap has stopped running yet!"

Gathering in the scattered goods was more than worth the trouble. After the delicacies had been brought from the fields and stored away, the camp had a feast the like of which none of us had had for years: soup, meat, tinned fruits—even fruitcake from home!

These visits of the B-29's continued for the next three or four weeks. Every four days or so the big birds would be seen again; the warning bell would sound, and the women and children herded back into the camp. Then, with mingled expectancy and dread, the men would go out again into the fields. The delivery improved steadily. Small wooden cases replaced the oil drums, and so fewer objects hurtled down without parachutes. Still the possibility of miscalculation remained; in every drop, there were three or four one-hundred-pound cases that came down without the aid of parachutes.

There appeared to be little communication between the air

force at Saipan and the army from West China who bossed us. For that reason, signals were always getting crossed. Once the none too bright captain in charge of our morale, Captain Spofford—who will be described later—had, in preparation for a children's party, spread a yellow parachute over the backstop of the soft ball diamond. It was on this open space that all the women and children of the camp used to gather to watch breathlessly "the drops on daddy," as one child put it. Evidently the pilot of a B-29 took this yellow marker to be the drop signal, and let go with a large load right on target. To the horror of those of us looking on helplessly from the fields, we saw twenty or so cases crash among the terrified mothers and children and ten more go singing through the roofs of several rooms. Again, by some astounding miracle, no one was injured. Each time this sort of thing happened, one could not help saying, "This luck just can't hold!"

When the next flock appeared, those of us in the countryside almost got ours. We had now learned to wait on the edge of the fields while the vultures swooped twice. After two drops, they always turned east and fled home to Saipan. As usual, after the second run, we moved out to forage for the dropped supplies. Suddenly we all looked up. There, coming right at us was one lone plane that had turned back and was just about to open up for a final drop. It was too late to try to run anywhere so, for whatever reason, we all stretched out flat in the grain and cowered there waiting for the end to come.

Seven free boxes and many more gallon-sized tins came down. They fell with great earth-shaking thuds all around us—one of them about twenty feet from me. But none of us was hit. When at last, shaking in every limb, I lifted my head, I saw with relief the great plane winging east. I also saw crouching near me and white as a sheet, a large Scot named John McCracken, a man whom I admired very greatly as one of the wisest and strongest in the camp. I said to him, "That was the closest call of the whole damn war for me. This is the last time I go out among the corn to forage for Spam!"

"Yes," he replied, panting. "I don't think I'd mind dying protecting my country or someone I love. But I'll be damned if I want to be killed by a can of Del Monte peaches!"

To our great relief, this was the last we saw of the B-29's. In all fairness to the energetic and generous souls who sent them and who flew the planes, it should be added that those same peaches had the best taste of anything I ever put in my mouth.

In the first days after the rescue, we were ruled by the god kings: so, despite the bombings, we lived in a paradise of excitement. But such an ecstatic level of life can never last for long in this imperfect world. Ten days after our liberation, we heard with dismay of a coming change: our rescuers were to replaced by a regular army unit. Poor souls, I thought. I would not want to be one of these merely human rulers, fated to succeed the gods!

Their entrance into our midst was befitting this pedestrian destiny. They came in by truck, rather than from the clouds. As we watched the thirty or forty of them clamber rather stiffly and glumly out of these mundane vehicles, it was plain to every disappointed internee that they represented the ordinary, run-of-the-mill G.I. rather than the Apollos of our liberation. In the thick-set, heavily mustached Colonel Brooks we had an able but—in comparison to the Gary Cooper who preceded him—unglamorous leader.

The G.I.'s never understood the resentment that greeted their arrival—how could they? It was inherent in the situation and mood of the camp, even before they set foot on the ground.

After all, we still had to remain in the squalor, the inconvenience and innate confinement of internment camp life. Shortly after he got there, the colonel had to announce this to us in a sober speech. There was, he said regretfully, no hope of the immediate repatriation by plane promised by our first rescuers. Most of us were far too healthy for that luxury. Unhappily, guerrilla bands had cut the railroad lines to Tsingtao so that there were, for the present, no means available of transporting us to a coastal port. The dismal result was we would have to remain in camp for at least another month, and possibly two, while the colonel tried to arrange some sort of transportation for us to our homes.

In spite of our additional supplies and freedom, the camp became suddenly more distasteful than ever. Now its tawdriness and drudgery were seen in contrast to a hope of immediate repatriation and long-forgotten tastes of civilization. What we had accepted as necessities of war became now unbearable irritations stemming from the inefficiencies of peace. As we listened to this dreary news on a chilly, gray afternoon, feelings of letdown burst in all their fury over the camp morale.

Apparently Colonel Brooks had already sensed the growing disenchantment; like every good officer, he was prepared with the army answer. Sagging spirits in the armed forces called for a trained morale booster. After he had made his sobering speech about repatriation, the colonel called Captain Spofford to the stand and introduced him to us as the man who would make our lives happier by bucking us up.

The good captain, in consequence, had most of us against him in advance. With his first words, he quickly lost more ground.

We all felt by this time a kind of alumni loyalty for "our camp." We were proud of the way the place had been organized and run; of how well it looked with its flowers and awnings, of what we had made with our equipment, and above all, of the ingenious ways we had found to entertain ourselves. We all found ourselves resenting it deeply when a newly arrived soldier would look at our compound and mutter, "God, what a dismal mess," or "How could you live in such a dreary place?"—in spite of the fact we had been making similar remarks ourselves for over two years.

When Spofford announced that he knew we'd had no good entertainment, and that his job was to bring us some "real amusement straight from Uncle Sam," our backs went up. He promised to get for us "as soon as humanly possible" baseball bats and balls, to organize checker tournaments for "oldsters and youngsters alike," and to run a father-and-son track meet the next day. He ended this part of his speech on a note of high passion—"And if I carry any weight at all with the higher-ups in the army, you'll have rubber horseshoes before the week is out!"

At this astounding promise, we looked at one another in wonder. One Belgian importer near me whispered to an English friend, "But zees man ees crazy!"

More was yet to come. He commented sadly on the fact that we had enjoyed no radios in camp, and that therefore, "You have not heard any music since the war began." Apparently in the captain's world, music came only from radios and phonographs. He continued, saying that he had a final surprise for us, one we would find "unbelievable." He could not have been more correct.

"At this very moment, I am having my man put up a public

address system that will bring gags and pop tunes to every corner of the camp. Private Bodkins, turn on the P.A. equipment!"

At this command, the pitiless blare of popular music sounded out over the camp. We shuddered. His promise to reach every nook and cranny was more than fulfilled. One would have had to climb the walls to escape that screech! "This is the greatest horror of the war!" muttered one British lawyer to an elderly man next to him.

The strange fact of the matter was that Spofford's speech really did buck us all up: it gave us something to laugh about. Poor old Spofford, he became the favorite topic of every conversation and the butt of every joke. Two days afterward, the B-29's roared once again above us. Faces grim with no little trepidation, we marshaled our courage to go out again after the goodies. Just as we were leaving the dorm, the lordly Cal Coolidge gave us his reassuring blessing from his high bed in the corner, where he was perusing a copy of *True Confessions*.

"Don't worry about your heads this time, boys. The packages will bounce. They're full of rubber horseshoes!"

The most hilarious result of Spofford's efforts on our behalf occurred about a week later. One rather demonic soul among the internees approached the innocent G.I. in charge of running the new P.A. system. After talking in friendly fashion for a few minutes with the ingenuousness of the serpent in Eden, he asked, "You want to do something to make these people happy, don't you?"

"Yeah, sure," said the soldier eagerly, "tell me what to do."

"Well," said our Mephistopheles, "these poor folks haven't wakened in the morning to popular music since they got here. No radios, no nothin'! They'd just love it if you'd put on a real peppy record just when they are getting up—say about 6 A.M."

The eagerness on the soldier's face was momentarily clouded, "Gee, do you think they'd *really* like that?"

"Oh, yes, I've talked to lots of them, and I know they would."

The next morning was all that a practical joker's soul might desire. Sharp at six, the quiet air of the camp was rent by the blare of "Oh, What a Beautiful Morning!" As soon as I realized what was happening, I went out on the balcony of our dorm to enjoy the fun. The camp was a chaos of furious inmates. After three years of rising at seven for roll call, in rain, sleet, or snow,

on Sundays, Christmas, and weekdays alike, everyone had luxuri-
ated in lazy risings since August 16.

Everywhere I looked, angry people were rushing about. Enraged fathers poured out of the little rows of family rooms;
elderly women in curlers, hurriedly putting on their bathrobes,
stumbled from their dorms. Each of them charged out looking for
blood! Then, some of them, realizing they hadn't the least idea
where the music was coming from, began, each in a dazed and
blind sort of way, to go off in different directions. Some kicked
the loudspeakers in helpless fury. Still others stood there holding
their heads and trying to think out calmly where the ultimate
source of the blare might be. Soon, stopping up their ears, all
marched off to the section commandeered by the army. I
laughed as I imagined the scene when that irate throng of
bathrobed internees finally located the good-hearted G.I. in
charge of the record player. He said to me later with some awe,
"It was a strange experience to face so many really crazy people,
all mad at you! My gosh, hadn't I played the latest popular tune,
one they hadn't even had the chance to hear before? You know I
honestly think all of you must be a little touched in the head by
all your troubles. I hope you can get back to normal again all
right."

If this G.I. was troubled by our "strangeness," Spofford was
tortured by it. His face took on a baffled, almost haunted look.
No one appeared to want to cooperate with him on his many
morale-boosting schemes. As he said one night over some bour-
bon, very close to tears, he just couldn't understand it. People
kept complaining about his loudspeaker. Sas Sloan had called
out one night as Spofford walked by, "Bring back the war—we
want some peace!" Another time somebody managed to cut the
main line to the loudspeaker just outside Spofford's door!

"My God," he continued, shaking his head sadly, "anybody'd
think we were your enemies! Why, when I read to them the
United States Army lectures on world affairs, it is unbelievable
but true that these foreigners called it propaganda! What makes
it all so puzzling is that these same games, contests, and lectures
went down so well with the kids in the service. You should have
heard them cheer when I put a loudspeaker for popular music in
their barracks! Why, for God's sake, is everyone so upset? Folks
keep telling me that Europeans—especially older ones—don't
really want the same things that American G.I.'s do. If that's
true—and I still find it hard to believe—then people are a lot

stranger than I thought, and I'm not even sure I understand
them any more."

It was not only Spofford who found the new world of peace
strange, disillusioning, and even bitter. To the permanent British residents of China, who made up more than half our number,
the glorious end was like waking from a bad dream to discover
that reality was worse. (Their situation resembled that of the
resident of New Haven who, his eyes and ears having been
buffeted by the film *The Hurricane,* staggered out into the night
to find himself tossed about by the famous New England hurricane of 1938.)

Like all of us, these people had lived through the war in hope,
buoyed up by the conviction that Weihsien camp was not "real
life," but only an accidental and temporary incursion into
experience, a nightmare which would of course vanish with the
dawn of peace. When the war ended, *real* life—a life of prosper-
ing business in the treaty ports, of comfortable homes and chatter
on the club porch, of weekends in the hills—would begin once
more. The hardest part for them came when the war was over,
and that day of promise arrived. What it brought was the
resumption—but in real life now—of the same utter absence of
life's usual security and meaning.

On a chilly gray day in mid-September, some four weeks after
our rescue, a British colonel showed up to address the British
subjects. As he said at the opening of his speech, this would be a
sobering hour for them, since his purpose was to tell them with
all possible candor what the reality they had now to face would
be like.

"Your small businesses in the cities of China, in the three years
since you left, have been almost all destroyed beyond repair.
Shops have been looted of their stock; Chinese merchants have
moved into the premises; go-downs have been ransacked,
wrecked, and abandoned, and are almost useless. Everything that
has not been shattered has passed into Chinese hands. There is
little or no hope of reparations with which to get started again.

"Above all, I must say to you with all the force and authority
at my command, that the days of 'colonial life' in Asia are over.
Our rule in the treaty ports is a thing of the past; favored
treatment of foreign firms under British law is gone; our control
of residential areas has become impossible.

"Those of you who worked for firms worldwide in scope can probably find work in your company's other offices. Although you, too, must move from China, you are among the luckier overseas British.

"Those of you, however, whose roots lie in China alone had best resign yourselves to the loss of the old life. We cannot force you now to leave China; you may still find work here and there for the time being in Tientsin, in Shanghai, or as advisers to Chinese firms. But the future here is a bleak one for the self-employed Britisher. Our official advice to you is to give up in East Asia, find what refuge you can with relatives in England or seek new jobs in Australia, New Zealand, Canada, and the other places where British life is still going on. An era has ended, and with it has ended your own past lives. I'm sorry, but these are the facts."

The British people listened to the colonel with rapt attention. Not a word was lost on that silent, stunned crowd. Quite unprepared for this by their own vivid dreams and hopes, they found what he was saying to them completely unbelievable. It was a terrible world they were hearing pictured, emptied of all familiar security and meaning, devoid of all ground or "place" to stand on and of all recognizable structure for life, and one without possibilities. Immediately they felt cold, adrift and alone in a directionless void. Some were quiet, in a state of shock; others wept openly; still others merely clung together mute, emptied of life. Yet at the same time, try as they might, they could not argue with patent and obvious truth. This was, as the colonel had reiterated, reality. I said to one middle-aged man, ashen and almost in tears, who had had a small goods shop in Tientsin, "But surely you *can* go back to England. You have people there, don't you?"

"No, I have no people there. I have never been there, and I know no one. My entire life, and that of my father before me, was spent in North China. When that is taken from us, we have no place on earth that is ours."

When those China residents glimpsed the real future, as they did for the first time that afternoon, it was as void of place and of meaning as had been their "unreal" life in camp. But beyond it there was no further hope of a glorious day of release. The precariousness of all historical life had rudely thrust itself upon those poor Westerners in Asia by the devastation of their colonial world when peace had come at last and they were free.

XIV ✐ After It Was All Over

Not all of us faced the same grim destiny as the permanent China residents. Many of us could return to an un-scarred and prosperous America. For us the end of the war meant, in fact, the freedom and opportunity for which we had all longed.

About the middle of September, three weeks after he had arrived among us, Colonel Brooks announced that at last he had been able to arrange rail transportation to the coast for those Americans and British who wished to return to their homelands. He told us that soon after we reached Tsingtao, ships would take us to San Francisco or to England, as the case might be.

We left the camp on September 25, 1945, and a strange, dreamlike, overwhelmingly exciting day it was. How could I say goodbye under such circumstances? I knew the parting was for good; that the world was too big and our lots too diverse for us ever to meet again; that even if we did meet through some chance encounter, the relationship we had enjoyed would have vanished with its context. Both context and relationship would be at best old memories rehearsed over a drink, but never relived in any depth or intensity. The farewells were too ultimate even to be sad.

Besides, those of us who were walking out the gate for the last time were looking eagerly ahead to the trucks that waited to carry us into the promising future, and not particularly heeding our disconsolate friends waving from the wall. Many of these had little future and were now losing their one firm reality, the recent past of internment life. Glancing back for a moment at those waving hands, the thought came to me that only when destiny gives us the great gift of an open future are we able fully to live, for intense life in the present is made up in large part of expectancy. Whenever we are alive and excited, it is the future and not the past that enlivens the present moment.

As the army trucks lumbered across the plain to the city, we could *see* that past receding in proportion to the diminishing size of the camp compound; with each yard forward, we could feel an increment of freedom and with each mile the patterns of normal life seemed to flow back like refreshed blood into our veins.

I felt gloriously alive when I walked into a comfortable railway coach, picked out my own seat next to a window, and watched the countryside flash by. Here were towns and villages, animals and birds, people waving, and the delights of a changing landscape. Each one of us felt himself to be alive and real again. We had left the bloodless life of camp and each had become once more a participating part of the interrelated system of things and people that make up our universe.

Life is participation, I thought, and as it dies when that participation is cut off, so it lives again when the world is re-entered. I think the leisurely picnic lunch which we all enjoyed as the train rushed along through farmlands and villages to Tsingtao was the happiest and most completely carefree meal of my life. Not even for a moment could we keep our eyes off the world of which we were now a part.

Perhaps the most moving aspect of that day's ride was the sight of countless Chinese—farmers, merchants, peddlers, women, children—who lined the tracks in towns or ran from their fields in the countryside toward us, cheering and waving at the train as we passed. We were their allies; we had been captured by our common enemy; now our forces had defeated the hated invader of their country. They stood for hours to give us that momentary expression of their support as our train flashed past.

How variable and transient the most genuine of political sentiments are is shown by the ironic fact that the same group of American and British residents would now be booed, if not attacked, by these same Chinese. The only friendly reception for which such a group might now have some feeble hope would be from the villages and farms of Japan.

We reached Tsingtao in the late afternoon. Again an immense crowd lined the streets to greet us; we were whisked in cabs through these cheering throngs to a luxurious Western-style hotel on the bay commandeered for us by the United States army. We could not but laugh happily at the contrast to our burdened march through Peking two and one-half years before on March 25, 1943.

The hotel was out of this world, a galaxy of wonders to our unaccustomed senses. I stopped short after I had gone through the revolving doors—what *was* I standing on? I laughed at myself when I looked down and saw a thick carpet under my feet. A large room for two was stranger still. There was space to move about in, a dresser for clothes, and hot water that came out of the faucet when one turned it on! These elements of civilized life greeted us from every side; we said "Hello" to them with a most intense delight. The normal patterns of existence were falling into place one by one.

The final touch to this amazing day came when, showered and shaved, we went down to dinner. A head waiter greeted us at the door of the grand dining hall, ushered us to a table set with tablecloth and silver, and presented us each with an immense menu replete with every delicacy. After we had ordered varied combinations of seafood, steak, and wine, we turned in our chairs to listen to a jazz band, from a visiting American battle cruiser, playing for us the newly popular song, "Don't Fence Me In!"

All too soon we became accustomed to luxury. After a few days, we were itching to be off and home. At the end of ten days, early in October, a troopship arrived to take the Americans in our group to the States. We were bundled aboard with a couple of thousand marines, and we set off for Shanghai, Okinawa, Hawaii, and the west coast of the United States. It was hardly a comfortable or memorable passage. Having been completely closeted from the action of the war, our communication with the soldiers fresh from combat was minimal. They seemed surprised and a little resentful when we prisoners admitted that we had not been badly mistreated—as if a person were a bit of a phony if he hadn't suffered in a camp. We, too, began to feel a touch uncomfortable about our relatively easy lot at Weihsien.

To ease the boredom, one of my friends from camp and I volunteered to work one shift in the ship's bakery, run by a regular navy baker of twenty-three, assisted by a pickup crew of homebound marines. The difference from our camp bakery was laughable: with inexhaustible supplies and mechanized equipment, we could turn out bread, cakes, and pies for two thousand people almost between smokes. I shall never forget our feelings when the young cook, upon discovering there were lumps in the filling for his two hundred and fifty lemon meringue pies, calmly pulled the release lever and sent the whole lot into the Pacific!

After four and one-half weeks at sea, we arrived at San Francisco, and debarked into the midst of a bustling and sumptuous America. One of the few really unpleasant experiences I have had was when the State Department man who came aboard to interview us asked me if I had stayed in China deliberately to escape the draft. Looking at his well-fattened jowls and rotund middle, I asked him why he had chosen "diplomacy" as his contribution to the war effort, and heard no more about the matter.

A week or so later, on March 11, 1946, I was home in Chicago. America was a dream world. All the familiar sights, sounds, and smells, the well-loved people, the buildings and the streets of the university community were there. Yet inwardly, I was a man from another planet.

Everything was absolutely normal—and totally strange. I did not know how to go about finding my place in it. People would tell me how much they had suffered from the rationing. "Why there were times when we had barely enough sugar or butter. Steaks were scarce, and gas was so hard to get that we had to form car pools." I would murmur some word of sympathy. Then they would remember where I had been, and would say, "Oh, but how silly, when you suffered so gravely."

I had in honesty to reply, "On the contrary, we didn't suffer very much." Then our estrangement would be complete, neither of us understanding the world that the other had experienced.

One day shortly after my return, I went with my mother to the grocery on the corner of 55th Street and Woodlawn Avenue in Chicago. It was by no means a supermarket—only an ordinary corner grocery. And yet it completely overwhelmed me. I stood in the middle staring at those shelves piled high with food, cereals, breads, canned vegetables, fruit, and meats, layer on layer of food, spilling over, piles of it in corners, and beyond the butcher's counter, there was more piled high in unopened crates and boxes.

I felt engulfed in food, drowned in immense and inexhaustible wealth, stuffed and bloated with so many fats, calories, and vitamins that I wanted to run outside. Meanwhile, people in the store were talking of their relief that the rigors of rationing were over. I understood then what real affluence meant. The break with our life in camp, which obviously still dominated my consciousness, seemed infinite. What possible bond was there between that life and this?

The next morning at breakfast the cartoon in the paper caught my eye. It was the time when UNRRA (United Nations Relief and Rehabilitation Administration) was embarking on its program; people in Washington were beginning to talk about American aid to devastated countries, the talk that ultimately flowered in the Marshall Plan. Sensing what it termed the misguided "do-goodism" involved in these humanitarian schemes, the Chicago *Tribune* was already mounting its attack. The cartoon that morning pictured a benevolent but naïve figure labeled UNCLE SUCKER, who was being milked of his possessions by wily and well-fed foreigners. The caption read: DON'T LET THEM GIVE AWAY WHAT IS OURS.

Suddenly a bell rang in my mind: I heard the voice of Rickey Kolcheck saying, "These are my parcels, and no one's going to take a single one from me"—and I felt at once completely at home. Amid all our plenty we, in overstuffed America, faced precisely the same crisis over which we had struggled with our seven and one-half parcels in a starving camp. The level of material wealth at issue was vastly different. But the human problems remained identical—except that now the stakes were higher.

Could we summon the moral strength, as well as the wisdom and prudence, to share our wealth with a now famished world? Or would we hoard it to ourselves, stuffing ourselves with surfeit but in doing so demolishing all hopes of achieving a humane and peaceful world community?

With a sinking heart, I realized that nowhere could one escape these deeper issues of life: on every level the same choice remains, for the same moral problem is posed to us.

A week or so later I was asked to speak on my experiences. The notion of the continuity of moral problems through the variables of situations fascinated me. I built the speech around that subject. I gave that talk about twice a week for the next six months, at service clubs, women's clubs, schools, and churches around Chicago, in the midwest generally, and later in Virginia and Tennessee.

The reactions illuminated the thesis of the speech and the themes of my thoughts concerning the human condition. Everyone was quite genuinely horrified on hearing the story of the Red Cross parcels. All found it hard to believe that "Americans" could have acted so selfishly. But when the parallel was drawn, and the similar choice that faced the audience as Americans in today's world was described, most persons in the audience would draw back. My listeners seemed to find the two situations quite dissimilar. They argued with me afterward that whereas to share with one's fellows in a camp was a human necessity, to give those foreigners free food that belonged to us was immoral.

One meeting of a women's church group especially fascinated

me. We met in a mammoth suburban residence outside Chicago, the expansive driveway lined with black Cadillacs and Lincolns. This group contained some forty middle-aged women, elegantly dressed and adorned.

As I spoke to these smiling and gracious ladies in the living room, out of the corner of my eye I could see two or three maids putting sandwiches, cookies, and towering chocolate cakes on the dining room table. I suppose I stressed the problems of hunger and the need for sharing even more than usual as my eye traveled from minks to gentle, round faces, to chauffeurs pacing outside, and then back to the cakes again. When I had finished, the president, whose face had worn a slight frown during the latter course of my talk, called for questions. When none was proffered, she rose and addressed the following remarks to me.

"I think our visitor, for all his good intentions, does not understand our point of view on these matters. You see, we don't believe at all in the value of material things. It is the spiritual values of life that *we* feel are significant. We believe that what America has to offer the world is her spiritual superiority, not any advantage she may have in the realm of mere material goods. Thus we would like to encourage the export to Europe and the rest of the world of our great spiritual ideals, our religious faith, our sense of morality and of the value of the inner life. So *we* send moral and religious writings abroad, and do not approve of concentrating on the things that are not so important to the welfare of the soul. That is why we do not support UNRRA; we think it is a shame that more of the churches, which should represent the spiritual and not the material, do not share our views. If there are, then, no more questions, let us adjourn the meeting. I can see our hostess has provided us with tantalizing refreshments in the dining room."

Thirty minutes later, as I walked past the long line of elegant limousines, my mouth still filled with the thick sweetness of whipped cream and chocolate, I tasted in all its bitter comedy the irony of the human condition. This girdled and minked group was surfeited in material comfort, and yet they saw themselves as believers solely in the spiritual! It was this very self-deception, necessary for conscience' sake, that allowed them to ignore the claims of their neighbors on their comfort, that made them delight in sharing their "faith" but not their food with a starving world, and that caused them to be the most totally unspiritual and insensitive group I had addressed in a year's time!

Only those, so I mused, who can understand, if not by experience then by sympathy, the full weight of material want and so the value of material goods, can possibly comprehend what the real spiritual issues of life are. For to wish and seek for justice in material things for one's neighbor is perhaps the highest of spiritual attainments, since it is the expression in social relations of what it means to love one's neighbor.* A healthy spirituality, to be spiritual and not callous, must affirm the material order, and concern itself with it—with housing, food, warmth, and comfort. At the same time, a healthy material order is possible only where there is enough moral strength to maintain a responsible integrity with regard to property, a just distribution with regard to goods, and as free an exercise of each one's creativity as is possible. So do the material and the spiritual realms, the secular and the religious, not exclude but cry out for each other. They are but different aspects of our one created, organic human life. And woe betide the philosopher, the theologian, or the society that seeks to sunder them!

Still fascinated by the continuity I discovered between the problems in camp and those which any wider society faced, I spent the winter of my twenty-seventh year pondering what I thought I had learned about man. Eagerly I devoured a good deal of philosophy, psychology, and theology, trying to check each discipline against the experience I had just quitted, since I was now sure that it was a valid sample of our human condition. In this interchange between theory and experience, I began to see some glimmering of answers to the questions which camp life had raised.

The most obvious dilemma had been the moral one: men must be just, fair, and generous if a creative and stable society is to be possible at all, and yet apparently this is for us a supremely difficult if not impossible task. How are we to understand ourselves; why does such an obvious necessity seem so unattainable and even unnatural to our present nature? As in camp, I continued to find both the humanistic and the rigidly pietistic answers to these questions unsatisfactory.

Those humanists who insist that men are naturally wise and good enough to be moral seemed to me to be continually refuted by the patent persistence of dangerous selfishness among people

* As Nicholas Berdyaev once wrote: "To eat bread is a material act, to break and share it a spiritual one."

whose intentions were good. Those religious perfectionists who believe that pious Christians are holy and holy people are good were refuted by the intolerance and lovelessness of many of the pious. Against both, therefore, the evidence revealed that it is above all things difficult to be good, and that in all of us—the wise, the idealistic, and the religious alike—lie deep forces beyond our easy control which often push us seemingly in spite of ourselves into selfish acts.

Liberal humanists often express amazement that their apparently intelligent Christian friends believe many things about God which cannot be proved. At least the Christian can answer that what he believes about God cannot be disproved. But the main article of faith of the humanist, namely, the goodness of mankind and man's consequent capacity to be moral, is refuted by any careful study of human nature. If it is unreasonable to hold a religious faith that cannot be demonstrated, surely it is irrational to defend a humanistic faith that the evidence so universally contradicts.

Our camp experience demonstrated that two things can safely be said about mankind. First, it seemed certain enough that man is immensely creative, ingenious, and courageous in the face of new problems. But it was also equally apparent that under pressure he loves himself and his own more than he will ever admit. Furthermore, both the universality and yet the puzzling "unnaturalness" of this self-love were certainly established by our experience, for men consistently denied the motivations which equally consistently determined their conduct. If men were just plain "good," this self-love would not have been so clearly pervasive in all they did. If, on the other hand, they were just plain "bad," if this self-love were simply "natural" to man, those who acted upon it would not have been so intent to deny its presence and to claim that their acts flowed instead from moral intentions.

The camp experience indicated, moreover, that a man's morality or immorality stems from the deepest spiritual center of his life—from what has been called by Paul Tillich his ultimate loyalty or concern—that center of devotion in a man's existence which provides for his life its final security and meaning, and to which, therefore, he gives his ultimate love and commitment.

Every man has such a spiritual center of security and meaning. It gives his activities purpose and significance, and thus provides his existence with coherence and direction. If anything should happen to this center, a man feels that his life is radically insecure and totally incoherent, that its pieces fall apart into uncoordinated bits. Existence then degenerates into a series of events and actions that lead nowhere, produce nothing, and so mean nothing.

Like the gods of primitive religion, this ultimate concern is something which a man worships with his whole being because it is the source of all value to him, that is, of all security and significance to his life. So, like the god of any worshiper, it determines in turn the decisions a man makes and ultimately the way in which he behaves.

These centers of ultimate concern vary greatly. For a great many men the preservation and advancement of their own power, be it financial, political, military, or social, may be what provides them with a sense of security and meaning. Such men will feel radical anxiety and the threat of insignificance until their own position and wealth are advanced to a point where it appears they cannot be threatened by competition. For others it may be their job or profession—be it music, art, scholarship or science—for which they will sacrifice everything, because from it they receive all their meaning. Still others find this sense of security and meaning in the status of their families or of their social group, such as their class, nation, or race, through whose wider success their own precarious security and fragmented meaning gain status.

When, in this sense, a man gives his ultimate devotion to his own welfare or to the welfare of his group, he is no longer free to be completely moral or rational when he finds himself under pressure. Whenever the security of the object of this commitment is threatened, he is driven by an intense anxiety to reinforce that security.

If the total meaning of his life depends upon his own welfare, a shortage of food will threaten the one thing significant to his whole existence and, whether he would ordinarily approve of his actions or not, he will do almost anything to make sure he is fed. His moral interest in the security of others will recede in importance before this challenge to the central concern of his life; and his rational sense of what is just and fair will lose its power to determine his actions.

Although under this kind of pressure he does, as we have seen, act immorally and unjustly, these moral and rational powers do not completely disappear. They remain, but as the servants of his greater concern, his own welfare. Thus, while he still finds himself demanding the seven and one-half parcels for himself, or desperately hanging onto his own living space, he uses moral and rational arguments to justify his self-concern. In this situation, no amount of intelligence or of ideals and good intentions will change his behavior or free him from his selfishness so that he can be good. The more acute mind of the intelligent man may well fashion more plausible rationalizations than can the slower mind of his neighbor. In each of our crucial moral issues this pattern repeated itself: over and over the more educated and respectable people defended their self-concern with more elegant briefs. We came, indeed, to have a grudging respect for the open rascal. He, at least, was forthright in admitting his selfishness.

When a man's basic security is not in danger, when he deals, as in research, with problems that do not concern his own welfare, a man's moral and rational powers are free to function with benevolence and wisdom. Out of experiences in such situations arises the humanist's faith in man's moral self-sufficiency and in his capacity for moral progress. But when man's self is basically threatened, when *he* is involved in the crisis, a new power enters the scene, a power seemingly stronger than either the moral consciousness or the objective mind. It is the embattled ego fighting with every weapon at its disposal for its own security.

The ethical issues of human community life are, therefore, the outward expression in action of deeper, more inward issues, we might say religious issues. For religion concerns men's ultimate loyalty; those things, be they gods or idols, to which men give their final devotion and commitment. It is what we can only call the religious worship of a finite creature—that creature being one's own life or that of his group—that causes the disruptions and conflicts of society. When our ultimate concern is directed to some partial or limited interest, we can, as I found, scarcely avoid inhumanity toward those outside that interest.

Injustice to other men, as Reinhold Niebuhr has said, is the social consequence of an inward idolatry, the worship of one's own self or group. The moral problems of selfishness, the intellectual problems of prejudice, and the social problems of dishonesty, inordinate privilege, and aggression are all together the result of the deeper religious problem of finding in some partial creature the ultimate security and meaning which only the Creator can give.

This then is the religious meaning of sin, far different from the usual meaning given it by the legalist mentality. Sin may be defined as an ultimate religious devotion to a finite interest; it is an overriding loyalty or concern for the self, its existence and its prestige, or for the existence and prestige of a group. From this deeper sin, that is, from this inordinate love of the self and its own, stem the moral evils of indifference, injustice, prejudice, and cruelty to one's neighbor, and the other destructive patterns of action that we call "sins."

Religion does not seem to be, as Matthew Arnold said, "Morality tinged with emotion." Rather, the reverse appears to be truer. A man's morality is his religion enacted in social existence. The rare power of selflessness, what we call true "morality" or "virtue," arises only when a life finds its ultimate devotion to lie beyond itself, thus allowing that person in times of crisis to forget his own concerns and to be free to love and help his neighbor.

The religious dimensions of man's existence can be, therefore, not only the ground of its only hope, but the source of life's deepest perversion. For man's sin is *religious* in character as is his selflessness, if by religion we mean, as we do here, the ultimate concern or commitment of a man's life.

This is why human religion is so ambiguous and has been the seat of history's greatest fanaticisms and cruelty as well as of its transcendent spiritual grandeur.

This religious dimension of life, giving it its demonic and its self-sacrificial character, permeates our personal, communal, and political existence. The presence of this dimension more than anything else renders false any purely secular account of man's problems and hopes. At the very moment man declares himself most proudly to "have come of age," and so to be free at last of "religion," he falls prey to some new personal, political, or racial idolatry which plunges his social life again into turmoil.

At the religious level of existence both our sin and the possibility of our salvation appear, for there our ultimate loyalty is determined. The question in human life is not whether a person, or a society, is religious or not, for no human can escape some ultimate commitment. The question is: To what sort of deity are we ultimately loyal, and what kind of god claims our deepest love and devotion?

While all men are thus religious, by no means are all forms of religion equally creative or uncreative. The common idea that a man's religion is a purely subjective and personal matter, without relevance to his behavior or character is, I believe, quite false. It separates inward commitment and outward behavior, which are intimately related. It is, in fact, the otherwise admirable trait of loyalty to one's family, one's group or nation which, when it becomes central, is the root of much of the injustice, pride, and selfishness we have described and with which we are surrounded.

The only hope in the human situation is that the "religiousness" of men find its true center in God, and not in the many idols that appear in the course of our experience. If men are to forget themselves enough to share with each other, to be honest under pressure, and to be rational and moral enough to establish community, they must have some center of loyalty and devotion, some source of security and meaning, beyond their own welfare.

This center of loyalty beyond themselves cannot be a human creation, greater than the individual but still finite, such as the family, the nation, tradition, race, or the church. Only the God who created all men and so represents none of them exclusively; only the God who rules all history and so is the instrument of no particular historical movement; only the God who judges His faithful as well as their enemies, and loves and cares for all, can be the creative center of human existence.

The ultimate concern of each man must raise him above his struggles with his neighbor instead of making these conflicts more bitter and intense. Given an ultimate security in God's eternal love, and an ultimate meaning to his own small life in God's eternal purposes, a man can forget his own welfare and for the first time look at his neighbor free from the gnawings of self-concern.

From this we can perhaps now see what the man of real faith is like. He is the man whose center of security and meaning lies not in his own life but in the power and love of God, a man who has surrendered an overriding concern for himself, so that the only really significant things in his life are the will of God and his neighbor's welfare. Such faith is intimately related to love, for faith is an inward self-surrender, a loss of self-centeredness and concern which transforms a man and frees him to love.

The Catholic world calls this depth of self-surrender *caritas*, the total love of God, and through that love the love of man. The Protestant world calls it "faith," an ultimate trust in God's love and power as the sole basis of the self's life and status. And rightly in both of them this principle of self-surrender to God, which is always the gift of grace, is the basis of what has traditionally been called "salvation." We would probably more easily define the latter reality—so far as we experience it—as an inner serenity of spirit, the capacity for healthy and real relations with others, and a creative concern for the world around us and for our neighbors.

This sort of faith is far different from what we usually associate with religious "belief." To most people "faith" means belief in a set creed or in a list of biblical fundamentals. Moreover, the sort of freedom from anxiety about the self we have mentioned is far different from a rigorous adherence to any particular rule of piety. A man may assent with his mind and lips to even the greatest truths, and practice in his acts all the rules of piety and holiness, and still keep the center of his concern fixed selfishly on his own bodily or spiritual welfare.

Only this is certain: If a man is *too* sure that he has, through his religion, surrendered his concern for himself and achieved virtue, it is fairly safe to conclude that his security no longer rests in the love of God but in his own holiness. His life then merely re-enacts the sin of self-idolatry in a Christian garb. The final pinnacle of faith, therefore, is to recognize our continuing self-concern and thus to trust our inner peace to the love of God alone. In this way even our anxiety about our own holiness and our own salvation is surrendered. The insight that the man of real faith knows he is justified by a grace from beyond himself and never by his own works is the heart of the message of God's love in the New Testament. It is the deepest answer to the dilemmas of man's moral life over which my thoughts that winter puzzled.

The other problem, arising from the camp experience, that often occupied my mind was that of meaning in a time of social chaos. At first it seemed as if this one at least had been left behind me in China. What kind of social chaos did postwar America face with its preponderant power in the world, its booming economy, and its seemingly stable political and social order? How in America could "meaning" be a problem to any person of education and energy who had a bit of luck? Were there any grounds for comparison between the fate of those British residents of China dislodged rudely from all their structures of value and the success that seemed to beckon those of us Americans who had lived through the war?

I realized anew that the continuities of experience are as great as its discontinuities, and that life under stress, while more vivid, was not necessarily atypical. For as the first postwar year developed, rumblings of trouble could be heard on the edges of our "stable" culture. The dismemberment of the older Western empires in Asia and Africa proceeded apace, and European society drew in sharply to its home ground, gearing itself to a new mode of life in a world where voices other than its own could be heard. But more to the point, another form of society, antithetical in its fundamental principles and hostile in at least its present intentions to the West, began to move into the newly vacated spaces, gaining ground month by month.

During that year, the Iron Curtain was lowered over Eastern Europe, a bitter struggle took place for Greece, and even Italy, near the center of Western life, seemed vulnerable. Above all, China changed from the leading Asiatic ally of the West to its most implacable antagonist. With this development, the whole future of a vast portion of Asia, Africa, and even South America became infinitely problematical. The West had to face the possibility that, far from ruling the rest of the globe, she might soon find herself isolated and even besieged by it. It seemed to be only a matter of time until this new hostile or semihostile bloc would possess the same weapons which the West now controlled. The nuclear strength that had been the very basis of American security rapidly became the prime symbol of a new insecurity.

America and the West faced a totally new situation. Its long-lived and powerful cultural life had been threatened from the inside before, by internecine wars among its own members and by home-grown fanaticisms such as Nazism. Now, however, it confronted a newly risen world outside its own orbit and so beyond the influence of its own deepest traditions and values. To be sure, Western experience and thought had provided the Marxist ideology with which this new world was fashioning itself. But when Marxism was transplanted to the alien soils of Asia, Africa, and South America, it might well lose many of the ties with European tradition which it still maintained, say, in parts of Eastern Europe and in present-day Russia.

Faced with this combination of an alien cultural substance armed with an accelerating power, the West suffered a new inner experience: it became cognizant of its own potential mortality in history. The future no longer seemed to guarantee an extension of the values and social structures which gave Western life its meanings. Rather, the future might now bring the diminution and even the extinction of these values.

Only a few pessimists prophesied the decline of the West—but hardly an aware person did not sniff this new possibility in the air. Wondering what the next decades might bring, he could sense history and the place of the West in it in a different and anxious way. Perhaps Western values would be destroyed. Perhaps change was *not* always for the best—and perhaps historical change led to no meaningful place at all. And possibly in some not too distant future, Western man would stare at a world in which he was no more at home than were those China residents when they walked out of Weihsien camp with resigned hopelessness—the world of the treaty ports forever lost to them.

The postwar American world was by no means plunged into despair by this new climate. These possibilities were merely that—possibilities, not certainties—and the chances of maintaining the social order without wars seemed steadily to improve as Europe moved back to health. Nevertheless, the older *certainty* that the future would be structured by Western values had vanished almost without trace; a meaningful history for us was now at best only a possibility. As a direct consequence, the confidence each person felt in the security of the meanings of his own life had vastly diminished.

Out of this new awareness of the relativity of all things human in history has arisen the question of a larger meaning in history as a whole. I had often heard secular philosophers ask with some impatience, "Is there a legitimate question about *the* meaning of history? Why not be content with small meanings? With social betterment, with the gradual growth of freedom, equality, and order—why ask about the ultimate nature of history when a perfectly full life can be enjoyed among these natural social values?"

Why indeed? Because such "small meanings" or "natural values" are by no means "natural" in history. Rather, they depend upon a stable social order dominated by democratic values and preserved by a vigorous technology under humanitarian control. Just as the meaning of life for a Westerner in the treaty ports of China depended upon the social order that Western dominance had established there, so the values so apparent in America's secular culture depend upon a particular historical order grounded in Western democratic and humanitarian ideals.

Such a social order is by no means certain or dependable in history—unless one assumes on faith that history will necessarily progress along Western humanitarian lines. But it is precisely that assumption that recent history has made dubious. In another sort of social order, on the contrary, such as Fascism projected, and such as the "harder" forms of Communism seem to promise, these democratic "small meanings" or "secular values" are practically impossible and their future questionable indeed. The question of *the* meaning of history is thus nothing more than the question of whether those "small meanings" that the democratic naturalist seems to take for granted are permanently available to man. Only in terms of an answer to that question can we have any confidence in the smaller meanings of life within which each of us must live to be creative. By saying he is content with the small meanings, the naturalistic philosopher is merely saying he has already answered the question of *the* meaning of history in terms of the progressivist faith that values *are* becoming increasingly available.

The uncertainty of the present situation has unsettled our faith in the permanence of Western culture and its values, and thus it has inescapably raised for us the question of the direction of history as a whole. We are being forced to ask whether the rise and fall of cultures constitutes the whole of history, or whether a thread of purpose may run through its course, giving it meaning even if our own order and values are mortal, as we fear.

The question of the ultimate meaning of life, and so of its historical context, is always posed when the mortality of human schemes of order is revealed, and when as a consequence the normal meanings of daily life are threatened or destroyed. With the asking of this question comes the sober realization that it is easy for us to be afraid and anxious in such historical uncertainty, when the threat of total loss or meaninglessness looms ahead of us. It is also obvious that the temptation to fanaticism in such circumstances is indeed great. Finally, it follows that to live with courage, serenity, and a real love of life in the midst of such uncertainty is a difficult task. To be aware of our contingency, of the mortality of all we love and value, and yet to love life and act creatively in it, requires a deeply rooted sense of the ultimate goodness and meaningfulness of life.

It has thus become apparent that a sense of creative freedom in life is bound up with a sense of dependable order in our social structures. When these structures of life are seen to be vulnerable, and our own activities incapable of establishing meaning in the face of uncontrollable forces of historical destruction, the sense of "Fate" grows. And with that sense comes a feeling of helplessness and despair, of having no freedom in the face of implacable Fortune.

To most humanists, living in a stable culture, the belief in the Providence of God seems to be antithetical to the belief in human creativity and freedom—because the established social order already provides a context for that creativity. When culture itself is unstable, and Fate, that ultimate threat to all meaning, seems to rule everything—as the experience of the Hellenistic world showed—all this changes. Then a belief in Providence, in a structure of meaning in which the individual's freedom and acts have value and so can make sense, becomes the foundation of human creative action, and man can believe in himself again.

Such a view of the vulnerability of life's meanings was one of my deepest experiences in camp, and it helped to prepare me for the even deeper abyss into which the postwar Western world has been forced to stare. The universal problem of selfishness, I found, called for the grace and forgiveness of God—both in camp and in the affluent society of America. Similarly, the problem of the fragmentariness of every human meaning seemed now to me to call for the answer of God's Providence, for that unity of divine power and meaning in the course of events that is not threatened by the historical catastrophes that overwhelm us.

Can we make more sense of our historical destiny than merely to speak of Fate and its designs, to say that at times the promise of fulfillment given to one age is inscrutably withdrawn for the next? Is there any steady meaning to which a man in *any* age or situation can relate himself and which will give significance and so creative zest to his life? What, if anything, is the Providence of God; where does it appear in the experience of mankind's turbulent and uncertain history? Have I, I wondered, found any answers to these questions from the experiences of an internment camp? I thought I had, although what I had learned was admittedly only the barest beginning.

The first lesson concerned what might be called the negative coherence of history, or, alternatively, the partial intelligibility of the meaningless. What is meaningless in the course of events is the fate that destroys the little systems of value and order which buoy us up, and that sets us adrift in a rootless sea of directionless events. The destruction of the whole established order of treaty-port life is one example. But this incoherent Fate is by no means completely unintelligible or blind. It follows its own logic, and that logic leads back to ourselves, to human choices and human freedom, and so it can become understandable to us.

Fate in history is not sheer fate; it is usually in part the consequence of sins in which we share communally if not personally, the effects of some former misuse of freedom. Fate is thus the mask God's judgment in history wears to those who do not know Him. History is blind only to those unfortunate communities that are blind to their own sins. To those who know and repent, there is both intelligibility and the hope of renewal in the ambiguities of time. Providence is then at least partly the divine judgment, enacted in the course of events. Insofar as this is one aspect of Providence, we can be empirically aware of its presence and inwardly certain of its justice.

The fate that overtook the white residents of China was neither arbitrary nor blind. Rather, it represented the slow but certain unraveling of the consequences of the greed and intolerance which accompanied the imperialism of their forerunners. In the same way the peril that threatens Western values is neither the old age of Western culture nor a remorseless Bad Fortune. It is the peril sown by our own sins of omission and commission which have driven men to hostility against us and to ideas antithetical to the ones we espouse. It is, in other words, the betrayal by our culture of the very values we cherish that in our day endangers the life-span of those values. To realize this, and act upon it, is already to make Fate more comprehensible, and to grasp its opportunities.

If to know the Providence of God is first of all to know in part the long-term justice of one's fate, then it is even more to know the universal opportunity which every fateful situation offers to us. For the man who knew nothing of divine Providence, coming to camp was an arbitrary fate that separated him from every familiar meaning by which he had lived his life. To those—and there were many—who found this new situation to be a strange work of Providence, however incomprehensible these purposes were, there could be no such loss of significance in the new and unexpected situation. Here, too, there could be an opportunity and a significant task to be performed—it might not be that of teacher or architect, but it could be that of stoker, cook, or master baker. A sense of significance that is rooted in the purposes of God cannot be lost in any situation. So it is not relinquished when one moves from Tientsin to Weihsien or from a Western-dominated society to another sort apparently shorn of values.

> If I ascend up into heaven, thou art there:
>> If I make my bed in hell, behold, thou art there. . . .
> Even there shall thy hand lead me,
>> and thy right hand shall hold me.
>
> Psalm 139:8, 10

The familiar psalm, often repeated but seldom experienced by most of us, had new import for many who found themselves suddenly plunged into a strange and grim existence, separated from all the usual comforts and goals of life—and yet faced with a new opportunity for creative life. For the man of faith, therefore, his most fundamental career, the service of the God who is ever present, remains in every contingency of an unstable history. *This* structure of meaning is not removed by any historical Fate, for I believe God rules the Fates that appear to rule so powerfully over us.

Even more, what we are called to do in this service also is ever present, a task that no Fate can remove from us. Our particular jobs of salesman, professor, or senator may prove useless in a camp or even in the next historical moment. But our neighbor is always with us, in the city, in the country, or in the camp. If the meaning of life on its deepest level is the service of God—which in turn means the service of the neighbor's needs and fellowship with him—then this is a task that carries over into any new situation. The creation and preservation of life so that it may be enjoyed by all, the development of community in the direction of justice, the satisfaction of the needs of all our fellows through some practical work well done, and finally the creation of fellowship with others—these fundamental tasks, communal expressions in each case of the love of one's neighbor, are present in any historical situation. In each circumstance they call for courage, integrity, self-sacrifice, energy, and intelligence; and on them depends the life of civilization.

On these two bases, therefore—the universal lordship of God and the universal presence of the neighbor with whom we can establish community—a significant vocation or task with religious roots cannot be removed by the ups and downs of historical fortune. On these terms, it is possible to be realistic without fear about our own mortality and that of the things we love, and to affirm without fanaticism our life and its values. Such deep-seated security about our own fate in God, plus a forthright allegiance to what we value and support in the world, will be increasingly necessary for our culture in the years ahead.

One of the strangest lessons that our unstable life-passage teaches us is that the unwanted is often creative rather than destructive. No one wished to go to Weihsien camp. Yet such an experience, resisted and abhorred, had within it the seeds of new insight and thus of new life for many of us. Almost because of its discomfort, its turmoil, and its boredom, it eventually became the source of certainties and of convictions with which life could henceforth be more creatively faced. This is a common mystery of life, an aspect, if you will, of common grace: out of apparent evil new creativity can arise if the meanings and possibilities latent within the new situation are grasped with courage and with faith.

This common experience—that the Fate which we did not welcome has become nevertheless the ground for future creativity —has, more than anything else, led men to speak of the Providence of God and to believe in His universal creative presence. I did not come to believe that God determined all aspects of the events in which I participated. But the experience of creativity in a circumstance neither intended nor wanted, has led me to believe that God works in and through each situation. And strangely, this divine activity provides the possibility of a new departure, a more vivid life, and a deeper joy than could have been provided by the life I had myself intended.

Men need God because their precarious and contingent lives can find final significance only in His almighty and eternal purposes, and because their fragmentary selves must find their ultimate center only in His transcendent love. If the meaning of men's lives is centered solely in their own achievements, these too are vulnerable to the twists and turns of history, and their lives will always teeter on the abyss of pointlessness and inertia. And if men's ultimate loyalty is centered in themselves, then the effect of their lives on others around them will be destructive of that community on which all depend. Only in God is there an ultimate loyalty that does not breed injustice and cruelty, and a meaning from which nothing in heaven or on earth can separate us.

12, 17, 19 & 20, 21, 23, 24*, 27, 33, 41 (45-6*), 4?

48-50, 58, 60, 65, 66, 72, 79, 81, 84, 89

90*, 92, 105, 110*, 112, 114, 118-9, 122

134, 136*, 141, (163) 165 w/B&W, 167, 168, 171

172*, 177, 197, 201, 203, 205, 207, 213, 217

221*, 222, 226, 229 30 232

(227*)